COMPETITIVE ECONOMICS: EQUILIBRIUM AND ARBITRATION

Advanced Series in Management

Volume 1

Series Editors

A. BENSOUSSAN

University Paris-Dauphine
and INRIA
Paris, France

and

P. A. NAERT

European Institute for
Advanced Studies in Management
Brussels, Belgium

NORTH-HOLLAND PUBLISHING COMPANY
AMSTERDAM · NEW YORK · OXFORD

Competitive Economics: Equilibrium and Arbitration

Ki Hang KIM

and

Fred W. ROUSH

Kiro Research Group
416 Arrowhead Drive
Montgomery
Alabama 36117
U.S.A.

1983

NORTH-HOLLAND PUBLISHING COMPANY
AMSTERDAM · NEW YORK · OXFORD

ISBN: 0 444 86497 0

Publishers:
NORTH-HOLLAND PUBLISHING COMPANY
AMSTERDAM · NEW YORK · OXFORD

Sole distributors for the U.S.A. and Canada:
ELSEVIER SCIENCE PUBLISHING COMPANY, INC.
52 Vanderbilt Avenue
New York, N.Y. 10017

Library of Congress Cataloging in Publication Data
Main entry under title:

Competitive economics.

(Advanced series in management ; v. 1)
Bibliography: p.
Includes indexes.
1. Economics, Mathematical. 2. Game theory.
3. Welfare economics. 4. Equilibrium (Economics)
I. Kim, Ki Hang. II. Roush, Fred William.
III. Series.
HB135.C63 1982 339.5 82-14393
ISBN 0-444-86497-0 (Elsevier)

PRINTED IN THE NETHERLANDS

DEDICATION

The first author dedicates this book to his mother Mrs. Mi-Ran (Hong) Kim. The second author dedicates this book to his parents Mr. and Mrs. J. Fred Roush.

PREFACE

This book is intended as a survey of some of the most important results in a number of active areas of recent mathematical economics research, and a discussion of their relevance to current situations. The two main themes are game theory and social welfare.

Game theory is the theory of what happens when n agents have an input into a process, and each tries to maximize a different function of the resulting output. This is a very general formulation of the traditional picture of economic agents who maximize utility. It is a basic representation of human beings acting in groups.

Social welfare theory is mathematical treatment of normative questions in economics, going beyond Pareto optimality. *What is best for a group ?* Under assumptions of cardinal, interpersonally comparable utility (and by Arrow's theorem this is more or less needed) reasonable social welfare functions exist. Axioms similar to the conditions of Arrow's theorem can characterize uniquely various evaluations of the well-being of society. We use in particular what we call *social arbitration functions*, closely related to the Nash bargaining solution. This provides a method of scientifically studying previously unanswerable questions.

The study of the market system by models of equilibrium has achieved new results since 1970. The theory of the core and results in strategyproofness (and information spaces, which we do not cover) help clarify the uniqueness of the market system and the question: *is there an alternative, other than rationing by force ?* Studies of market demand functions, of nonexistence of noncooperative equilibrium, and of the number of equilibria show that previously unknown phenomena may occur. New Models such as temporary general equilibrium and rational expectations equilibrium show the role of expectations. With game theory, the theory of oligopoly has advanced.

Governments face the principal-agent problem in deciding how to allocate public goods, a problem for which nothing so simple as the private goods market exists. The principal's problem is that he depends on various agents for information and for performing certain things, but that the agent's goals do not coincide with his. Thus he must design a system in which their self-interest as much as possible is in doing what he wants.

The final chapter is concerned with potential applications of this material to certain current economic problems: the environment, financing of public facilities, energy and resources, the business cycle, inflation, and unemployment, income distribution and welfare.

Ki Hang Kim
Pyongyang, Korea

Fred W. Roush
Montgomery, Alabama

NOTE ON THE USE OF THE BOOK

This book is directed simultaneously at graduate students, professional economists, and management scientists, mathematicians and others with mathematical skills, and government and private planners and administrators as well as the lay public. Professional economists and management scientists will probably be interested in Chapters 2-8 which survey a number of topics in modern mathematical economics from a game-theoretic viewpoint. Mathematically inclined readers can also read this material with no economic prerequisites. Non-mathematically inclined readers should skip the heavy mathematics in Chapters 2-7. From chapter summaries, conclusions, and non-mathematical portions of the text they may still be able to obtain a good knowledge of the concepts involved and the results which have been proved. Chapter 1 and Chapter 8 are less mathematical, more directed at the reader who is not a specialist in this area, and are a discussion of some current economic problems.

ACKNOWLEDGEMENT

The authors would like to acknowledge the assistance of Philippe Naert, Alain Bensoussan, and Herbert Glejser who read portions of the manuscript and Hervé Moulin who read most of it and making very useful comments and suggestions. However, we alone are responsible for any remaining errors and shortcomings.

TABLE OF CONTENTS

CHAPTER 1

HISTORY AND BACKGROUND

1.1 INTRODUCTION

Since the United States is representative of market system economies, we shall only discuss briefly the economic history of the United States. This very brief summary is to give some idea of the stages the U.S. economic system went through. In brief, the U.S. started as small colonies on the brink of starvation. It then become a thriving largely agricultural economy. Britain viewed America as existing for its economic benefit, especially as a supplier of raw materials, and introduced corresponding restrictions on our economy. The American feeling that we were economically exploited played a large role in the American revolution.

The nineteenth century was noted for conflicts between regions over tariffs, slavery, and banking and monetary practices. In addition manufacturing, and trade flourished in an atmosphere of few restrictions on the capitalist. Monopolists could drive their rivals out of business and forget the public interest. Farming expanded to the West but farmers had serious economic problems. Every twenty years or so there would be a panic.

The most notable event in American economic history is the *Great Depression*. The reforms of the New Deal did not solve it, although they may have helped prevent a recurrence. Instead the solution was the massive government spending of World War II.

After World War II there were about twenty years of great prosperity. Then came the Vietnam War. Since it was unpopular with a sizable proportion of the population, as were the anti-poverty programs of the Great Society, there was some deficit spending. By about 1970 there began a combination of low growth and high inflation called "stagflation," which lasted throughout the decade with varying degrees of intensity. Concern about the environment, about oil prices and energy, declining productivity, the plight of the small farmer, illegal strikes by public employees, the decline of the dollar, special unemployment problems among the young and minority groups, housing problems, and the near bankruptcy of New York City was typical of the decade and still continues.

The failure of existing economic concepts to explain a situation of both unemployment and high inflation seems to call for new economic concepts. Game theory is relevant to a situation in which a few powerful competitors bargain for shares of markets and income. Such situations occur because of the power of giant corporations, unions, and other organizations.

The problem of balancing interests in protecting the environment seems also to call for another type of new concept, a practical way of aggregating the utilities of an action to different members of society.

The advantage of the market system is in theory that in it everyone has an incentive to work towards what is for the good of everyone. Yet these two problems indicate problems for it. As we will later find there are some impossibility theorems which can be interpreted as saying ideal performance cannot be realized. Yet there are also positive results, and we will stress these latter.

1.2 THE U.S. ECONOMY TO 1930

The principal motive for European colonies was economic, although official pronouncements gave equal weight to conversion of the native inhabitants. Colonies were thought of as sources of raw materials, first gold and silver, then furs, lumber and naval stores, and agricultural products such as indigo and sugar. Especially important in the future U.S. was tobacco, without which the Virginia colonies would perhaps have failed.

The American Revolution grew in part out of American resentment at British taxes and economic regulations. It was financed largely by printing paper money, as were the French and Russian revolutions. J. K. Galbraith (1975) speculated that all those revolutions would have been impossible without inflated paper money.

In effect this means, that as the revolutionary government incurred debts, it simply printed more paper money to pay them. This increase in the money supply caused inflation. A suit of clothes eventually cost a million dollars. Other American wars have been financed in the same way as the Revolution by continentals, so the Civil War by greenbacks. World War I was financed mostly by selling bonds which could be bought with borrowed money, again expanding the money supply and causing inflation. (An increase in income taxes paid about one-third of the cost). World War II was financed about half by taxation and half by bonds sold under more restrictions. Price controls and rationing were used to limit inflation, which was 63% over the total war and post-war period, mostly afterwards.

The American economy and population grew rapidly in the first half of the nineteenth century. The economic situation of the ordinary people was better than in Europe.

The banking and monetary systems were chaotic, especially in the West. Foreign coins and bank notes of hundreds of banks were commonly circulated. Western banks frequently had very dubious policies, for instance very little cash to cover their deposits and loans made to poor credit risks. However these practices were actually beneficial to the region. The inflated money and easy loans were liked by farmers in debt and those who borrowed to set up new industry.

The East on the other hand opposed these practices, and managed to get a Bank of the United States created (1791-1811 and 1816-1836) to control the monetary system. One of Andrew Jackson's major concerns was to eliminate this bank, and he succeeded in doing this.

The other major economic conflict prior to the Civil War was over the tariff. The Southern economy was dominated by export agriculture, especially cotton, grown on large plantations by slave labor. The Northern economy was more oriented towards manufacturing. Thus a high tariff, a tax on imports, helped the North by reducing competition with European manufacturers, but hurt the South by increasing the price of imports it received in the return for cotton. Actually, if there is no danger of dependence on another country, and trading is competitive, it can be shown in principle that tariffs are harmful. In practice, there is some danger in being economically dependent on another country which can use its economic strength for political ends. Moreover export economies have frequently been associated with situations in which a few rich plantation owners exploit many poor laborers.

The North managed to keep a high tariff in force much of the time, and this was a significant source of division between the two regions.

After the Civil War the South became a region of backwardness and poverty, characterized by tenant farming and malnutrition, up to the time of the New Deal.

Elsewhere there was great industrial expansion in the United States. This was the era of laissez-faire, or unrestricted capitalism. Great business empires were built by methods which seem dubious. Labor unions were not effective and the government did not regulate business activity significantly. This was the era of social Darwinism, when the rich justified their wealth and the ruthless competition through which it had been obtained as "survival of the fittest."

In the West, soft money was a major issue. The U.S. was on a gold standard. Opponents of hard money argued for free coinage of silver at a fixed ratio. Since silver was much more abundant than gold in the United States, this would have increased the money supply and thus caused inflation, and eased problems of debt among farmers and those starting new businesses. The gold standard was somewhat deflationary, since the American economy grew more rapidly than the supply of gold.

An income tax was first passed at the time of the Civil War. In the 1890's a 2% income tax was passed but was vigorously opposed and later declared unconstitutional. At this time about 1% of the American people had 50% of the wealth. In 1913 an amendment was passed making income taxes constitutional, and shortly after, another income tax. During the later New Deal, income taxes became much more progressive. Today the top 1% of the population has 25% of the total wealth (Pen, 1971).

Much of the economic expansion was financed by foreign capital. Only with World War I did the United States reverse this position of being a borrower. The railroads in particular required heavy investment which never really paid off, although fortunes were made by individuals in the railroad business.

About every twenty years there was a panic, when banks would collapse, business was poor, and wages were very low. These were times of severe suffering, though they lasted only a year or two. J. K. Galbraith links these to the collapse of intense speculation in the time immediately preceding. Other possible causes include agricultural failures and a continuing business cycle.

At the turn of the century it became evident that capitalism had to be regulated by law in order to prevent monopoly and to eliminated unfair, dishonest, and harmful business methods. Such regulation begain in the administration of Theodore Roosevelt, and has greatly increased since.

1.3 THE DEPRESSION AND WORLD WAR II

For business, 1921-1929 was a time of prosperity in the United States, although farmers and working people did not share much of the benefits. According to J. K. Galbraith, productivity increased 43%, but wages were nearly constant, so that nearly all the increase in productivity went to corporate profits, which tripled. Since profits went to the rich, who do not consume all their wealth for supply to balance demand, this money had to be re-invested. Investment takes place only in a climate of optimism and confidence, which was lost during the stock market crash of 1929.

Speculation is a case of positive feedback. The more rapidly prices rise, the more desirable it is to hold things temporarily to make a profit. There is no limit within the system, but psychological factors cause an eventual collapse. Positive feedback systems are unstable.

There were also widespread dishonesty and unsound practices connected with the building up of stock prices. There was much consolidation of businesses. Half of all nonbanking corporate wealth was in 200 companies in 1930, controlled by about 2,000 individuals. People were allowed to buy stock on small margins, that is they put down only a small share of the stock price, to buy and sell. However naturally they were responsible for the whole price if it later fell. Issues of stocks were made for no other reason than to profit from speculation. The Federal Reserve System contributed to the increase of speculation by lowering interest rates, in order to ease the financial problems of Britain and France.

After the stock market collapsed came the Great Depression. Its severity is illustrated by the following figures from the Bureau of Labor Statistics, where 1926 figures are 100.

	Prices	Employment	Payrolls
1929	95	97	100
1930	86	84	81
1931	73	72	61
1932	60	60	41
1933	65	64	44

Seventeen million people were at one time on relief. Moreover the nation did not recover until World War II. President Hoover's policies were aimed mainly at restoring confidence, although his relief efforts and Reconstruction Finance Corporation were probably helpful.

President Roosevelt attacked the depression by a wide range of programs known as the New Deal. Although these programs did not cure the depression, they have become a lasting part of the American system, and have helped make the distribution of income more equitable as well as possibly preventing a recurrence of the depression.

The figures above indicate a 35% deflation in four years. Deflation is very hard on debtors and reduces business activity. So the administration tried to inflated the currency by raising the price of gold from $20.67 per ounce to $35 per ounce in 1933-34. However since the government had previously called in all gold and forbidden its private ownership, this did not greatly affect domestic prices.

The Securities and Exchange Commission was formed to regulate the stock market. One of the most effective measures came from Congress and not the administration, and was the Federal Deposit Insurance Corporation, which insured bank deposits against failure of the bank. Moreover the FDIC regulated banks more closely to prevent failure. The Federal Reserve System was reformed.

In agriculture, programs were undertaken to restrict production so as to raise prices, and to conserve soil from erosion. Crop insurance, and government supports of the price of agricultural goods were initiated. Since that time, agriculture has essentially been removed from the market system. It could be said that in the United States, agricultural policy is a mild form of socialism. It became a policy for the government to maintain and store food surpluses, and to distribute surplus food by what is now the Food Stamp Program. To ease the burdens of debt, loans were refinanced at low interest rates, and there was also legislation on mortgages. One of the most successful projects was the Tennessee Valley Authority a combination of water control, electric power production, and other activities. Rural electrification was done elsewhere.

In industry minimum wages and maximum working hours became standard. There was also a program to encourage fair competition, but it was later found that the results had hampered competition. Unions, which were very weak in the 1920's, became much stronger. Social Security was begun with programs of old age and unemployment benefits (in cooperation with the states) and provisions for dependant children and the disabled.

The Works Projects Administration was able to employ about a third of the unemployed on public works projects. It constructed 122,000 public buildings, 664,000 miles of roads, and 77,000 bridges, as well as doing many other things.

Why was the Great Depression so much more long-lasting than earlier ones ? Proposed explanations include Dust Bowl agricultural problems, the international depression, the high indebtedness in proportion to income, and the extent of previous overinvestment, especially in durable goods. As previously mentioned, the prosperity of the twenties had gone more to capital than workers. Instead of increasing consumption, those who had it re-invested the money. As a result capacity was built up far above the levels of consumption. Even in 1926 there was excess capacity.

Economists today feel that to end the depression what was needed was much greater levels of government spending. World War II quickly ended it. The average government budget during World War II was roughly 75 billion dollars, where as the highest government budget during the depression years was less than 9 billion (in 1930 only 1.4 billion). In a computer model of the depression economy, H. Theil found a program of taxation and spending that ended it in four years. Much of this material on the depression has been taken from H. Scheiber, H. Vatter, and H. Faulkner (1976).

Conceivably the excess capacity built up in the twenties and the reduced living standard of the thirties helped the economy to make the remarkable effort needed in World War II. The government spending which eliminated the depression as in earlier wars, caused pressure for severe inflation. In principle this problem could be solved by taxation, but this did not prove to be so in practice. A six-fold increase in taxes did not nearly match the increase in spending. Instead rationing and price controls were instituted. These were effective to the extent that the average inflation rate during 1943-1945 was less than 2%. The savings rate went up to 25%, the highest level in American history. J. K. Galbraith attributes part of the success of wage and price controls to the monopoly (oligopoly) power of giant corporations. There was much more difficulty in regulating the more competitive food and clothing markets.

Immediately after the war there was high inflation (about 15%) and instead of the depression many expected to resume, a continuing prosperity.

1.4 THE POST-WAR ERA

The period from 1948 to 1967 was one of prosperity, growth, and low inflation rates. Recessions occurred in 1949, 1954, 1958, and 1961. These appear to be mainly due to the normal course of the business cycle, in which investment grows too rapidly and there develops excess capacity and equipment. In the post-war period the idea of J. M. Keynes expressed in 1936, was the dominant view among professional economists, though only in the Kennedy administration did the U.S. government adopt them. Say's law is that supply creates demand for it. Hence there should be no unemployment: the demand for labor should equal the supply. Keynes theorized that in depressions Say's law breaks down, that instead there is disequilibrium, inequality of supply and demand. His original explanation for this, "liquidity preference," that people prefer to have ready cash instead of investments when the interest rate is too low, is no longer generally held. Galbraith suggests market or monopoly power as a substitute reason for disequilibrium. The way for government to fight depression and recession, according to these ideas, is to increase its spending, and in particular to incur deficits. Such deficits can be paid off by increasing taxes during years of prosperity after the recession has ended. This would also have the desirable effect of restraining the positive half, or boom, in the business cycle. Government spending has its effect on the economy more than its actual amount by a multiplier which equals $\frac{1}{s}$ where s is the marginal propensity to save, the proportion of an increase in income which will be saved instead of consumed.

That government deficits can promote recovery from a recession has been demonstrated by actual events. But there are problems. One is politics. It seems to be impossible to increase taxes when Keynesian theory says they should be increased. Moreover there is a tendency to have a large deficit every election year in order that those running for re-election can point to a prosperous economy.

Another, somewhat related problem is that Keynesian methods seem to be helpless against inflation. About the only instance in which a majority of economists agree they were successful is in the 1964 tax cut, intended to stimulate the economy.

Some see the economic problems of the seventies as a result of the Vietnam War, which was undertaken while attempting to maintain the social programs of the Great Society. The Vietnam

War cost about $25 billion a year at its peak. In 1968 a 10% tax surcharge was enacted, called by Campagna "too little and too late." On the other hand Galbraith feels that the deficits of President Johnson were relatively small, and did not have a major effect in the seventies.

In 1970 there was another recession for which Galbraith blames the end of the stock market boom, which may have come close to being a crash, and the use of monetary policy to fight inflation. Campagna blames inflationary expectations and the 1969 Tax Reform Act, which was less favorable to investors than preceding tax laws.

This recession was the first real instance of stagflation, the simultaneous occurrence of stagnation and inflation (6%). In August 1971 President Nixon reversed his earlier position and instituted wage and price controls because of the inflation. Prices were relatively stable and the GNP resumed increasing. Campagna attributes the recovery to easing of inflationary expectations, increases in defense spending, and in costs of the price support program. Galbraith was one of the proposers of wage and price controls.

The strict controls were ended in November 1971, and a period of more flexible guidances put into effect. Inflation was about 3%. But there were serious foreign trade problems at this time.

Previous exchange rates had become obsolete with increases in European and Japanese productivity. There was a 2 billion dollar trade deficit in the fourth quarter of 1971. People abroad tried to convert dollars into gold. In August 1971 the dollar was taken off the gold standard for international trade by suspending redemption in gold (Roosevelt had earlier done this for trade within the U.S.). A purely symbolic price of gold was still stated. The dollar was also devalued in the fall by various amounts, the largest 17% for yen, relative to foreign currencies. Also exchange rates were made more flexible and reductions in tariffs negotiated.

Phase III, voluntary compliance with guidelines, began in January 1973. It lasted only six months because of a 9% inflation rate when mandatory controls were lifted. Phase IV, roughly the same as Phase II, lasted about a year. Campagna attributes the inflation partly to the recovery to the end of the Vietnam War, and to Watergate.

In the fall came the oil embargo, followed by large increases in the price of oil. Controlled prices and depletion allowances had kept the price of energy artificially low so that the U.S. economy was based on the premise of cheap energy. Energy intensive processes were used instead of labor instensive ones, cities were surrounded with miles of suburbs, and inefficient methods used.

In 1974 there was another recession. Inflation was 11%, unemployment 8%, and the GNP declined 1.3% in real terms. A budget deficit of $45 billion stimulated a business recovery in 1975. The inflation rate was 9% but unemployment remained at 8.5%. Recovery continued in 1976.

During the administration of President Carter unemployment went down to 6%, but inflation became worse. Investment was low, because of the low rate of factory capacity utilization. The growth rate in productivity of the American worker had gradually fallen from 3.4% after World War II to less than 1% in 1977-78.

Our actual productivity as of 1981, is the highest in the world but its increase is quite small. This is a problem because workers have come to be optimistic about wage increases, to expect an ever higher standard of living. Real wage increases can only occur in two ways (1) increases in productivity and (2) by capital and management taking decreases equal to the increase in wages. Companies do not favor the second method. Instead they tend to pass any increase in wages on to the consumer, which causes inflation, and leaves the workers where they were.

The decline in productivity may be due to aging equipment, expenditures on pollution control and safety, less research, more expensive energy, less saving, and a decline in morale illustrated by a 20% absenteeism rate in the automobile industry.

President Carter's voluntary wage and price controls program failed. Inflation was the main problem but economists predicted a recession, which did not come until 1980 and then was mild. There were more problems with oil in 1979, and sales of grain to the Soviet Union, previously the main hope of balancing international trade and keeping up farm prices, were terminated. Inflation was 13% in 1979 and about 11% in 1980. Interest rates reached 20% in an attempt to control inflation by slowing the growth of the money supply.

President Reagan proposes to severely cut the budget, hoping eventually to balance it, ease pollution standards, practice supply-side economics in encouraging business to rise to the level of demand, restore grain sales to the Soviet Union, and encourage domestic oil production. Down to the middle of 1981, inflation has gone down to 8%, possibly partly due to a surplus of oil.

Other economic aspects of the decade include the near bankruptcy of New York and other cities, and of Chrysler, the general problems of the cities, unemployment of young people and minorities, the problem of farmers with low prices, high inheritance and property taxes, and competition between family farms and corporations, international economic problems, bank loans to developing nations which are in danger of default, immigration from Latin America and of refugees, attempts to limit defense spending, the increasing proportion of older people and possible bankruptcy of Social Security, an increase in personal credit, rising medical and housing costs, and continuing technological progress.

1.5 THE NEED FOR NEW CONCEPTS

It appears that the classical concepts of economics may not be adequate to describe and perhaps solve today's economic dilemmas. People are unemployed, yet there is demand for goods they could produce. Instead of perfect competition, monopoly and oligopoly are present in various industries, and in labor. Inflation seems inversely related to unemployment, but the relationship changes over time. Inflation is related to related to expectations of future inflation, not just the current economic state. Keynesian methods of stimulating an economy by deficit spending appear to cause more inflation instead of providing a real solution. A monetarist solution to inflation seems to require a great price in terms of recession.

Some economies such as France, Germany, Sweden, Japan are planned by the government to a considerable degree, and have been quite successful. Everywhere government plays a role comparable to if not greater than the private sector. People are impatient with inequality due to an impersonal market system in which the farmer, for instance, is highly productive but gets deeper and deeper in debt. Yet income transfers by traditional standards distort incentives and cause inefficiency.

As technology becomes more complex, the world is more closely linked together, and man's effect on nature becomes more powerful, it becomes unrealistic to consider only goods produced, bought and sold without the side effects of production or consumption, known as externalities. Pollution is the best-known such side effect. There are other situations in which firms each seeking to maximize profits, engage in behavior that is harmful or inefficient, because of externalities, things not reflected directly in monetary transactions. A study of public goods such as education cannot use only the idea of a market. In development of new energy sources, basic research is a public good, which only the government or a cooperative group can effectively provide, since its benefits extend to those firms who don't pay for it, the free-riders. But technology, some feel, should be decided by the market system.

Campagna noted that neither monetarism nor Keynesianism seems to have a method of overcoming stagflation. The question of distribution seems very important, yet it is not one that earlier mathematical economics readily deals with. Major forces in modern economies include oligopoly, or competition of a few large companies, the struggle between corporations and unions for income shares, government, the desire of the public to preserve the environment, the question of how much should be spent on social programs, public expectations.

There are two types of concepts which can be used to study such questions of distribution (1) social welfare functions, giving the normative or ideal aspect of a distribution, and (2) game theory, answering the positive or objective question, what distribution will actually result from a power structure.

Social welfare functions and their variants, social choice functions, social decision functions, social arbitration functions express the idea of group preference, what does an entire group prefer, if the preferences of its members are not unanimous. If the possible individual preferences can be arranged suitably along a 1-dimensional scale (single-peaked preferences), then majority rule is a social welfare function. With the major role played by government, the study of majority rule has importance in economics as will as political science.

Yet for many purposes majority voting is not a satisfactory method of deciding the value of a proposal to society. It ignores a minority, is not always consistent, and does not take into account questions of intensity of feeling. A theorem of Kenneth Arrow shows that these problems cannot be solved without supposing something like interpersonal comparison of utilities, or values. That is, the value of one thing to one person can be said to be greater, or equal, or less than the value of another thing to another person.

Given interpersonal comparison of utilities, several types of social preference functions can be constructed. The simplest, basically Jeremy Bentham's utilitarianism, adds the utilities of the members of society. It has been uniquely characterized by John Harsanyi in terms of probabilistic rationality. Another is the leximin relation, in which the welfare of the worst off individuals are the basis for comparison between two social states. A third is the Nash social welfare function, in which minimum utilities are assigned in some way and the socially most desired state is considered as the outcome of such that the product of utility gains over some fixed base state, is a maximum.

Game theory does not consider the relative merits of social states but rather which social state will emerge from the actions of individuals who are rational and motivated by self-interest. Classical economics is one special case of this idea, the case in which there are so many agents that the effect of each on the total is insignificant.

No solution concept has been formulated which is for all types of games. For non-cooperative games the basic idea is that of (Nash) equilibrium: a set of strategies for which no individual would desire to change his strategy, given the strategies of the other players. Other fundamental ideas include dominant strategies, ones which are best regardless of what the other players do, and maximin strategies, which minimize the loss in the worst possible case.

For pure bargaining games, the Nash bargaining solution follows from simple assumptions, as do two alternative theories of Raiffa, Crott, Germeier, Kalai and Smorodinsky, and Kalai. For games in which coalitions can win specified amounts, and divide it arbitrarily the $M_1^{(i)}$ bargaining solution is perhaps the simplest behaviorally justified solution concept which always exists. Various refinements include the kernel, nucleolus, and $M_1^{(im)}$ solutions.

A committee game is a cooperative game in which certain subsets of the players, called winning coalitions, can achieve any outcome they agree on. For instance a winning coalition could be defined as a majority or as a $\frac{2}{3}$ majority. This is a model of a committee which makes its decisions by majority rule, or some similar method. Solutions have been formulated which use such factors as the number of winning coalitions who prefer some other outcome, and sets of coalitions and outcomes each prefers, related to one another.

John Harsanyi developed a quite general cooperative solution concept related to the Shapley value, which was generalized by Shapley in a different way, the λ-transfer value. There is an ordinal bargaining set generalizing $M_1^{(i)}$. The core is defined very generally but does not exist for many games.

Recent economic applications of game theory, primarily the Nash equilibrium, include the theories of noncooperative equilibrium, of incentive compatible mechanisms, and of the principal agent problem. In addition the market has been characterized as the solution to various games. Noncooperative equilibrium deals with the problem of a small number of economic competitors, each of whom can affect the total market, and can raise prices. One problem in studying this phenomenon is that equilibrium generally fails to exist, that is the situation is unstable. This can provide on explanation of inflation. Difficulties in making this quantitative are to fix a time-scale, and the extent to which players anticipate each other's actions.

Incentive compatible mechanisms are those in which self-interest causes the participants to act "honestly," according to the system. Examples include majority voting between two choices, the market under perfect competition, and strictly hierarchical systems. Frequently Nash equilibrium is required to exist and give a Pareto optimum, that is an outcome from which there is no way for everyone to improve his utility. One important problem is to devise incentive compatible mechanisms which deal with public goods, for which the market is inadequate. A second is to study incentive compatibility of welfare capitalism with Pareto optimality only within the set of incentive compatible schemes.

The principal agent problem is a reformulation of basically the same question. Consider an organization headed by a "principal" who has incomplete knowledge about the situations of his subordinates. The subordinates will react to any structure he chooses so as to maximize their own welfare levels. How can the principal design a system so that this behavior has the best results for him ?

These questions are also relevant to the question of market versus centralized economies. Strong point of the market system is basically its incentive compatibility, together with simplicity and ease of administration. On the other hand a weakness of most centralized economies is that firms and individuals have incentives to conceal the true amount they can produce, lest this become a quota. One type of centralized economy has been shown unstable (Ericson, 1981). Possibly these defects can be overcome.

1.6 CONCLUSION

The U.S. economy has a history of exuberant growth and flexibility, but also panics and depressions. Prior to the effects of the New Deal and the growth of strong labor unions there was much economic inequality between farmers and workers and management and capital. The experiment of laissez-faire capitalism in the nineteenthe century had undesirable results, and government now plays a very large role in the economy.

From World War II there was steady growth and prosperity until about 1970, interrupted about every five years by a small recession. The Keynesian method of deficit spending could pretty much have prevented even these. In 1970 a near-collapse of the stock market began an era of stagnation and inflation. It is not clear how much the Vietnam War had to do with this, since by current standards deficits were not large. Attempts to control modern inflation by monetary policy may have played a role. Wage and price controls were instituted but as soon as they were made voluntary, inflation started up again. There were foreign trade problems. The oil embargo and other factors led to a recession in 1974. During the remainder of the decade unemployment was reduced at the expense of higher inflation. A mild, delayed recession occurred in 1980 accompanied by 11% inflation. The current administration proposes to reduce federal spending and encourage the supply side of the economy. The present economy involves powerful giant corporations and labor unions, a decreasing rate of productivity, much credit, fights over the environment and energy, and problems in the cities and among farmers.

Older economic concepts do not adequately explain stagflation or show how to deal with public goods. In this book we intend to show how newer concepts of social welfare functions, noncooperative equilibrium, and incentive compatibility may help.

CHAPTER 2

EQUILIBRIUM

2.1 INTRODUCTION

The first section deals with the famous law of supply and demand for prices, wages, rents on land and resources, profits, and the interest rate. If supply is less than demand, any producer will find it profitable to raise prices. If supply is greater than demand, in the absence of monopoly new competitors will find it profitable to enter the market and lower the price. Supply is determined largely by costs of production.

The second explains demand in terms of individual preferences for different goods. These preferences can be conveniently represented by what is called utility. Consumers choose so as to maximize utility, and this gives rise to demand. Demand for a specific good must be estimated from actual data about it. Three mathematical formulas are commonly used to approximate total demand: the linear expenditure system, the Rotterdam model, and the addilog model.

The third section presents an informal version of the equations for prices of all goods in a simple market economy. Fairly recent methods in mathematics including fixed theorems and differential topology are needed to study existence, uniqueness, and stability of prices.

The fourth section discusses the advantages of the market system. It is efficient and under perfect competition is the only system for which it is to the advantage of every individual and group to support the system.

2.2 SUPPLY AND DEMAND

Adam Smith in 1876 argued that supply and demand determine the prices of goods, the wages of workers, the rents on land, the rate of profit, and the interest rate, in essentially the same way. The prices of goods are such that supply of a good at that price equals its demand at that price. When supply equals demand, the economy is said to be in equilibrium. This is an idealization, since the two will never be exactly equal. The case of disequilibrium occurs in inflation caused by decreased supply or excess demand, in unemployment, and under legal restrictions on trade.

The argument is that if prices for a good are too high, so that supply exceeds demand, then sellers will lower prices in order to sell their goods. If prices are too low, so that demand exceeds supply, sellers can raise their prices and sell all they have, and increase revenue, so they will do this. Quantitative versions of this process are called *tatonnement processes*, and the exact mechanism is a subject of debate.

This type of equilibrium will not hold true under conditions of oligopoly, when competitive sellers can make greater profits by raising their prices, perhaps restricting or destroying part of their production. Instead it is relevant to situations close to perfect competition, when no one can raise his price without losing business to another.

Under any form of competition, prices will not remain too low. However under some conditions it will be more profitable for a seller to sell all of his good at a high price than all of it at the equilibrium. One argument that prices will not be too high at equilibrium is that if there are many sellers and prices are such that demand is short of supply then some sellers on a statistical basis will almost surely sell none of their goods. So it would certainly be to the advantage of these to lower prices. Unless everyone follows suit, some seller's high-priced goods will not sell, and it will be to his advantage to reduce prices.

Easley and Ledyard (1981) give a specific model of this nature for an auction, which yields convergence to the equilibrium price. There are buyers and sellers, of a single good.

Each buyer and seller has a schedule telling the value to him of any number of units of the good. Sellers sell only at prices at least as great as the values of the goods to them. Each time period in theory there is a new supply of goods. As longs as it is possible buyers make no bids higher than the highest bid of the previous time, and sellers accept no prices lower than the lowest price of the previous time. Within this range trading is random. When all possible such trades have been made, if further trades can be made without loss, buyers will raise prices and sellers lower them. Theoretically the price will converge to equilibrium, and convergence according to theory occurred also experimentally.

The best-known example of near-perfect competition is in agricultural goods, where there are many small, independent producers (though the distribution system is one of oligopoly). It is a well-known problem of farmers that if crops are good, there is an oversupply and prices fall. It is also noteworthy that agriculture is an economic problem in most countries. Clothing is also fairly competitive, as is housing.

There is disagreement as to how far from competitive various markets are in which a few large companies predominate: automobiles, television, energy, computers, appliances. There seems to be fairly keen competition in some of these on the basis of consumer appeal and stylistic distinction, for instance television ratings, and advertisements for cigarettes. But price competition seems less prevalent.

The numerical values of prices can in principle be calculated from supply and demand functions. The supply function gives the quantity of a good that producers will find it worthwhile to produce and sell at a given price. This is usually illustrated by a curve in which price is plotted against supply.

Under perfect competition, price will generally equal marginal cost, the cost of producing 1 extra unit of the good. The reason is that if price exceed marginal cost, a competitor could enter the industry, make price closer to marginal cost, and make a profit.

Adam Smith concluded that in a static economy without unions or minimum wage legislation the same would be true of the wage of labor. The basic wage would be the minimum amount on which a man could support himself and his family. Unusually difficult, unpleasant, or dangerous work would pay more. He attributed the higher wages at that time in American than in England to the fact that our economy was expanding very rapidly. An expanding economy will have wages above the subsistence level. If it is true that in a static economy, market forces tend to reduce wages to a minimum, this could partly explain the present dilemma of stagflation. Productivity increases are slight, and the efforts of labor to resist the downward market forces on wages may cause inflation. But this is only one aspect of the noncooperative equilibrium problem we will consider later.

Adam Smith anticipated Karl Marx in considering labor as the basic standard of value (although as productivity increases this standard must also change). But to Marx, labor was the only source of value. He did not, like Smith, take into account rents on land and other resources. That is, if one person allows another to farm his land, the owner expects payments in return. In poor agricultural countries, the share cropping system has been the main alternative to serfdom. Smith predicted that shares would be such that the farmer would keep the minimum needed for his family to subsist and to continue his operations. Frequently shares have been as high as 50% in various countries. A major purpose of land reform is to alleviate this problem. While ethically there seems some reason to agree with Marx that the landlord does not deserve pay for letting someone else farm his land, rents are a necessity in a market system in order to allocate scarce resources efficiently. That is, land that is best for growing wheat should be devoted to wheat production and land that is best for growing grapes to vineyards. The market system should in general do this. Land that is very good for growing a certain crop will have such a high price that only that crop can profitably be grown on it. In a similar way, timber, oil and other resources should in principle be used efficiently in a market system. There are some exceptions. First, externalities occur, in which one person's activity affects others in ways not accounted for by the market system. For example in fishing, no one owns the world's breeding stock of fish. So it may be profitable for private enterprise to fish a certain species to extinction, even if this is contrary to national welfare. The market system may encourage immediate exploitation instead of conservation, since future goods are not financially as valuable as those today. The market value of almost anything payable 100 years from now would not be great today. There are questions of pollution. Regarding energy, government policy has kept its price artificially low. And there is the question in economies, efficient for whom ? If the wealthy own provide most of the demand for a good, its allocation will be efficient in providing benefits mainly for them. By the standards of more impartial social arbitration functions we will later develop the market allocation might not be as good as others.

The expected return on investments varies with the degree of risk. However for a given risk investors will seek the most profitable investments, so that profits should be more or less constant, a rent on capital. In practice, profits are highly unpredictable. Profits are the mechanism of development and growth in a capitalist economy. A major problem faced by countries wishing to industrialize is to acquire the necessary capital or facilities: factory equipment, electricity, transportation, communication, education. In capitalist countries this is performed by the wealthy. They have no need to consume all their income and may prefer to invest the portion they save, expecting more in return, to simply hoarding it. Centralized economies accomplish this by forced saving. In all cases some agricultural surplus is needed.

The interest rate is determined by the supply and demand for monetary loans. It can be kept high by actions of the Federal Reserve Board. It is also related to the rate of profit since in the absence of risk a person with surplus wealth would invest or loan it according to which gave the highest rate of return. Thus high interest rates will very much reduce investment in activities whose expected returns are less. If interest rates are low, as sometimes they have been by law, money for loans may be scarce in a market system.

Numerically, prices are derived from supply and demand curves. Let $s(p)$ be the quantity of a good supplied at price p

and d(p) the demand for it at price p. Then the equilibrium price p will be the solution to the equation s(p) = d(p). Let c(s) be the cost of producing the quantity s of a good. Then net income from producing it is c(s) - ps. This will be a maximum if $\frac{dc}{ds} - p = 0$, or $\frac{dc}{ds} = p$. By definition $\frac{dc}{ds}$ is marginal cost. Approximately it can be viewed as the cost of producing 1 extra unit of a commodity. Thus marginal cost and price should be equal. If net income were not a maximum, under perfect competition, someone would find it profitable to enter the market to increase supply. This reasoning does not hold under conditions of monopoly or oligopoly, since prices will not be constant but can be affected by the actions of individual producers.

So in principle, marginal cost explains supply.

We now study utility and substitution.

The more mysterious of the two is demand. Total demand for a good at a given price is the sum of the demands of each individual for it at that price. The demand of an individual is determined by substitution with other goods. If no other good could replace it, like oxygen to breathe, his demand would be a constant. At any price he would require the same amount. However in general substitutes can be found. If one form of food or recreation is too expensive then many people will consume more of a cheaper form.

Consumer preferences are the underlying determinants of demand. Specifically for all possible amounts of different commodities that can be bought with a given amount of money, which does a consumer most prefer ? This, given his income, is his contribution to the total demand. Technically, a specified amount of each of a collection of commodities is called a *commodity bundle*. For instance 5 pounds of sugar and two loaves of bread is a commodity bundle.

The preferences of a rational individual with perfect powers of discrimination should have two properties: transitivity and completeness. *Transitivity* means if one bundle is considered at least as good as a second and the second at least as good as the third, then the first bundle is at least as good as the third bundle. Intransitivity can happen for actual people, due to lack of perfect discrimination, or arbitrary decision procedures.

Many results of economics are valid even without transitivity. *Completeness* means that for any two bundles, either one is preferred, or both are equally good.

On a finite set, any relation having the properties of transitivity and completeness can be assigned a numerical scale. There will be some alternative or alternatives which are equally good among themselves, but are preferred to all others. These can be assigned the highest number. In turn the less preferred groups can be assigned lower numbers. Infinitely many different assignments are possible. For instance if a is preferred to b to c, the following are all valid utility functions.

$$\begin{cases} u(a) = 3, & u(b) = 2, & u(c) = 1 \\ u(a) = 10, & u(b) = 5, & u(c) = 0 \\ u(a) = 100, & u(b) = 99, & u(c) = 1 \end{cases}$$

In the case of commodity bundles there is an infinite range of possibilities to be considered. That is the quantity of each good is considered as being any real number (perhaps less than a certain maximum). In this situation preferences should ordinarily have a third property, continuity. That an individual's preferences are *continuous* means, if he considers $x_1, x_2, x_3, \ldots$ at least as good as y (or no better than y) and $x_1, x_2, x_3, \ldots$ approach x as limit, then he regards x as at least as good as y (or no better than y). It is a theorem of G. Debreu (1959) that if an individual's preferences are continuous, transitive, and complete, then there exists a continuous function u such that $u(x) \geq u(y)$ if and only if the individual considers x at least as good as y. For example he might prefer x_1 units of food and y_1 units of clothing to x_2 units of food and y_2 units of clothing if and only if $x_1y_1 > x_2y_2$. In this case xy would be a utility function for him.

Again utility functions are not unique in this situation. If u is a utility function and g is a continuous, monotone increasing function from the real numbers to the real numbers, then g(u) is also a utility function. For example for any real number p, the utility function $(xy)^p$ represents the same preferences as xy. This situation will be changed in later chapters when we take up expected utility and interpersonal comparison.

Consider a market with n individual and m goods. Then a commodity bundle is a vector, or n-tuple, $(x_1, x_2, \ldots, x_m)$ where x_j is the quantity of good j in the bundle. Let x_i be the set of possible consumption bundles of individual i.

DEFINITION 2.2.1. A *binary relation* on X_i is a set of ordered pairs from X_i, i.e., a subset of $X_i \times X_i$.

EXAMPLE 2.2.1. The relation $x = y$ on the real numbers is represented by the set of all ordered pairs (x, y) such that $x = y$, such as (1, 1) and (5, 5).

The *preference relation* is similarly the set of all pairs (x_1, x_2) such that individual i considers x_1 at least as good as x_2.

DEFINITION 2.2.2. That a binary relation r is *transitive* means if $(a, b) \in r$ and $(b, c) \in r$ then $(a, c) \in r$. That it is *complete* means for all (a, b) in the domain either (a, b) r or $(b, a) \in r$. A transitive complete relation is called a *weak order*.

EXAMPLE 2.2.2. The relation $x = y$ is a weak order. The relation $x = y$ is transitive but is not complete.

DEFINITION 2.2.3. A set of points in n-dimensional space is *closed* if it contains all its limit points. A preference relation r is *continuous* if for all $a \in X_i$ the sets $\{x: (a, x) \in r\}$ and $\{x: (x, a) \in r\}$ are closed.

EXAMPLE 2.2.3. A circle or square with its boundary and interior is closed. The relation $x \geq y$ is continuous.

DEFINITION 2.2.4. A *utility function* is a continuous real valued function u such that $u(x) \geq u(y)$ if and only if (x, y) belongs to the preference relation of an individual.

EXAMPLE 2.2.4. For any continuous real-valued function u, u is the utility function of the relation $\{(x, y): u(x) \geq u(y)\}$.

A utility function corresponds to a unique binary relation. However for any monotone increasing function g, u and g(u) represent the same binary relation.

DEFINITION 2.2.5. A subset X of n-dimensional space is *compact* if it is closed and for some real number m, no coordinate of a point of X has absolute value larger than m. It is *convex* if for all u, v in X the line segment with endpoints u, v lies in X.

EXAMPLE 2.2.5. The disk $\{(x, y): x^2 + y^2 \leq 1\}$ is compact and convex.

THEOREM 2.2.1. *Any continuous weak order r on a compact convex subset X can be represented by a utility function. (This theorem is also true without compactness and convexity).*

Sketch of Proof. We first show any closed subset K of X has a point which is maximal in the weak order. Following Hildenbrand and Kirman (1976), let $C_z = \{x: (x, z) \in r\}$. Then for any finite collection $z_1, z_2, \ldots, z_k$ there is a largest member of $z_1, z_2, \ldots, z_k$ in r, by induction on k. (This uses transitivity and completeness). This element belongs in $C_{z_1} \cap C_{z_2} \cap \ldots \cap C_{z_q}$. Thus any finite family of sets C_z has nonempty intersection. By a property of compactness, since the C_z are closed, $\cap C_z \neq \emptyset$. An element a in $\cap C_z$ has $(a, z) \in r$ for all r and is therefor a largest element. Likewise there is a smallest element.

Let b, a be largest and smallest elements of X. By convexity every element of the segment L from b to a lies in X.

We will show that for any element $x \in X$ there exists $x_1 \in L$ which is equivalent to x in the sense that (x, x_1) and (x_1, x) both belong to r. Every element of L belongs to either $\{y \in L: (y, x) \in r\}$ or $\{y \in L: (x, y) \in r\}$ by completeness. So these two closed nonempty sets have union L. Since L is connected they have nonzero intersection. It suffices to let x_1 be a point of the intersection.

It will suffice to define v on the line segment L, since elsewhere v can be obtained by setting $v(x) = v(x_1)$. This will first be done for a set of midpoints. First define v on a, b so that the ordering is correct. Now divide L into two equal parts. If the midpoint m is between a, b in r, set

$$v(m) = \frac{v(a) + v(b)}{2}$$

If m is equivalent to one of a, b, let that give the definition. At the next stage divide each half of L in two. Map the midpoint to the image of an equivalent point if there is one already defined, or to the midpoint of v(s), v(t) where s, t are the closest point in r above and below on which v has already been defined. Continue this process. This will give a function v from the set M of midpoints and a, b to the real numbers which represents correctly the r-ordering.

Moreover v(M) is dense in [v(a), v(b)]. Suppose not. Let c be a point of the interval not in $\overline{v(M)}$. Let $e = \inf \{v(x): v(x) > c\}$, $f = \sup \{v(x): v(x) < c\}$. Choose points y_1, y_2 of M such that $e < v(y_1) < e + \frac{e - f}{3}$, $f > v(y_2) > f - \frac{e - f}{3}$, and so that no point of M occurring earlier in the midpoint process lies in $[v(y_2), v(y_1)]$. Consider the first point of M which lies strictly between y_1, y_2 in the r-ordering. Then v on this point is

$$\frac{v(y_1) + v(y_2)}{2}$$

which lies strictly between e, f. This contradicts the definition of e or f. This proves density.

For $x \notin M$, let $v(x) = \inf \{v(y): y \in M, (y, x) \in r\}$. For $x \in M$ this agrees with the previous definition.

From the definition in terms of inf it is immediate that if $(x, y) \in r$ then $v(x) \geq v(y)$. If $(x, y) \in r$ but $(y, x) \notin r$ we can find some elements $z, w \in M$ with $(x, z) \in r$, $(z, w) \in r$, $(w, y) \in r$, and $(w, z) \notin r$. Thus $v(x) \geq v(z) > v(w) \geq v(y)$.

By the order property just proved any discontinuity of v has a gap form, i.e., x_n converges to x in the r-ordering and is increasing but $v(x) > \sup v(x_n)$ or the reverse. But this contradicts the fact that v has dense image, since there will exist a point $v(y)$ of $v(M)$ between $v(x)$ and $\sup v(x_n)$. But then some x_m will exceed y in the v ordering by convergence. So $v(x_m) > \sup v(x_m)$, a contradiction. Therefore v is continuous. And these properties on L imply the extension to all of X also has them. This completes the proof. □

As an example of the passage from utility to demand function, consider the linear expenditure system.

$$v = \Sigma \mu_i \log (q_i - \gamma_i)$$

To find demand, maximize this subject to the constraint $\Sigma p_i q_i = n$. This can conveniently be done by the method of Lagrange multipliers. Let λ be the Lagrange multiplier. Then

$$\Sigma \mu_i \log (q_i - \gamma_i) - \lambda \Sigma p_i q_i$$

is to have zero partial derivative with respect to each q_i.

$$\begin{cases} \dfrac{\mu_i}{q_i - \gamma_i} = \lambda p_i \\ (q_i - \gamma_i) p_i = \lambda^{-1} \mu_i \end{cases}$$

Thus as mentioned earlier the expenditures $(q_i - \gamma_i)p_i$ above the minimum γ_i on the ith good are proportional to μ_i.

Several additional assumptions are typically made on utility functions: that they are twice-continuously differentiable, monotone increasing in each variable, and quasi-concave. The first assumption is made largely for mathematical convenience, and is not very restrictive. Monotonicity means that if all goods but one are hold constant, a person would always prefer that good be increased, in other words there is no maximum amount he wants. Within a certain range, this is reasonable in economics. The last is that if a person considers x at least as good as z and y at least as good as z, then for him the $\frac{x + y}{2}$ is at least as good as z. For instance, a person would typically prefer a mixture of food and clothing supplies to all food and no clothing or all clothing and no food. Strict quasi-concavity means that $\frac{x + y}{2}$ is considered strictly better than z where x, y, z are as above.

Suppose the individual receives income M. The set of commodity bundles $(x_1, \ldots, x_m)$ he can purchase are those such that

$$p \cdot x \leq M$$

where $p = (p_1, \ldots, p_m)$ represent prices of the items in question and $p \cdot x$ is

$$p_1x_1 + p_2x_2 + \cdots + p_mx_m$$

in other words, the total expense of buying the bundle. Under the assumptions mentioned above, the problem of maximizing u(x) for $p \cdot x \leq M$ will have a solution, which is unique if u is strictly quasi-concave. This solution is the individual's choice as to what goods he most prefers (maximum u) in other words, those he will try to purchase. This gives the amount of each good which he demands. It will depend continuously on prices and income. The sum of all the individual demand functions give aggregate, or total demand.

Individual demand can be shown generally to be the point $(x_1, \ldots, x_n)$ such that the ratios of prices of any two goods equals the ratio of their marginal utilities (increase in utility obtained by adding 1 unit of each commodity). If this were not so, by increasing the amount of the good with higher utility to price ratio, and reducing the other, total utility could be increased. Since $(x_1, \ldots, x_n)$ makes u a maximin, this cannot be.

Demand depends on utility in a complicated way. If the price of a good is increased (assuming income increases enough to make the original purchase possible, or else that it does not affect the assortment of goods selected) then the marginal utility/price ratio will decrease. Then the amount of it in the purchase bundle will decrease and the amount of the other goods increase until the marginal utility/price ratios again are equal. Thus the demand depends on degrees of satiation for goods in various combinations, reflected in marginal utility ratios.

The effect of a price change in demand can be split into two parts. An income part reflects the fact that a higher price means money to buy other goods. A substitution part means that if the price of one good is raised people will increase consumption of other goods as substitutes.

More precisely, for an individual, let x_j be his demand for good j, u utility, p_j price of good j, M income. The *demand* is a function $x_j(p, M)$ of prices and income. However it can also be taken as a function of prices and utility.

DEFINITION 2.2.6. Let $C(p, u_0) = \inf \{p \cdot y: u(y) = u_0\}$.

In other words $C(p, u_0)$ is the minimum amount of income needed to attain utility level u_0.

Let $x_j(p, u_0) = x_j(p, M)$ such that $M = C(p, u_0)$. This expresses demand in terms of price and utility.

LEMMA 2.2.2. $\dfrac{\partial C}{\partial p_j} = x_j$.

Proof. For any small increase h in the price of good j,

$$C(p + h, u_0) \leq C(p, u_0) + hx_j(p, u_0)$$

since with the amount of money on the right, the individual could purchase the same bundle as with $C(p, u_0)$ to obtain utility level

u_0. But also

$$C(p, u_0) \le C(p + h, u_0) - hx_j(p + h, u_0)$$

since with the amount of money on the right, the individual could purchase the same bundle as with $C(p + h, u_0)$.

Assuming x_j is continuous, these two inequalities imply the lemma. □

This lemma means that the effect of change in prices on income needed to sustain a certain utility can be calculated as if the consumption bundle were constant.

THEOREM 2.2.3. $\dfrac{\partial x_i(p, M)}{\partial p_j} = \dfrac{\partial x_i(p, u_0)}{\partial p_j} - \dfrac{\partial x_i(p, M)}{\partial M} x_j$.

Proof. We differentiate the equation

$$x_i(p, u_0) = x_i(p, M) = x_i(p, C(p, u_0))$$

to obtain

$$\frac{\partial x_i(p, u_0)}{\partial p_j} = \frac{\partial x_i(p, M)}{\partial p_j} + \frac{\partial x_i(p, M)}{\partial M} \frac{\partial C}{\partial p_j}$$

The theorem follows from the above lemma by rearranging terms. □

The first term on the right is considered to be the substitution effect and the second is considered to be the income effect.

The matrix (s_{ij}) given by

$$s_{ij} = \frac{\partial x_i(p, u_0)}{\partial p_j}$$

is called the *Slutsky matrix*.

Let

$$u_{ij} = \frac{\partial^2 u}{\partial x_i \partial x_j}$$

and $U = (u_{ij})$. Since marginal utilities will be proportional to prices we have

$$\frac{\partial u}{\partial x_i} = \lambda p_i \tag{2.2.1}$$

for some λ, for all i.

THEOREM 2.2.4. $s_{ij} = \lambda(U^{-1})_{ij} - \frac{\lambda}{\xi}\frac{\partial x_i}{\partial m}\frac{\partial x_j}{\partial m}$, $\xi = \frac{\partial \lambda}{\partial m}$

Proof. By differentiating (2.2.1) with respect to m and p_i we have a matrix relation

$$\begin{cases} U\left(\frac{\partial x}{\partial m}\right) = \left(\frac{\partial \lambda}{\partial m}\right)p \\ U\left(\frac{\partial x_i}{\partial p_j}\right) = \lambda I + p\left(\frac{\partial \lambda}{\partial p}\right)^T \end{cases}$$

Here I is an identity matrix. By differentiating the formula $p^T x = M$ with respect to m and p_i we have

$$\begin{cases} p^T\left(\frac{\partial x}{\partial m}\right) = 1 \\ p^T\left(\frac{\partial x_i}{\partial p_j}\right) = -x^T \end{cases}$$

These give the *Fundamental Matrix Equation of Consumer Demand Theory*,

$$\begin{bmatrix} U & p \\ p^T & 0 \end{bmatrix}\begin{bmatrix} \frac{\partial x}{\partial m} & \frac{\partial x}{\partial p^T} \\ -\frac{\partial \lambda}{\partial m} & -\frac{\partial \lambda}{\partial p^T} \end{bmatrix} = \begin{bmatrix} 0 & \lambda I \\ 1 & -x^T \end{bmatrix}$$

The first matrix has the explicit inverse, where $\alpha = p^T U^{-1} p$

$$\alpha^{-1}\begin{bmatrix} U^{-1} - (U^{-1}p)(U^{-1}p)^T & U^{-1}p \\ (U^{-1}p)^T & -1 \end{bmatrix}$$

This gives

$$\begin{cases} (\frac{\partial x}{\partial m}) = \alpha^{-1}U^{-1}p \\ (\frac{\partial \lambda}{\partial m}) = \alpha^{-1} \end{cases}$$

$$\begin{cases} (\frac{\partial x}{\partial p^T}) = \lambda U^{-1} - \lambda\alpha^{-1}(U^{-1}p)(U^{-1}p)^T - \alpha^{-1}U^{-1}px^T \\ (\frac{\partial \lambda}{\partial p^T}) = -\lambda\alpha^{-1}U^{-1}p - \alpha^{-1}q \end{cases}$$

This gives

$$\begin{cases} (\frac{\partial x}{\partial m}) = (\frac{\partial \lambda}{\partial m})U^{-1}p \\ \alpha(\frac{\partial x}{\partial m}) = (\frac{\partial \lambda}{\partial m})^{-1}(\frac{\partial x}{\partial m}) = U^{-1}p \end{cases}$$

And we have

$$\begin{cases} (\frac{\partial x}{\partial p^T}) = \lambda U^{-1} - \lambda(\frac{\partial \lambda}{\partial m})^{-1}(\frac{\partial x}{\partial m})(\frac{\partial x}{\partial m})^T - (\frac{\partial x}{\partial m})x^T \\ S = \lambda U^{-1} - \lambda(\frac{\partial \lambda}{\partial m})^{-1}(\frac{\partial x}{\partial m})(\frac{\partial x}{\partial m})^T \end{cases}$$

This proves the theorem. □

COROLLARY. *The Slutsky matrix S is symmetric.*

Proof. Since U is symmetric, so is U^{-1}. □

This means that the substitution effect of good i on good j equals the substitution effect of good j on good i.

EXAMPLE 2.2.6. For utility function of the form $\Pi x_i^{\mu_i}$ demand is given by $x_i p_i = \mu_i m$. Thus the total price effects

$$\begin{cases} \frac{\partial x_i}{\partial p_j} = -\mu_i m(p_i)^{-2} & \text{for } i = j \\ \frac{\partial x_i}{\partial p_j} = 0 & \text{for } i \neq j \end{cases}$$

and the income effects are

$$x_j \frac{\partial x_i}{\partial m} = \frac{\mu_i \mu_j m}{p_i p_j}$$

The difference gives the Slutsky matrix, which will be symmetric.
□

EXAMPLE 2.2.7. Suppose the utility function is $ax + \frac{h}{2} x^T x$ where a is a constant vector, h is a constant scalar. It can be shown that demand is given by

$$hx = -a + \frac{p^T a}{p^T p} p + \frac{mh}{p^T p} p$$

$$\frac{\partial x}{\partial m} = \frac{1}{p^T p} p$$

Thus the income effects are

$$h^{-1}\left(-a + \frac{p^T a}{p^T p} p + \frac{mh}{p^T p} p\right)\left(\frac{p^T}{p^T p}\right)$$

which is not in general symmetric. But by the theorem, the substitution effects are

$$\lambda h^{-1}(I - (pp^T)(p^T p)^{-1}), \quad \lambda = \frac{p^T a}{p^T p} + \frac{mh}{p^T p}$$

and this is symmetric.

There does not exist a general theoretical formula for demand in terms of price. Instead from statistical studies of particulars goods, numerical approximations are found. Three types of approximating formulas are generally used for utility: *CES*, *quadratic*, and the *addilog indirect utility model* (Theil 1975). Klein-Rubin utilities generalizing the CES (constant elasticity of substitution) are

$$u = \Sigma \mu_i \log (q_i - \gamma_i) \quad \text{or} \quad \Pi (q_i - \gamma_i)^{\mu_i}$$

where u is utility, q_i is the quantity of good i, γ_i is a constant equal to the minimum purchase of good i, and μ_i is a constant related to elasticity of substitution.

In this system, income expenditure on good i equals the minimum expenditure plus an amount proportional to μ_i. Thus above the minimum expenditure, demand of good i is inversely proportional to its price. This type of demand function is called the *linear expenditure system*. CES or *Cobb-Douglas utilities* result when $\gamma_i = 0$.

The price elasticity of demand is the most important single quantity associated with the demand function, other than demand itself. It is the rate of increase of demand in terms of price, expressed as a proportion of current demand. From it changes in demand resulting from price changes can be predicted, if price changes are not too large.

The quadratic utility function expresses utility as an arbitrary second degree function of quantities. Since any twice-differentiable can be approximated by a quadratic function, this is a completely general approximation. Demand is then a ratio of quadratic functions in the prices. The *Rotterdam model* is an approximation to this for small changes.

The addilog model deals with the indirect utility function, which expresses an individual's utility in terms of income and price. It assumes this is given by

$$u = \Sigma A_i \left(\frac{p_i}{m}\right)^{\alpha_i}$$

where u is utility, A_i and α_i are constants, p_i is the price of good i, m is income.

One way to regard demand is as analogous to the output of a manufacturer. If the price of some input rises, it may be more productive to adopt a different process which uses a smaller proportion of this input. If there are a continuous range of available processes, a continuous demand function might arise. Yet the form of the demand function seems to depend on the specific processes involved.

Preference independence, the hypothesis that u has the form $\Sigma\ u_i q_i$, is frequently a valid simplifying assumption.

2.3 THE MARKET

Supply and demand for a single good determine its price. Yet each good influences other goods directly and indirectly by substitution. Moreover most persons in an economy are both suppliers (workers) and demanders (consumers). Leon Walras was the first to show how equations could be written for a total economy.

In a simplified model without corporations, we imagine that each person brings certain goods to market: his labor, talents, and resources in producing some item, or in a more simple picture, perhaps, his own production of food, clothing, and so on. He sells these at the market price and with the resulting income he purchases goods for consumption. Savings and debt are also ignored in this model.

The given quantities are each individual's utility function u_i, and the quantity y_{ij} of each good j he brings to market. From these are calculated prices p_j and the consumption or purchase bundles consisting of the quantity x_{ij} of good j purchased by individual i.

There are three sets of equations by which these are found.

(W1) $\sum_i y_{ij} = \sum_i x_{ij}$ for each j.

The total quantity of good j brought to market equals the total amount brought away.

(W2) $\sum_j p_j x_{ij} \leq \sum_j p_j y_{ij}$ for each i.

Each individual spends at most what he receives as income by selling his goods. (In general, equality holds here).

(W3) $u_i(x_{ij})$ is a maximum subject to (W2).

Each individual purchases that bundle of goods he most prefers for his income. If the u_i satisfy assumptions mentioned in the last section, the last is equivalent to

$$\text{(W3')} \qquad \frac{\partial u_i(x_{ij})}{\partial x_{ij}} = \lambda_i p_j$$

for some numbers λ_i.

In these equations prices, and hence the value of money are determined only relative to one another, as ratios. If all prices are doubled or tripled, this model remains unchanged. This paradoxical feature that it is not prices and wages which matter at a given point in time, but only their ratio makes inflation and deflation possible. The economic effect of inflation is essentially to savings and debt, which have been ignored here.

Existence of solutions, and uniquenss and stability are deep problems with which the mathematics of Walras's time was unable to deal. The first proofs were given by Abraham Wald about 1935. Modern proofs generally use fixed point theorems of topology. For example the Brouwer fixed point theorem asserts that any continuous mapping, or function from an n-dimensional cube to itself has a fixed point, a point mapped to itself. This can be applied to a function on the set of prices which suitably raise prices for excess demand or lowers them for excess supply. A fixed point will give prices at which supply equals demand. The Kakutani fixed point theorem generalizes the Brouwer theorem to multi-valued functions or relations.

A set of points in n-dimensional space is called *convex* if it has no "indentations" but always bulges outward, more precisely if all line segments joining two points of the set are in the set. An orange or ice cube is convex but not a banana or, near the stem, an apple. A set of points is called *closed* if it includes its boundary. It is called *compact* if it is closed and lies in a bounded region of space. For instance circles, spheres, cubes, and regular polygons with their interiors are compact and convex.

If the utility functions are *strictly quasi-concave* then the maximum in (W3) is unique. Equation (W3') is standard calculus, but follows most elegantly from the method of Lagrange multipliers. That is, to maximize u_i subject to $\Sigma\, p_j x_{ij} = c$, where c denotes the constant, we let λ_i be unknown constants, and set all partial derivatives of $u_i - \lambda_i(\Sigma\, p_j x_{ij})$ equal to zero.

If the utility functions are quasi-concave only, so that $\frac{1}{2}(x + y)$ may be indifferent to, as well as strictly preferred to the indifferent bundles x, y then the maximum in (W3) may not be unique, but may occur over a convex set.

It is a little surprising that in either case a fixed point theorem apparently must be applied not merely to a function, but to a binary relation, to prove existence of equilibrium. Around the turn of the century, L. E. J. Brouwer had proved that every continuous function from a compact convex set in n-dimensional space to itself must have a fixed point. For example, a rotation of a sphere and its interior fixes the center of the sphere. A continuous function f(x) from a finite closed interval of real numbers to the same interval has as fixed point the least real number x such that f(x) - x is nonnegative.

In the general case, the proof involves deep concepts of topology, see Courant and Robbins (1941), or Spanier (1966). The basic idea is that if f is a mapping from a sphere to itself without fixed points, then the mapping h from the sphere to its boundary defined by intersection of the ray from f(x) to x with the boundary of the sphere maps the boundary of the sphere by the identity mapping. It is what is called a *retraction* from the sphere onto its boundary, and this cannot exist. Recent proofs in the American Mathematical Monthly (1981) based on n-dimensional integration, are perhaps the simplest. Or see Burger (1963), Scarf (1973).

A refinement, the Lefschetz fixed point theorem, attaches an integer called an *index* to each fixed point, and shows that these integers must sum to 1. It applies to many spaces which are not topologically equivalent to convex ones.

The Kakutani fixed point theorem is a generalization of Brouwer's which replaces the function f by a multi-valued funtion f (equivalently, a binary relation). That is f(x) is an entire set of points, not a single point. Kakutani's theorem is derived from Brouwer's by approximating the binary relation by continuous functions (Hildenbrand 1976).

Suppose we have strictly quasi-concave preferences, so that demand is uniquely defined. We will define a mapping from the set of prices to itself which will have a fixed point if and only if excess of demand over supply (excess demand) is zero. Roughly speaking, this will tend to raise prices if there is excess demand and lower them if there is excess supply. Then we apply a fixed point theorem. The main complication is what happens if some prices are zero. We will show that as some prices tend to zero, but others remain positive and bounded, demand for each person tends to infinity for each good having zero price.

Suppose not. We can find a sequence of price vectors p<k> which converge, some to zero, such that the demands for all goods also converge. Let x be the limit demand vector, and t be obtained from p by increasing the quantities of all goods with zero prices. By monotonicity, the individual prefer t to x. Let s be obtained from t by decreasing the quantity of all goods by a small positive amount ε. Then for ε small enough s is still preferred to x. Then for k large enough s is feasible at prices p(k) and s is preferred to the demand vector (close to x) for these prices. This is impossible, since the demand vector represents the most preferred feasible bundle of goods.

THEOREM 2.3.1. *If utilities are strictly quasi-concave and monotone, nonzero equilibrium prices exist.*

Proof. To a set of positive prices p_j we associate the new prices, following Nikaido (1970)

$$\frac{p_j + \max(z_j, 0)}{1 + \sum_{j=1}^{n} \max(z_j, 0)}$$

where $z_j = \sum_i x_{ij} - \sum_i y_{ij}$ is the total excess of demand over supply for good j. This function is continuous. It preserves nonnegativity of prices and the equation $\sum p_j = 1$. To extend it to the case where some prices are zero, we allow multiple values. In fact send a point p having some zero prices to the set of price vector t which satisfy $\sum t_j = 1$, $t_j \geq 0$, $t_j = 0$ if $p_j > 0$.

This extension will have the continuity and convexity properties needed to apply Kakutani's fixed point theorem on the set $\{p: p_j \geq 0, \Sigma p_j = 1\}$. Thus there will be a fixed point. By definition of the mapping when some prices are zero, no fixed points can occur in that case. So all prices are positive. If supply did not equal demand for all goods, there would exist $z_j > 0$ and $p_k > 0$. Then p_k will be reduced which is impossible. So $z_k = 0$ for all k. This completes the proof. □

The price-ratios giving equilibrium are not always unique. In fact Debreu (1974) proved that any continuous function z(p) satisfying $p \cdot z = 0$ and $z(p) = z(kp)$ on a compact set, can be an excess demand function for some economy. Such functions can readily be constructed such that $z = 0$ has more than one solution.

It has been shown by methods of differential topology developed in the 1950's that there are generally a finite, odd number of equilibrium points. Moreover if the Jacobian matrix

$$\left(\frac{\partial z_i}{\partial p_j}\right)$$

of the economy is positive definite then equilibrium is unique. Positive definiteness, and hence uniqueness, will occur either (1) if all goods are gross substitutes for each other, that is, an increase in the price of any good causes an increase in total demand for every other good or (2) each good has more influence on its own demand than all other goods combined. These same conditions are sufficient for local stability of equilibrium prices. Mathematically they correspond to computing the topological degree of the excess demand function in terms of the Jacobian, a standard procedure.

It is not known whether this type of nonuniqueness and instability occurs in actual economies or has any impact on inflation, but it is not generally thought to cause inflation. The theory of regular economies was originated by Debreu (1970). See also Dierker (1974), (1977). Balasko (1980) studied a converse question, to what extent is an economy determined by the number of equilibria it has ?

EXAMPLE 2.3.1. Economies with multiple equilibrium exist even for the case of only two goods and two agents. This case is illustrated by what is called an *Edgeworth box*. Choose the units in which the goods are measured so that the total amount of each good is 1. Then allocations of goods can be represented by points of the square with vertices (0, 0), (0, 1), (1, 0), (1, 1). A point (x, y) means that agent 1 receives an amount x of the first good and an amount y of the second good. Then agent 2 will have amounts (1 - x, 1 - y) of the two goods. In effect agent 1's allocation is measured upwards from (0, 0) and agent 2's allocation for the same point is measured downwards from (1, 1).

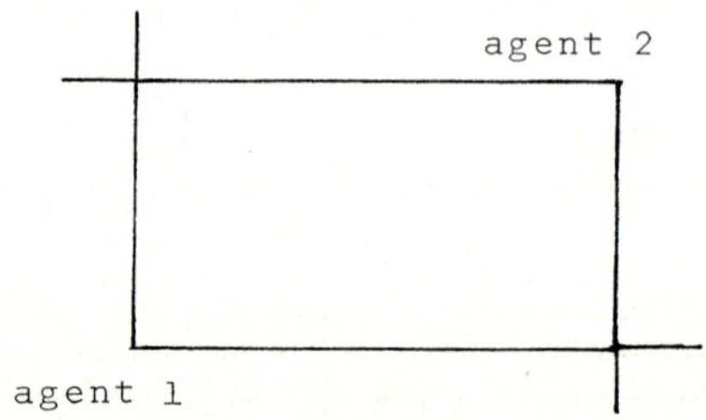

Edgeworth box

The utility function of each agent can be indicated by the indifference curves $\{(x, y): u(x, y) = c\}$. These will be disjoint concave curves with respect to (0, 0) for agent 1, and for agent 2 the curves will be concave with respect to (1, 1).

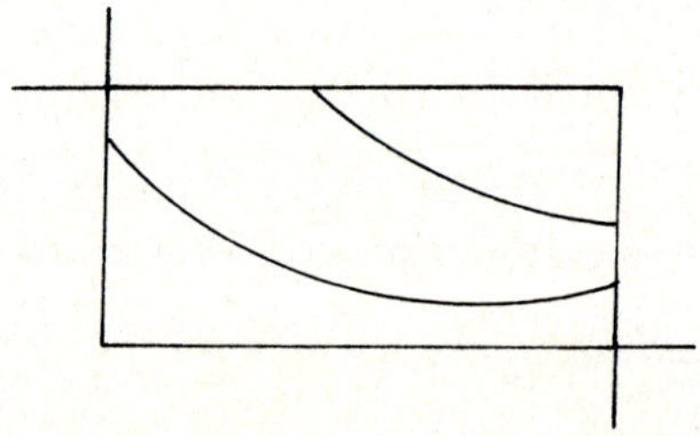

Indifference curves for agent 1

We assume the utility functions are monotone, strictly quasi-concave, and have continuous second derivatives.

The set of Pareto optimal points forms a curve called the *contract curve*, which stretches from (0, 0) to (1, 1) and is increasing in each variable. For example if the two utility functions are equal, the contract curve will be the line segment $y = x$.

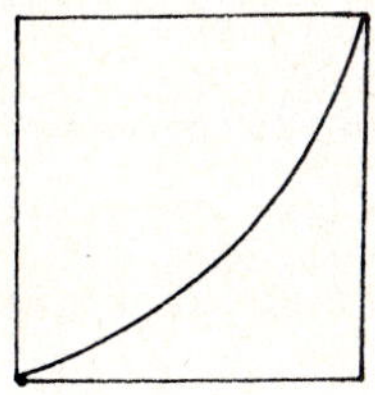

Contract curve

The contract curve consists of those points (x, y) such that

$$\frac{\dfrac{\partial u_1(x, y)}{\partial x}}{\dfrac{\partial u_1(x, y)}{\partial y}} = \frac{\dfrac{\partial u_2(1-x, 1-y)}{\partial x}}{\dfrac{\partial u_2(1-x, 1-y)}{\partial y}}$$

since the condition is that ratios of marginal utilities are equal. The ratio in question is the negative of the slope of the indifference curve of either players through the point (x,y).

The competitive equilibria for various initial allocations can be determined from the contract curve together with the marginal utility ratio r at each point of it. That is for an initial allocation (a, b) the competitive equilibrium points are precisely those points (x, y) on the contract curve such that

$$\frac{y - b}{x - a} = -r$$

since the budget equation is $rx + y = ra + b$ because r equals the ratio of prices.

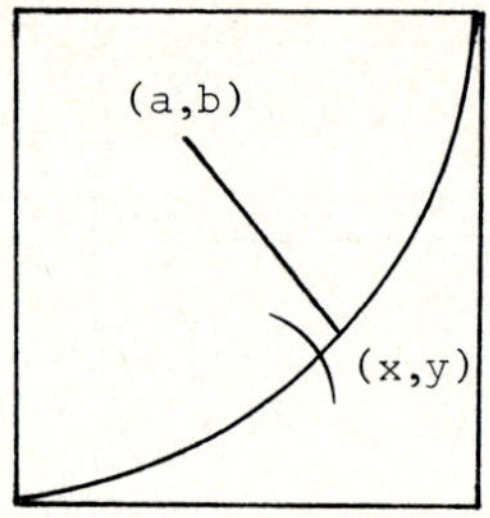

Equilibrium for initial allocation (a, b)

This means the line from (a, b) to (x, y) is tangent to the indifference curve of either player at (x, y).

The indifference curve and ratio of marginal utilities can be any sufficiently differentiable curve and function such that the indifference curve increases from (0, 0) to (1, 1) and r is positive. To prove this it suffices to construct a utility function for a player which has an arbitrarily prescribed slope at each point of the contract curve. To do this it essentially suffices to construct the family of indifference curves. Choose a function $\varepsilon(x, y)$ small enough that the line segments through (x, y) with slope -r have no intersections within distance $\varepsilon(x, y)$ of the contract curve. Extend these vertically a horizontally to the edges of the square with a little smoothing. This gives the required indifference curves.

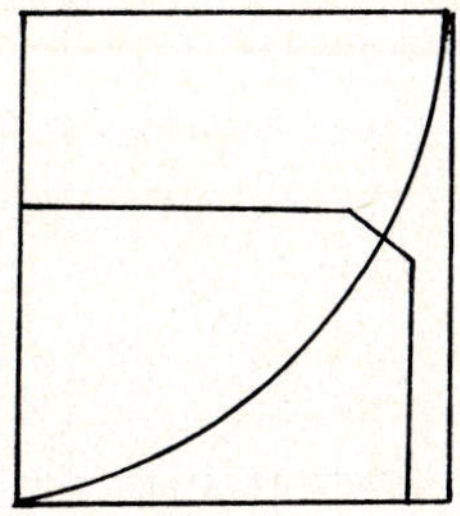

Indifference curve before smoothing

Now examples can easily be constructed of economies with multiple equilibria, as below

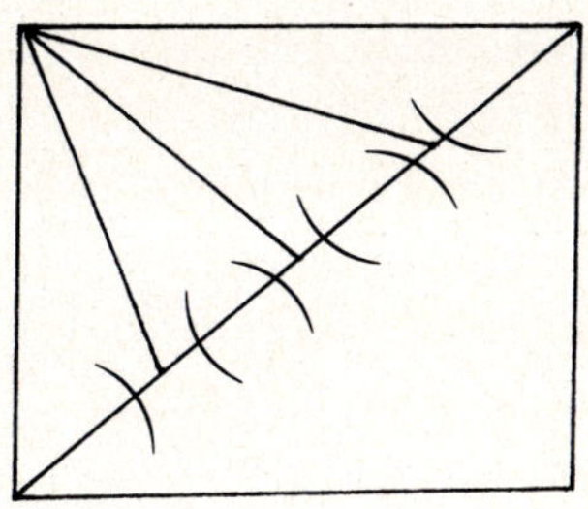

Economy with multiple equilibria

2.4 PARETO EFFICIENCY AND CORE

Is the market system desirable ? Are there any alternatives other than government-imposed rationing ? Here we will consider some advantages of market economies. Disadvantages will be taken up later. The most obvious advantage is that a market economy runs itself. The government in principle need only take care of public goods and prevent crime.

Adam Smith conjectured that *any nation could attain prosperity by free trade and a reasonably good enforcement of laws.* Mathematically the market system has a property named Pareto optimality or Pareto efficiency after the Italian social Scientist Vilfredo Pareto. A state is called *Pareto optimal* if there is no other state in which everyone would be better off. This does not mean everyone is well-off; politically a dictatorship is Pareto optimal, as are many other forms of social choice. If one person realizes his maximum utility the state is Pareto optimal regardless of the conditions of others. But it is possible also for there to be various degrees of equality and Pareto optimality. That is, Pareto optimality is a necessary, but not a sufficient condition for an ideal social system. A wide variety of economic distributions may be Pareto optimal, some equal, some unequal. If there is a fixed amount of a single good, any distribution of it will be Pareto optimal, since to make everyone better off requires a larger total of the good. But Pareto optimality does imply efficiency. If the production or distribution is inefficient, making it more efficient and distributing the gains equally would make everyone better off.

Geometrically if pairs of utilities are plotted to form a region such as that below

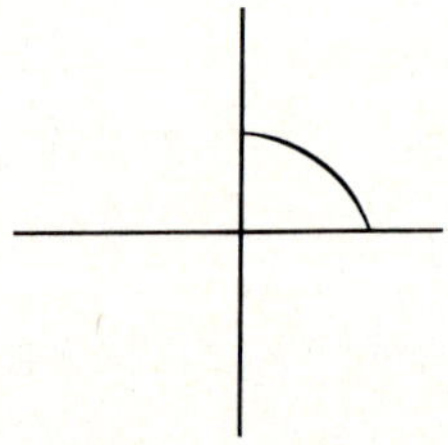

the Pareto optimal points will usually be those on the upper-right boundary of the region (here the curved boundary line). The other points are not, since if a line is extended upward and to the right it will intersect the boundary in a point with both coordinates larger.

Adam Smith's argument for efficiency was based on competition. An argument from the model above goes as follows. Suppose there was an alternative distribution of goods so that everyone's utility were higher. Then since everyone purchased their most preferred bundle before, everyone must now have purchased more total value measured at the market prices. But this would require a larger amount of at least one good, otherwise the total value cannot be larger. This proves trading gives a Pareto efficient distribution of goods.

This argument can be extended to the case in which we have manufacturing corporations as well as individual agents. In this case equilibrium involves each firm maximizing profits at the given prices. Individuals who own shares of the firms receive corresponding shares of income. Their other income equals what they receive from selling the goods they bring to market. Suppose there was an alternative set of manufacturing processes by the corporations and distribution of the goods which gives everyone a higher utility. Then at the market prices everyone has a greater value of purchased goods. The corporation profits cannot be greater at these prices. Thus everyone has a greater value of goods purchased with the sale of his own goods. Thus the total quantity of some good brought to market is greater. This is impossible.

Thus the market system always, at equilibrium, gives a Pareto efficient allocation of goods. It follows that there can only be four main types of problems with the market system: *(1) public goods and externalities, (2) disequilibrium, including monopoly, (3) inequality, (4) time effects possibly including a business cycle or inflation.* The reason is that private goods, equilibrium, and a single time period were the only assumptions needed for Pareto optimality, and a Pareto optimal result is best except for the resulting distribution.

It was a popular view earlier in the century that economics could not deal with questions of *inequality*, which may require "unscientific" value judgements, and consequently the sole purpose of economics is to assure a Pareto efficient outcome. This viewpoint makes the market system, of a *laissez-faire* variety, look outstanding, but today this view is less prevalent. Instead explicit assumptions can be made about the desirability of various income distributions.

There is converse result on efficiency. Every Pareto efficient allocation of goods can be realized by the market system for some initial allocation of goods. The following is an argument for this, under certain assumptions of differentiability, quasi-concavity, and monotonicity of utilities. At a Pareto efficient allocation of goods, the ratio of marginal utilities of two goods must be the same for everyone. If not, then the person who has a lower marginal utility proportionalitely of one good can trade some of it for the other. Both persons' utilities will be higher. A tiny amount can be taken from them and distributed to the rest, making everyone's utility higher. Thus the ratio of marginal utilities of two goods is the same for everyone. Then set prices proportional to marginal utilities. Give each person an allotment of money, or of raw materials and company shares which will enable him to pay for the goods distributed to him.

This has an application to centralized economies, that it is sufficient to choose prices, production processes, and incomes to achieve any optional economic allocation. In practice there are a couple of problems. First is the actual computation of optimum prices and production in a modern economy of millions of different kinds of goods. This problem is significant in Soviet planning, which calculates with 1,000 groups of goods. Secondly, wages cannot be linear in quantity like prices, or the competitive equilibrium will be the only equilibrium. Moreover income cannot be an unconditional payment, if it is to be a motivation. Instead each worker must be assigned a quota and receives his full calculated income only if he produces this quota. Otherwise he receives much less. Then there is the problem that workers can pretend they are able to produce much less than they actually are able to produce, a form of manipulability. This has also been a serious problem in the U.S.S.R.

One answer to the second question at the beginning of this section grew out of a conjecture of F. Y. Edgeworth (1881) proved in the 1960's in a limit as the number of agents tends to infinity. The *core* of a game is the set of allocations for which no coalition among the players has the ability to do better by its own actions indenpendently of the others. In economics the core has the meaning of all allocations such that no coalition of the agents could improve on all of their utilities by withdrawing from the group and trading solely among themselves. This concept implies both Pareto efficiency (coalition of all players) and individual rationality, that no individual has lower utility than his utility with his original goods (coalitions of only one player).

Equilibrium allocations always lie in the core. Suppose not. Let every member of a coalition C have higher utility from trading only among themselves than by the equilibrium. At equilibrium prices, they must all have higher monetary value trading among themselves only since their utilities are all higher. Thus the total monetary value of the goods of the group after trading is greater. But this equals the total monetary value of the goods before trading. So it cannot be greater. This contradiction proves the result.

The theorem mentioned is that as one multiplies the number of agents of each kind, every core allocation converges to the competitive equilibrium. There are a number of different versions of this theorem, all with complicated proofs. But what the theorem implies is that any allocation other than the competitive equilibrium must be imposed by the government. Any other allocation will result in a loss for some group compared to what they could do trading by themselves. So they would withdraw from the system unless they were forced to participate.

Next we express some of these concepts mathematically.

THEOREM 2.4.1. *Any equilibrium of a simple exchange economy is Pareto efficient.*

Proof. Suppose prices p_j and consumption amounts x_{ij} provide an equilibrium. Suppose an allocation w_{ij} gives each person higher utility. To be feasible,

$$\sum_i w_{ij} = \sum_i y_{ij} = \sum_i x_{ij}$$

If for some i, $\sum p_j w_{ij} \leq \sum p_j x_{ij}$ then w_{ij} could be purchased with the same income as x. Since x_{ij} is a maximum for u_{ij} the utility from the w_{ij} allocation could not exceed that from the x_{ij} allocation. This is false. So $\sum p_j w_{ij} > \sum p_j x_{ij}$ for all i. Thus

$$\sum_{i,j} p_j w_{ij} > \sum_{i,j} p_j x_{ij}$$

But equality must hold, since

$$\sum_i w_{ij} = \sum_i x_{ij}$$

This completes the proof. □

DEFINITION 2.4.1. The *core* of a simple exchange economy is the set of allocations x_{ij} such that there does not exist a coalition C, an allocation w_{ij} for $i \in C$ with

$$\begin{cases} \sum_C w_{ij} = \sum_C y_{ij} \\ u_i(w) > u_i(x) \text{ for } i \in C \end{cases}$$

EXAMPLE 2.4.1. An equilibrium allocation is always in the core, by an argument very similar to the last proof. For two traders there will usually be many core elements: all Pareto optimal outcomes for which each trader likes his final allocation at least as much as his initial allocation.

DEFINITION 2.4.2. The *r-fold replication* of a simple exchange economy is an economy having the same set of goods, in which each trader is replaced by r traders with exactly the same utility function and initial allocation.

An equilibrium is also an equilibrium for any replication of an economy, so it is in the core of any replication. One core theorem (Debreu and Scarf 1963) is that conversely any allocation in the core of all replications of an economy is an equilibrium. A stronger result in terms of finite economies is a theorem of Grodal (1975) which asserts that if a sequence of finite economies converges in a certain sense, as the number of agents tends to infinity, then the distance from the core to the set of equilibria converges to zero at a rate proportional to the reciprocal of the number of agents or faster. For a survey of results to 1975 see Hildenbrand (1977). An elementary treatment of the core can be found in Hildenbrand and Kirman (1976).

EXAMPLE 2.4.2. Suppose that instead of quantities of all goods being divisible, we have n sellers each selling a single horse and m buyers each wishing to buy a single horse. Everyone regards any two of the horses as equally good. Let b_i be the amount of money which for buyer i equals in value a horse and s_i the amount for a seller. Assume all s_i, p_i are distinct.

A trade can be described as follows. We have a subset S_1 of the sellers who sell their horses, prices p_i for which they are sold, and one-to-one function f from S_1 into the set B of buyers describing who will buy what horse.

In for this to be individually rational, we must have $p_i \geq s_i$ and $p_i \leq b_{f(i)}$ for each $i \in S_1$.

At price p, demand consists of $|\{j: p \leq b_j\}|$ and supply consists of $|\{i: p \geq s_i\}|$. The set of prices p such that these two quantities are equal is the set of competitive equilibrium prices. In the resulting allocation all sellers i such that $s_i \geq p$ sell a horse at price p and all buyers j such that $b_j \leq p$ buy a horse at price p.

In the core no subset consisting of a set S_2 of sellers and a set B_2 of buyers can better the given allocation for all its members.

First we consider the condition for Pareto optimality. This condition is basically that the ones who wind up with the horses are the n players (buyers or sellers) having the highest utility for a horse (money transfers do not affect Pareto optimality). This is the case for the competitive equilibrium since those ending with a horse are the n players whose utility of a horse exceeds the largest s_i less than or equal to p. So the buyers and sellers must be the same as in the competitive equilibrium.

Next consider the core condition for all 2 player coalitions consisting of a seller i with $s_i \le p$ and a buyer b_j with $b_j \ge p$. Set utility scales so that the original utility of each buyer is 0 and each seller is s_i. Then this coalition by themselves can guarantee any distribution of utility whose total is b_j. Their actual total is

$$p_i - p_{f^{-1}(j)} + b_j$$

Thus

$$p_i - p_{f^{-1}(j)} \ge 0$$

for all i with $s_i \le p$ and all j with $b_j \ge p$. If any of these inequalities were strict then

$$\Sigma\, p_i - \Sigma\, p_{f^{-1}(j)} > 0$$

But $\Sigma\, p_i = \Sigma\, p_{f^{-1}(j)}$ since the right-hand side is a rearrangement of left-hand side. Thus $p_i = p_{f^{-1}(j)}$ for all i, j among those who actually trade. So all p_i are equal. By individual rationality they lie in the same range as p. This shows that the core is identical to the competitive equilibrium.

This example is sometimes known as a *Bohm-Bawerk economy*.

EXAMPLE 2.4.3. The core in an atomless economy with two types of traders and two goods. Let the first type of trader have utility function u_1 and initial allocation $w\langle 1\rangle$ and let the second type trader have utility function u_2 and initial allocation $w\langle 2\rangle$. Let the total populations of the two types of traders be in the ratio $r_1(r_2)^{-1}$ where $r_1 + r_2 = 1$.

In order to represent the case where there are a very large number of traders each having slight effect on the total market, we identify the traders of types 1, 2 with the points of the respective intervals $[0, r_1]$ and $[0, r_2]$. Thus there is an infinite number of traders of each type.

For a subset S of the real line, which can be explicitly defined without any arbitrary choices, there is defined a quntity called *Lebesgue measure* m(S) which gives the total size of S. If S is a union of finitely many disjoint intervals, m(S) is the sum of the lengths of S. For a point or finite set S, m(S) is zero. Thus

$$\frac{m(S)}{r_i}$$

will express the proportion of points of $[0, r_i]$ which lie in S.

More generally a measure is a function m on a family of subsets T of a set S such that

(i) T is closed under complements, countable unions, and intersections, and $\emptyset \subset T$.

(ii) m(S) is nonnegative real number or infinity for $S \varepsilon T$.

(iii) $m(\emptyset) = 0$.

(iv) $m\left(\bigcup_1^\infty S_k\right) = \sum_1^\infty m(S_k)$ if the S_k are disjoint members of T.

An allocation can be generally represented now by functions $f_i\colon [0, r_i] \to R^2$ on R^2 where f(v) is the allocation (x_1, x_2) received by trader v.

Assume utilities are strictly quasi-concave, monotone, and have continuous second derivatives.

A competitive equilibrium allocation is one satisfying these conditions, where $f_1(v) = (x_{11}(v), x_{12}(v))$ and $f_2(v) = (x_{21}(v), x_{22}(v))$.

$$(2.4.1)\begin{cases} \int_0^{r_1} x_{11}(v)\,dv + \int_0^{r_2} x_{21}(v)\,dv = r_1 w_1\langle 1\rangle + r_2 w_1\langle 2\rangle \\ \int_0^{r_1} x_{12}(v)\,dv + \int_0^{r_2} x_{22}(v)\,dv = r_1 w_2\langle 1\rangle + r_2 w_2\langle 2\rangle \end{cases}$$

$$(2.4.2) \quad \begin{cases} p_1x_{11}(v) + p_2x_{12}(v) = p_1w_1{<}1{>} + p_2{<}1{>} \\ p_1x_{21}(v) + p_2x_{22}(v) = p_1w_1{<}2{>} + p_2{<}2{>} \end{cases}$$

(2.4.3) Subject to the first equation of (2.4.2), $u_1(x_{11}(v), x_{12}(v))$ is a maximum. Subject to the second equation of (2.4.2) $u_2(x_{21}(v), x_{22}(v))$ is a maximum.

These three sets of relations express equality of supply and demand, each consumer's budget equation, and each consumer's preference. From (2.4.2), (2.4.3) and quasi-concavity it follows that x_{11}, x_{12} do not depend on v and that x_{21}, x_{22} do not depend on v. Thus the first equations, for instance, can be written

$$\begin{cases} r_1x_{11} + r_2x_{21} = r_1w_1{<}1{>} + r_2w_1{<}2{>} \\ r_1x_{12} + r_2x_{22} = r_1w_2{<}1{>} + r_2w_2{<}2{>} \end{cases}$$

For the core, equations (2.4.1) must still hold. Sets of measure zero are ignored since, subject to (2.4.1) any single trader could increase his utility. This will not be mentioned explicitly in the following.

All traders of type 1 must receive equal utility. Else take a set S_1 of traders type 1 of measure $\alpha > 0$ receiving less utility than the remaining type 1 traders. Take a set S_2 of traders of type 2 of measure receiving utility less than or equal to x where x is chosen so that $m(S_2)$ is

$$\frac{r_2}{r_1}\alpha$$

Then the groups S_1, S_2 could improve their utilities by trading as if they were scaled down copies of the entire set of traders. By symmetry, all type 2 traders must receive the same utility.

By strict quasi-concavity, all type 1 traders receive the same allocation. Else the outcome is not Pareto optimal since the type 1 traders could equally distribute the total goods they receive, and be better off. Likewise the type 2 traders all receive the same allocation. So x_{ij} does not depend on v.

A *vector of equilibrium prices* p has the property that at those prices any bundle the consumer would prefer is more expensive. We will show such a vector p exists. Let S_i be the set of vectors $y - w<i>$ such that a trader of type i prefers y to his core allocation $x<i>$. The *core property* implies that no convex combination of vectors from $S_1 \cup S_2$ is nonpositive, else if $\Sigma\, a_i r_i + \Sigma\, b_i t_i \le 0$, $r_i \varepsilon S_1$, $t_i \varepsilon S_2$ then we can have subsets of the traders proportional to the sizes of a_i, b_i who can obtain the vectors $w<i> + r_i$, $w<i> + t_i$. They will prefer this result to the allocation $x<i>$ by definition of S_i. This contradicts the definition of the core.

So no convex combination of vectors of $S_1 \cup S_2$ is nonpositive. This means by a theorem on convex sets that there exists a hyperplane separating a cone containing $S_1 \cup S_2$ from the set of negative vectors. Thus there exists a nonzero nonnegative vector p such that $p \cdot (y - w<i>)$ is always nonnegative whenever y is preferred to $x<i>$. By continuity

$$p \cdot (x<i> - w<i>) \ge 0$$

All coordinates of p must be positive (else we could let y increase $w<i>$ in one coordinate, decrease it slightly in the rest and y is preferred to $w<i>$ but $p \cdot (y - w<i>) < 0$).

If any of the inequalities just written were strict, then

$$p\, \Sigma\, r_i x<i> - p\, \Sigma\, r_i w<i> > 0$$

which is false. So

$$p \cdot x<i> = p \cdot w<i>$$

This verifies equation (2.4.2). Condition (2.4.3) follows from $p \cdot (y - w<i>) > 0$ for any y preferred to $x<i>$.

This argument extends to a proof of the equality of core and competitive equilibrium if the traders are of finitely many types.

Does the market optimize a specific quantity ? Recall the equations

$$\sum_i x_{ij} = \sum_i y_{ij}, \qquad \sum p_j x_{ij} = \sum p_j y_{ij}, \qquad \frac{\partial u_i}{\partial x_{ij}} = \lambda_i p_j$$

The first and last are the same equations obtained by maximizing

(2.4.4) $$\sum \frac{1}{\lambda_i} u_i$$

subject to

$$\sum_i x_{ij} = \sum_i y_{ij}$$

Equation (2.4.4) is maximized generally where λ_i is proportional to the marginal utility of any good for trader i. This in turn suggests that the more satiated, or richer trader i is, the more heavily the market weights his welfare. On the other hand, in this sum many small identical terms corresponding to middle or lower income groups might contribute a larger total than a few large terms for the rich. Intuitively this corresponds to the idea that the market serves monetary demand, of which the wealthy contribute more as individuals, perhaps less in total. Any Pareto optimum must maximize some weighted sum of utilities, by a general result in optimization theory.

Production can be added to the market model. We follow (Nikaido 1970). In addition to the individual traders, we have a set of production units, or firms. For each firm k we have a set of Y_k production processes. A production process is an m-tuple of real numbers like a commodity bundle, except that some numbers can be negative. The negative numbers are the inputs and the positive numbers outputs. Each Y_k is assumed to be a closed convex set containing zero, such that (1) $\sum Y_k$ has entirely positive vectors, i.e., all processes require inputs, and (2) $\sum Y_k \cap (-\sum Y_k) = \{0\}$, that is, processes cannot be reversed. (The latter is related to the laws of thermodynamics). It is assumed the economy can produce positive amounts of all goods.

The firms are owned by one or more traders each, and if α_{ik} is the proportion of firm k owned by trader i, then trader i receives a proportion α_{ik} of its profits in addition to what he receives by selling his commodities. Firms choose their production processes to maximize profits, which are the difference between the values of inputs and outputs at prices p_j. Equilibrium will exist by an argument similar to the preceding one without production. In fact continuity of excess demand, behavior as prices tend to zero, and $p \cdot z = 0$ were the only facts used, and will still be true.

THEOREM 2.4.2. *Every equilibrium of an economy with production is Pareto efficient.*

Proof. Suppose not. Let the initial allocations be w_{ij}. For the equilibrium let y_{kj} represent production of firm k, x_{ij} consumption. For an allocation which is better for each trader, let v_{kj} be production and c_{ij} consumption. Then since utilities are higher, each person receives more total value of goods at price p_j.

$$\sum_j p_j c_{ij} > \sum_j p_j x_{ij} = \sum_j p_j w_{ij} + \sum_k a_{ik}\left(\sum_j p_j y_{jk}\right)$$

We have

$$\sum_i c_{ij} = \sum w_{ij} + \sum v_{kj}$$

Sum the inequality on i and multiply the equation by p_j and sum. This gives a contradiction since

$$\sum p_j v_{jk} \leq \sum_j p_j y_{jk}$$

by profit maximization. This completes the proof. □

There is also a converse to this theorem (Debreu 1959).

2.5 CONCLUSION

Competitive prices can generally be explained as those at which supply equals demand. Wages, rents, profits, and interest can be explained in a similar way. Prices should not over the long run be such that demand exceeds supply, even without perfect competition. But in monopoly prices can be such that supply exceeds demand. On the supply side this means prices will equal marginal cost of producing a good, and on the demand side, that they will be proportional to the marginal utility of a good.

Utility is a number assigned to commodity bundles for a given individual, such that commodity bundles with higher utility are preferred to those with lower utility. It can be proved such numbers exist, but are not unique for rational individuals. Demand apparently cannot be predicted without actual statistics on a given commodity, but several formulas are frequently used to represent it in which constants must be found empirically.

A system of equations can be written out for supply and demand of all goods together in a simple market system. Solutions that is equilibrium prices, always exist, but are not always unique. Stability and uniqueness are guaranted if goods are gross substitutes for one another, that is, an increase in the price of one good increases demand for every other good.

A market system without externalities at equilibrium gives a Pareto efficient production and allocation of goods. This means there is no other process by which everyone could be made economically better off. Thus the main possible problems of a market system are (1) externalities and public goods, (2) disequilibrium, (3) inequality, (4) time effects. Conversely for some incomes and prices every Pareto efficient allocation can be realized by the market.

The core of an economy is the set of allocations for which no coalition consisting of part of the traders could all be richer by withdrawing from the group and trading among themselves. It has been proved in the last 20 years that as the number of traders of each type tends to infinity every core allocation tends to a competitive equilibrium. This means all allocations which differ significantly from the competitive equilibrium must be imposed by force.

Under certain conditions the market system seems to be the only one which is Pareto efficient and incentive compatible, that is, no individual has an incentive to be misrepresent his true situation and so disrupt the system. However in a condition of oligopoly, as will be discussed later, the market system itself is not incentive compatible. A more general result was proved by Satterthwaite and Sonnenschein (1979).

CHAPTER 3

NONCOOPERATIVE GAME THEORY

3.1 INTRODUCTION

Game theory is an attempt to describe situations where several agents try to optimize separate things, and each agent's actions affects the goal of every other agent. If the agents play one after another, and the maximum number of plays is known, and all agents are perfectly informed, there is a game of perfect information. This can in principle be solved by working backwards. We give examples of typical and important games widely discussed in the game-theoretic literature.

A game is said to be in *normal form*if each player must choose a single strategy, not knowing the choices of the others. These strategies simultaneously determine the outcome. Multistage games (*extensive form*) can be reduced to normal form. The strategies of the agents are said to be a *Nash equilibrium* if no single player could change his strategy to his own advantage. If players are allowed to randomize their strategies, finite games always have Nash equilibrium points. For 2 players, if whenever one gains the other loses, any two Nash equilibrium points are equivalent. For games not necessarily having this property, we describe a "*hybrid*" solution concept combining Nash equilibrium with maximin strategies. Maximin strategies are the idea of "playing it safe," avoiding risk. We relate the hybrid solution to those Nash equilibrium points which are Pareto optimal in the set of all Nash equilibrium points.

A *dominant strategy* is one which is best no matter what the strategies of the other players are. Most games considered in game theory do not have dominant strategies. A wider concept is *dominance solvability*. A strategy is dominated if there exists another strategy which is always at least as good, and sometimes better for a player. Such strategies may generally be ignored in noncooperative game theory. After all dominated strategies are deleted, it may be that new strategies become dominated. These are deleted in turn. The process is continued until a subgame is obtained with no dominated strategies. If every player is indifferent between any two payoffs in the subgame, the original game is said to be *d-solvable*. We briefly also discuss uniqueness of Nash equilibrium.

The last section is about the question when will a game be cooperative ? In *metagames* the players play conditional strategies "if you play x, I'll play y." In *supergames*, a game is repeated an infinite number of times, but future payoffs of player i are discounted at the rate α_i. Or there can be a probability α_i in the view of player i that the game will be played again, after each play.

Cooperative behavior can occur without communication in either case. Communication without any guarantee of truth frequently does not make a game cooperative. Specific mechanisms have been proposed for playing games cooperatively in a few cases.

3.2 ILLUSTRATIVE EXAMPLES

A game is a precisely defined situation in which each of a set of players chooses a strategy. The strategies of all players determines the outcome. Each player has a preference relation giving which outcomes to prefers to which others. Usually preferences are specified by the utilities of the outcomes to different players. For instance (1, 3, 2) means a utility of 1 to the first player, 3 to the second, and 2 to the third. The second player, but not the first, prefers this to (2, 2, 3).

Games are classified in may ways: the number of players, the extent of information, communication, and cooperative action allowed, whether the game will be repeated, whether randomized strategies (mixed strategies) are allowed. Noncooperative games are usually taken to be those in which no communication among players is allowed and in particular, no binding agreements can be made.

A game of perfect information is one, like chess or go, in

which the players play in sequence, each learning the previous moves before he plays. In theory such a game can be always solved by working backwards provided the length of the game is finite. Consider the possible games after k moves. Now analyze the possibilities for move k. Choose the move giving highest utility to the player making move k, if this is unique. Else consider the set of all moves giving highest utility.

EXAMPLE 3.2.1. *Tree game*. Suppose we have a 2-stage game represented by this tree

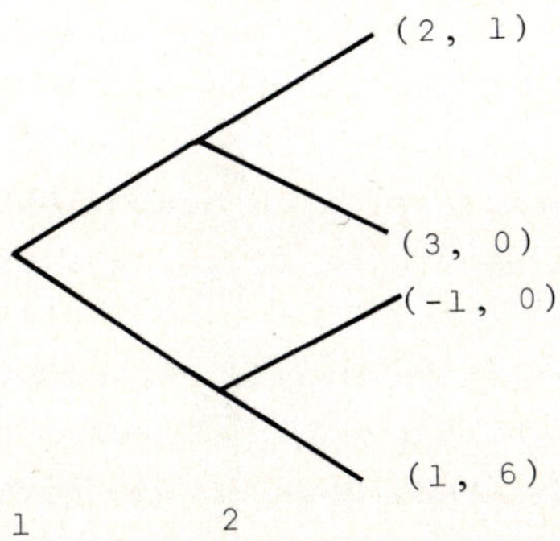

Player 1 choose the first branch, then player 2 chooses the second along whichever branch player 1 chooses. First we analyze the last move. Player 2 will choose his move according to which branch gives him the higher utility. Thus if player 1 chooses the upper branch of stage 1, he will choose the (2, 1) payoff. If player 1 chooses the lower branch, player 2 will choose the (1, 6) payoff.

Now we analyze the first move. Of the two payoffs, player 1 prefers (2, 1). So he will play the upper branch on the first move.

The solution concept of this example is called *perfect equilibrium*. Theoretically, it exists, but in practice, games such as chess or go are too complicated to solve. A number of simpler games of mainly mathematical interest have been solved.

In applications of game theory, it is more frequent that each player must make his moves in ignorance of what the others will do. They are thought of as acting at the same time. For example a military commander must make his plans without knowing those of the enemy.

The same is frequently true in economic competition and sports. Such games can in principle be reduced from an extended form, move by move description, to a single stage, called *normal form*. In doing so however the strategical features are hidden, so that this reduction is useful for theoretical analysis of the class of games but not for finding the best strategy in a particular game. For instance in chess a single move in normal form would if it were possible, represent a complete strategy in terms of moves and responses to any moves of the opponent for the entire game. This is not useful in actually deciding how to win a particular game.

In normal form, each player chooses a single move in ignorance of the moves of the other players, and this single move completes the game. Each move in the normal form game represents an entire strategy for the extended form game, that is his choice of a move at stage k for every sequence of preceding moves, for all k.

EXAMPLE 3.2.2. *Dominant strategy, nonoptimal outcome.*

Player 2

$$\text{Player 1} \quad \begin{bmatrix} (0,\ 0) & (4,\ 4) \\ (2,\ 2) & (5,\ 1) \end{bmatrix}$$

Here player 1's play is to choose a row, and player 2's play is to choose a column. The utilities of the outcome are found in the intersection of the chosen row and chosen column. Player 1 here has what is called a *dominant strategy*. In either column, the second row gives him a higher payoff. So he will play the second row. Knowing this, player 2 will play the first column, since he prefers (2, 2) to (5, 1). The reasonable outcome is therefore (2, 2).

If by deleting dominated strategies in turn for the different players, one obtains a unique n-tuple of utilities, the game is said to be *d-solvable*. Perfect equilibrium can be regarded as a special case of d-solvability.

Observe that in the game above, if the two players could make a binding agreement, they would likely play for (4, 4) instead of (2, 2). Thus dominant strategies may not be cooperative solutions. This is more strikingly true in the next example.

EXAMPLE 3.2.3. *Prisoner's dilemma.*

$$\begin{bmatrix} (-1, -1) & (-10, 0) \\ (0, -10) & (-5, -5) \end{bmatrix}$$

Here the second strategy is dominant for both players. So (-5, -5) will result instead of the preferable (-1, -1). This game is frequently invoked as a model of the harmful effects of individualism: arms races, pollution, farm prices, for instance. It is the "tragedy of the commons." The original story is that two criminals are arrested. They are suspected of a major crime (10 year sentence) but a lesser crime (1 year sentence) can be proved. They are kept completely separate. Each as an incentive to confess is told if he confesses and his partner does not, he will be freed. If both confess there will be a 5 year sentence for both.

A game is said to be *constant-sum* (*zero-sum*) if the sum of the two players' payoffs is constant (zero). The most important feature of such game is that the interests of the players are strictly opposed. If one gains, the other loses.

EXAMPLE 3.2.4. *Zero-sum game.*

$$\begin{bmatrix} (1, -1) & (0, 0) & (-1, 1) \\ (0, 0) & (0, 0) & (0, 0) \\ (-1, 1) & (0, 0) & (1, -1) \end{bmatrix}$$

Here the second strategy for each player appears the only rational solution. If either player did not play his second strategy, his opponent would logically play to gain, and he would lose as a result. Generally in game theory the opponent is assumed intelligent enough that one cannot win simply by figuring out what he will do and going one step further.

This example illustrates several principles. A *maximin strategy* is one which cuts one's worst possible loss to a minimum. Maximin strategies are not always reasonable: sometimes this worst case will not be expected to occur. Also frequently the opponent can take advantage of one who always follows this.

A *Nash equilibrium point* is a strategy n-tuple such that if any one person played something different and the others did not, the one who differs from the equilibrium cannot gain.

The above solution has both these properties and also has the property that if the game were played sequentially (with perfect information) with either player going first and his move known to the second player who then moves result would be the same. These properties generally hold for all 2-person constant-sum games, if mixed strategies are allowed. This means that instead of having fixed strategies, the players have fixed probabilities with which they choose between their two strategies.

The opposite case, where the players' interests are strictly agreed, does not occur too often but has a natural solution.

EXAMPLE 3.2.5. *Equal utilities.*

$$\begin{bmatrix} (5, 5) & (4, 4) \\ (3, 3) & (6, 6) \end{bmatrix}$$

Here (6, 6) is the solution. It is not a maximin strategy. It is one of two Nash equilibrium points. It would result from either player playing first. There are no dominant strategies.

If there is a unique Nash equilibrium point in terms of mixed strategies, it can be argued that it is the noncooperative solution. At any other point, one of the two players would not be doing as well as he could. Games with two Nash equilibrium points are more subtle.

EXAMPLE 3.2.6. *Brinksmanship or chicken.*

$$\begin{bmatrix} (-1, -1) & (-5, 5) \\ (5, -5) & (-10, -10) \end{bmatrix}$$

Here two drivers drive down the middle of the road toward each other. If either swerves to avoid the other, he loses face. But if neither does, they collide. The two Nash equilibria are (-5, 5) and (5, -5). But how can either be chosen ? The maximin strategies give (-1, -1). No better strategies are apparent however there is the problem that the opponent can take advantage of them. If it were known that the opponent could predict one's actions, this would be advantage, since then strategy 2 would be played.

EXAMPLE 3.2.7. *Battle of the sexes.*

$$\begin{bmatrix} (1, 2) & (0, 0) \\ (0, 0) & (2, 1) \end{bmatrix}$$

A couple is separated at a certain time and cannot communicate. The man and woman each have a favorite place to go which they like better than their mate's. However, if the two go different places, payoffs are zero. There are three Nash equilibrium points, with outcomes (2, 1), (1, 2) and $(\frac{2}{3}, \frac{2}{3})$. The last results from player 1 playing his first strategy $\frac{1}{3}$ of the time and player 2 playing her second strategy $\frac{1}{3}$ of the time. Again there seems no way to choose a specific one of these: the opponent might choose another. The maximin strategy for player 1 is to play his first strategy $\frac{2}{3}$ of the time. If both players play maximin strategies, the result is again $(\frac{2}{3}, \frac{2}{3})$. Since this is guaranteed, the maximin strategies seem as good as any in the noncooperative case.

The cooperative solution of this game would be different.

For such games a more refined analysis might be as follows: if the players are benevolent toward one another, choose the maximum point at which utilities are equal. (This might be the real-life outcome). If they are slightly malevolent, they might choose the Nash equilibrium, which the other player cannot take advantage of. But if they are perfectly neutral, the maximin offers more assurance of getting a reasonable payoff, even if the other figures out one's strategy, than any other point.

3.3 NASH EQUILIBRIUM AND MAXIMIN STRATEGY

A number of specific solution ideas have been mentioned in the previous section. In order to indicate when each is valid, we need to discuss the scope of noncooperative game theory, and to define general classes of games.

Game theory is a theory of rational behavior under self interest. We can consider a number of cases of what is meant by rational behavior under self-interest.

GT1. RATIONAL BEHAVIOR UNDER CERTAINTY. This amounts to maximization of a utility function representing one's preferences. A utility function exists provided preferences are complete and transitive.

GT2. RATIONAL BEHAVIOR UNDER PROBABILITY. Assume that a person has preferences over the set of all lotteries assigning various probabilities to each of a set of events. Let $tx + (1 - t)y$ denote a lottery which yields x with probability t and y otherwise. Suppose we have a complete, transitive preference R satisfying these axioms, where I is indifference and P is strict preference. Here t is assumed to satisfy $0 \le t \le 1$.

AXIOM 1. *If x I y then $tx + (1 - t)z$ I $ty + (1 - t)z$ for all z, t.*

AXIOM 2. *If x P y then $tx + (1 - t)z$ P $ty + (1 - t)z$ for all z, $t > 0$.*

AXIOM 3. *If x P y P z then for some t, y I $tx + (1 - t)z$.*

Axiom 1 states that indifferent outcomes may be substituted for one another. Axiom 2 states that if x is preferred to y a lottery between x and z is preferred to a lottery between y and z. Axiom 3 states that y is between x and z in its appeal, some probability mixture of x, z is indifferent to y. It reflects a continuity in t of the preferences.

THEOREM 3.3.1. *If Axioms 1, 2, 3 hold there exists a function u such that x P y if and only if $u(x) = u(y)$, and*

$$u(tx + (1 - t)y) = t(u(x)) + (1 - t)u(y)$$

If u is any other such function, $u(x) = a\,u(x) + b$ for constants a, b where $a > b$.

Proof. We only indicate how to define u. If all alternatives are indifferent, let u be constant. Otherwise let x, y be such that x P y. Set $u(x) = 0$, $u(y) = 1$. Let z not be indifferent to x or y.

Case 1. z P x P y. Let x I $tz + (1 - t)y$. Then let

$$u(z) = -\frac{1 - t}{t}$$

Case 2. x P z P y. Let z I $tx + (1 - t)y$. Then let $u(z) = (1 - t)$.

Case 3. x P y P z. Let y I $tx + (1 - t)z$. Let

$$u(z) = \frac{1}{1 - t}$$

It is straightforward to verify that u has the properties mentioned in theorem. □

EXAMPLE 3.3.1. Suppose y is indifferent to a 50-50 lottery between x, z. Then z should be assigned a utility of 2.

This type of utility is called *expected utility*. It can be measured experimentally by following the method used to define u. That is for given x, y we set u(x) = 0, u(y) = 1 and the subject is asked to give a probability t such that he considers y equivalent to a lottery between x, z where x has probability t.

It is also important in game theory, if probability mixture of strategies are allowed, called *mixed strategies*. The rule for decision making under uncertainty is then, maximize expected utility.

GT3. RATIONAL BEHAVIOR UNDER COMPLETE UNCERTAINTY. In some situations the possible outcomes may be known, but there is no way to estimate the probabilities of the different outcomes.

This type of problem is represented by a decision table, a sort of game against nature.

		Outcome 1	Outcome 2
Strategy	1	10	5
	2	6	6

The numbers inside the table represent the expected utilities resulting from strategies (actions) if various outcomes occur. Here strategies 2 guarantees a utility of 6 no matter what the outcome, and strategy 1 will give 10 if outcome 1 occurs but only 5 if outcome 2 happens.

DEFINITION 3.3.1. Strategy x *dominates* strategy y if the payoff u(x, i) ≥ u(y, i) for all outcomes i and the payoff u(x, i) > u(y, i) for some outcome y.

DEFINITION 3.3.2. Strategy x is a *maximin strategy* if for all y

$$\inf_i u(x, i) \geq \inf_j u(y, j)$$

The *security level* f is $\inf_i u(x, i)$.

EXAMPLE 3.3.2. In the table above, neither strategy is dominant, but strategy 2 is maximin.

A maximin strategy guards against the worst case. It reflects a sort of *risk-aversion*. In some situations it seems appropriate as guaranteeing a certain minimum payoff. Taking out insurance is a maximin strategy.

Maximin strategies are not consistent over *probability mixtures*.

EXAMPLE 3.3.3. Suppose we have a probability mixture with $t = \frac{1}{2}$ of the preceding table with

1	0	5
2	0	5

Then strategy 1 is maximin.

In fact Luce and Raiffa (1957) present a proof that no decision method under uncertainty can be consistent over probability mixtures, provided that decisions are not changed if columns are duplicated, i.e., there are two copies of the same outcome, and that there is symmetry in the strategies and outcomes.

EXAMPLE 3.3.4. Take the table

1	0
0	1

in which both outcomes are symmetric. Duplicate a column

1	0	0
0	1	1

Now consider a permutation of the outcomes

0	0	1
1	1	0

Take a random mixture of the two tables

$\frac{1}{2}$	0	$\frac{1}{2}$
$\frac{1}{2}$	1	$\frac{1}{2}$

Now the second strategy is dominant.

In practice, people seem to assign subjective probabilities no matter how inaccurate, to events, and go by expected utility more often than using a maximin strategy. But in some cases a maximin strategy may be either intrinsically valid or an approximation to the use of unknown subjective probabilities.

Dominant strategies on the other hand do not lead to inconsistencies, but also may not lead to the choice of any strategy, if none is dominant.

No ordinary noncooperative solution including dominant strategies is appropriate if the game is cooperative (as in the cooperative prisoner's dilemma) or if the other player knows your play before he moves.

A subtler case is *Newcomb's paradox*. Suppose a being from another planet claims (and evidence supports his claim) that he can predict human behavior with 99.9999% accuracy. He offers the human subject, x, a choice of taking an closed box or a closed box and an open one. The open one has \$10. He states, "I have predicted your behavior and used my prediction to determine how much I put in the closed box. If you take both boxes, the closed box is empty. If you take only the closed box, it contains \$1,000,000." There are two ways x can reason, and different people find different ones appealing.

NP1. No matter how much is in the closed box, I will get \$10 more by taking both. So I will take both. This gives a dominant strategy:

		Predicted closed	Predicted both
x	Closed only	1,000,000	0
	Both	1,000,010	10

The outcome will be \$10 plus a 10^{-6} chance of \$1,000,000, or \$11.

NP2. I will calculate the expected values. If I take both boxes, my expected payoff is \$11 again. If I take one box, my expected payoff is \$999,999. So I choose strategy 2.

We offer as explanation that dominant strategies do not apply here, since there is no clearcut distinction between a subject x and a state of nature. Instead the subject must be considered a part of the state of nature.

GT4. NONCOOPERATIVE GAME THEORY. A game against an intelligent opponent or opponents, with no communication allowed between the players.

DEFINITION 3.3.3. An *n-person game form* consists of strategy sets $A_1, \ldots, A_n$ and a function $F: A_1 \times \ldots \times A_n$ to T_0 where T_0 is the set of outcomes. An n-person game form together with weak orders $R_1, \ldots, R_n$ on T_0.

The relation R_i is the *preference relation* of player i over outcomes. Frequently it is replaced by an expected utility function u_i.

EXAMPLE 3.3.5. For most of the preceding games, A_i is {first strategy, second strategy}, and u_i is given by the ith number inside parentheses.

The only reason this differs from the (GT3) is that the predictability of the opponent reduces the uncertainty. Thus the opponent should be assumed as intelligent or more so than oneself. This means if a player adopts any strategy principle he must allow for the possibilities that the opponent will (1) use the same principle, (2) figure out that this principle is being used and play against it or (3) use a different principle more advantageous to himself. In general a principle can be evaluated by considering the minimum over the three types of responses.

However the idea of perfect rationality and self-interest along these lines seems contradictory except for a quite restricted class of games. Such rationality is well-defined for (a) games where both players' utilities are equal, (b) zero-sum games. More generally it may be true if either any two players x, y either never have strictly opposed interests or they never have strictly agreed interests, regarding two outcomes in which everyone but x plays the same strategy, and if no player can change another's utility without changing his own. In these cases the outcome should, for instance be Pareto optimal.

The reason for the difficulty is the idea of each player thinking about what the other thinks involves an infinite regression. In the prisoner's dilemma, for instance, perfect rationality with self-interest does not compel the (-5, -5) outcome. The players could reason this way "If I adopt dominant strategy as a criterion, the outcome I can expect is (-5, -5). If I instead try for a Pareto optimum perhaps my opponent will also." This reasoning is more plausible if the payoffs are:

$$\begin{bmatrix} (1000, 1000) & (-1, 1001) \\ (1001, -1) & (0, 0) \end{bmatrix}$$

But (-1, -1) does not seem compelling either. Instead the concept of perfectly rational self-interest may be contradictory.

For the game

$$\begin{bmatrix} (0, 0) & (1000, 1000) \\ (1, 1) & (1001, 0) \end{bmatrix}$$

also seems to go through. The above mentioned proof of Luce and Raiffa (1957) also seems to argue against a consistent concept of perfect rationality for 2 person games.

The following three concepts seem necessary for our concept of *perfect rationality with self-interest.*

PR1. STACKELBERG. Suppose the players are arranged in any order > and player i assumes all players j > i can figure out his play. Then $(x_1, \ldots, x_n)$ is an outcome.

PR2. PARETO. The outcome is Pareto optimal. (Otherwise the players could each play for a better Pareto optimum, if it assumed they think the same way).

PR3. EXCHANGEABILITY. If $(x_1, \ldots, x_n)$ and $(y_1, \ldots, y_n)$ satisfy (PR1), (PR2) then if for all i, $z_i = x_i$ or y_i, so does $(z_1, \ldots, z_n)$. (The first condition implies Nash equilibrium).

PR4. NASH. No player has a strategy yielding a higher payoff than a solution, if the other players play for the solution.

If the Stackelberg equilibria in (PR1) are sufficiently unique then conversely we have an equilibrium such that for any other strategy of any player, a plausible best reply by the others yields less utility to the player in question.

A similar concept has been considered (Aspremont and Gerard-Varet 1980) as an equilibrium in which the players can communicate.

EXAMPLE 3.3.6. In this game the properties above mentioned hold, but the interests of the players are not strictly opposed.

$$\begin{bmatrix} (0,\ 0) & (1,\ -1) \\ (-1,\ 1) & (-5,\ -5) \end{bmatrix}$$

Moulin has proved that the above properties hold for a pair of maximin strategies, if the security levels represented Pareto optimal payoffs.

Can a weaker concept of rationality be constructed which includes both the case of conditions (PR1)-(PR4) and games where 1 player has a dominant strategy but which is significantly stronger than Nash equilibrium by itself ? A comparison with normal forms of games of perfect information does yield a fairly strong argument for allowing dominant strategies, at least in a not-quite-perfect rationality in which Newcomb's paradox is disallowed. One motivation for Nash equilibrium is that it includes dominant strategies and equilibria of the type considered above.

THEOREM 3.3.2. *Any finite game has at least one Nash equilibrium point in terms of mixed strategies.*

Proof. For mixed strategies $x_1, \ldots, x_n$ let $f_i(x_1, \ldots, x_n)$ be the set of best replies of player i,

$$f_i = \{z: u_i(x_1, \ldots, z, \ldots, x_n)$$

$$= \max_{y_i \varepsilon A_i} u_i(x_1, \ldots, y_i, \ldots, x_n)\}$$

Then by definition f_i for each i is a convex compact set since if z_1, z_2 are best replies then the outcomes are indifferent, and $pz_1 + pz_2$ will also be indifferent. Therefore $f_1, \ldots, f_n$ is a convex-valued set function or correspondence from the compact convex set of mixed strategy n-tuples to itself. In order to apply Kakutani's fixed point theorem, it is only necessary to verify that f_i has a closed graph. That is, let

$x_1(k), \ldots, x_n(k)$ converge to $a_1, \ldots, a_n$ and let $y_1(k), \ldots,$ $y_n(k)$ converge to $b_1, \ldots, b_n$ where $y_i(k) \varepsilon f(x_1(k), \ldots, x_n(k))$ for each i. Then $b_i \varepsilon f_i(a_1, \ldots, a_n)$. Suppose not. Then there exists c_i for some i which is a better reply than b_i. But then for k large, c_i will be a better reply than $y_i(k)$ that is

$$u_i(x_1(k), \ldots, c_i, \ldots, x_n(k)) > u_i(x_1(k), \ldots, y_i(k), \ldots, x_n(k))$$

since the former is close to $u_i(a_1, \ldots, c_i, \ldots, a_n)$ and the latter is close to $u_i(a_1, \ldots, b_i, \ldots, a_n)$. This is a contradiction.

Therefore a fixed point exists. This will be a best reply to itself, or a Nash equilibrium. □

Stated in terms other than best reply mappings, the following is the definition of Nash equilibrium.

Suppose there exists a unique Nash equilibrium or a some Nash equilibrium point which is as good as or better for everyone than any other Nash equilibrium point. (Indifferent optimal Nash equilibria must also be interchangeable in a certain sense). Every other point if anticipated by the other player would be something else. And if there is a rational choice of some particular solution it is reasonable that the other player could anticipate it.

The class of games with this property includes 2-person games in which the interests of the players are strictly opposed such as constant-sum games in which Nash equilibria exist.

DEFINITION 3.3.4. That the *interests* of the players are strictly opposed in a 2-person game means for all x_1, x_2 and y_1, y_2 in $A_1 \times A_2$, $F(x_1, x_2)\ R_1\ F(y_1, y_2)$ if and only if $F(y_1, y_2)$ $R_2\ F(x_1, x_2)$.

DEFINITION 3.3.5. Two Nash equilibrium points (x_1, x_2) and (y_1, y_2) are said to be *exchangeable* if (x_1, y_2) and (y_1, x_2) are also Nash equilibria, and all four points give each player the same payoff.

The argument above can be called *semicooperative* in that the players must know each other's payoffs, and it is assumed they have insight into one another's thought processes.

There is also a noncooperative interpretation of the Nash equilibrium based on continuous or repeated play, important in economics. For example what are called *tatonnement processes* are means by which an economy out of equilibrium converges to an equilibrium. If by experience a player knows that other players will play strategies for a Nash equilibrium point, he should follow suit. But if a point is not a Nash equilibrium point, some player is likely to change things to improve his payoff. Kaneko (1981) has a more complicated theory based on repeated play.

Finally there is a cooperative interpretation of Nash equilibrium. If players agree on a strategy n-tuple which is a Nash equilibrium, this outcome is self-enforcing, since, again, no player would gain by changing his strategy.

However if none of the above fits the way in which the game is played, Nash equilibrium may not be an accurate model of rational behavior.

For example if a game is played only once, and players do not know one another's payoffs, then the dominant strategy and maximin strategy solutions discussed later are more reasonable.

The players' interests are strictly opposed if when one player gains, the other loses.

EXAMPLE 3.3.7. If all outcomes are strongly Pareto optimal, the interests of the players are strictly opposed. For a zero-sum game or constant-sum game, the associated game in terms of mixed strategies is also zero or constant-sum, and the interests of the players are strictly opposed.

Such games are models of competition or rivalry.

This concept can be generalized to the case when only one player affects the other in a competitive way.

DEFINITION 3.3.6. A 2-person game is *row opposed* provided that (1) for all x, y, z; $u_1(x, y) < u_1(x, z)$ if and only if $u_2(x, y) > u_2(x, z)$, (2) if $u_1(x, y) = u_1(w, y)$ then $u_2(x, y) = u_2(w, y)$ for all x, y, w.

The second player can be considered a sort of predator. That is he can make a gain by his own actions only if the other player loses like a predator who can only live by eating his prey.

THEOREM 3.3.3. *If x, y and z, w are Nash equilibria for a row opposed game, then they give both players the same payoffs, and x, w and z, y are also Nash equilibria.*

Proof. By Nash equilibrium, $u_1(x, y) \geq u_1(z, y)$, $u_2(z, y) \leq u_2(z, w)$, $u_1(z, w) \geq u_1(x, w)$, $u_2(x, w) \leq u_2(x, y)$. By row opposed, applied to the second and fourth inequalities $u_1(x, y) \geq u_1(z, y) \geq u_1(z, w) \geq u_1(x, w) \geq u_1(x, y)$. So all four are equal. The definition of row opposed also implies all four u_2 values are equal. It is straightforward then to show x, w and z, y are Nash equilibria. □

Even if (2) failed, (x, w) and (z, y) would be Nash equilibria.

Games satisfying the conclusion of this theorem are said to be solvable in the sense of Nash, and their Nash equilibria are said to be *interchangeable with one another*.

Suppose there does not exist a unique class of Nash equilibrium point which are more or less best for everyone, and interchangeable with one another. Then the players face uncertainty. There is no way for the players, if they know the payoffs to everyone, but cannot communicate to settle on unique strategies which have are "best possible" relative to one another, as are Nash equilibrium points. In repeated play, trial and error could lead to same particular Nash equilibrium. But in single play, no player can predict which Nash equilibrium should be chosen.

And any other strategy could be taken advantage of, if it could be anticipated.

Nevertheless, we argue that in such a situation a maximin strategy may be better than the alternative of having a completely unpredictable outcome. If no possibility is ideal, it seems better to choose one that has some merit rather than to choose one purely at random. Some experts may completely reject maximin strategies which are not a Nash equilibrium. It may be that the particular game should be studied. A pair of maximin strategies not in equilibrium can be valid essentially only if each player is not certain of the other's intentions. This appears justified in the battle of the sexes and chicken, for roughly equal players. Another paradox which illustrates pitfalls in being certain about some else's intentions is the hangman's dilemma. The hangman tells the prisoner "I will hang you either today, tomorrow, or the next day, and it will be on a day you do not expect it." The prisoner reasons by induction that he cannot be hanged on the last day, therefore also not on the next do last day, thus not on the first day either. He is then hanged the second day.

There is even a sort of paradox in the idea of probability. The probability of a coin coming out heads is $\frac{1}{2}$ but in an infinite number of tosses, the results could be all tails. Thus the hypothesis that the probability is $\frac{1}{2}$ is completely nonfalsifiable, and in fact gives no information at all. To be meaningful, probability would have to make some statement like, within a large finite number of tosses, the proportion of heads will be $\frac{1}{2} \pm \varepsilon$ for specific ε. Such a statement may be justified by ergodic theory, and on this basis we will continue to use probabilities. So we will assume that in this uncertainty players try to minimize risk, that is use maximin strategies.

Under conditions in which every strategy is maximin and there are no Nash equilibrium points or subsets, we claim every strategy is as good as every other.

EXAMPLE 3.3.8. Consider the 2-person game with pure strategies:

$$\begin{bmatrix} (1, -1) & (-1, 1) \\ (-1, 1) & (1, -1) \end{bmatrix}$$

By symmetry all pure strategies are equally good for both players. (There is a *mixed strategy Nash equilibrium*).

It can be proved that if the interests of the players are strictly opposed in a 2-person game, any Nash equilibrium strategy is also a maximin strategy.

PROPOSITION 3.3.4. *Suppose a 2-person game with $n \times m$ payoff matrices A, B and mixed strategies has an interior Nash equilibrium (x_1, y_1) and an interior pair of maximin strategies (x_2, y_2). Then these yield the same payoffs.*

Proof. The equations for Nash equilibrium give

$$\frac{\partial}{\partial x}(xAy - \lambda x \cdot (1, 1, \dots, 1))$$
$$= \frac{\partial}{\partial y}(xBy - \mu y \cdot (1, 1, \dots, 1)) = 0$$

Thus $Ay_1 = \lambda(1, 1, \dots, 1)$, $x_1 B = \mu(1, 1, \dots, 1)$.

A maximin strategy for player 1 is also maximin for the zero-sum game A, $-A$ and is then also a Nash equilibrium strategy of this game. Thus it satisfies $x_2 A = \delta(1, 1, \dots, 1)$, $By_2 = \sigma(1, 1, \dots, 1)$. But by computing $x_2 A y_1$ two ways $\lambda = \delta$. Also $\mu = \sigma$. The payoffs at (x_1, y_1) are $(x_1 A y_1, x_1 B y_1) = (\lambda, \mu)$. At (x_2, y_2) we have $(x_2 A y_2, x_2 B y_2) = (\delta, \sigma) = (\lambda, \mu)$. □

The authors have proposed a concept of *Nash equilibrium subsets* as a general noncooperative solution. The idea is to compare equilibrium subsets by their security levels.

DEFINITION 3.3.7. A set $B_1 \times \dots \times B_n \subset A_1 \times \dots \times A_n$ is called an *equilibrium subset* if whenever $(x_1, \dots, x_n) \in$

$B_1 \times \ldots \times B_n$, $y_j = x_j$ for $j \neq i$ and $y_i \in A_i \setminus B_i$ then $F(x_1, \ldots, x_n)\ R_i\ F(y_1, \ldots, y_n)$.

EXAMPLE 3.3.9. In the game below, {1, 2} × {1, 2} is a Nash equilibrium subset preferable to the only pure strategy Nash equilibrium point {3, 3}.

$$\begin{bmatrix} (9, 10) & (10, 9) & (0, 0) \\ (10, 9) & (9, 10) & (0, 0) \\ (0, 0) & (0, 0) & (1, 1) \end{bmatrix}$$

Every Nash equilibrium point is an equilibrium subset. The definition of equilibrium subset means that it is never beneficial for any one player to depart from the subset.

Next we assume that preferences are representable by continuous utility functions.

DEFINITION 3.3.8. The *security level* of player i in $B_1 \times \ldots \times B_n \subset A_1 \times \ldots \times A_n$ is

$$\sup_{b \in B_i} \inf_{x: x_i = b} u_i(x)$$

where x ranges over $B_1 \times \ldots \times B_n$.

EXAMPLE 3.3.10. In the finite or compact case, this will be the minimum payoff guaranteed by a maximin strategy.

DEFINITION 3.3.9. One equilibrium subset *Pareto dominates* another if the security level of each player is at least as great in the former as the latter but not conversely.

EXAMPLE 3.3.11. For Nash equilibrium points, utilities (3, 4) would Pareto dominate (2, 3) or (1, 4).

It can be shown that an intersection of equilibrium subsets again one.

DEFINITION 3.3.10. The *standard equilibrium subset* of a game consists of the intersection of all equilibrium subsets which contain every closed equilibrium subset which is Pareto nondominated and minimal under inclusion.

It can also be shown that if one equilibrium subset contains another, the security levels of the latter are at least as high for each player. However containment can hold true with equality of security levels.

EXAMPLE 3.3.12. Every finite zero-sum game with mixed strategies has security levels identical to any Nash equilibrium point in it.

EXAMPLE 3.3.13. For the games above, the standard equilibrium subset is the unique Nash equilibrium point if such exists and is otherwise the entire game except in the last preceding game when it is $\{1, 2\} \times \{1, 2\}$.

THEOREM 3.3.5. *For a finite game with mixed strategies every closed equilibrium subset Pareto undominated and minimal under inclusion is a Nash equilibrium point.*

Proof. Suppose not. Let $B_1 \times \dots \times B_n$ be an equilibrium subset for which the theorem is false. Let C_i be the convex hull of B_i. Then $C_1 \times \dots \times C_n$ is an equilibrium subset having the same security levels. There exists a Nash equilibrium point in $C_1 \times \dots \times C_n$ by the same proof as that of the first theorem of this section: the best reply to a point of $C_1 \times \dots \times C_n$ includes a convex subset of $C_1 \times \dots \times C_n$. This cannot Pareto dominate $C_1 \times \dots \times C_n$, so the security levels of the two must be equal.

It will suffice to show $B = B_1 \times \dots \times B_n$ has a Nash equilibrium point. If $B = C_1 \times \dots \times C_n$ then this has been shown.

If not then $D = C_1 \times \ldots \times C_n \setminus B$ is open in $C_1 \times \ldots \times C_n$ and contained in the convex hull of the closed set B. We claim that since B is an equilibrium subset, every point of B will be a Nash equilibrium within B, that no individual's action in $C_1 \times \ldots \times C_n$ will affect his own utility. It will suffice to show this is an open subset since u is linear in each variable. Suppose two points of D differ only by individual's strategy giving him different utilities. We can assume the line through them intersects B on either side. One side has lower utility than the two points in D, contracting the assumption B was an equilibrium subset. Therefore each point of B is a Nash equilibrium point within B. But since B is an equilibrium subset, it will be a Nash equilibrium in the whole game. This completes the proof. □

COROLLARY. *For finite games with mixed strategies, the standard equilibrium subset is the smallest equilibrium subset containing all Nash equilibrium points which are not Pareto dominated by other Nash equilibrium points.*

The authors have elsewhere suggested maximin strategies on the standard equilibrium subset as a universal noncooperative solution concept. There is little theoretical justification for this "*hybrid*" concept but it exists for all finite games, unifies a number of other solution concepts, and is reasonable for all examples we have studied.

In *Stackelberg equilibrium*, also called *leader-follower equilibrium*, one player, the leader, play first. The other players, given his play, play for a Nash equilibrium among themselves.

EXAMPLE 3.3.14. The first game of this section was essentially a Stackelberg equilibrium.

Rosenthal (1980) has considered solution concept for 2-person noncooperative games in which each player i at a pair (x_1, x_2) will either play x_i or will play the best reply to x_j, $j \neq i$.

The minimum over these two possibilities leads to a new game with modified payoffs.

Harsanyi (1977) gives a method for obtaining a mixed strategy equilibrium from a specified initial n-tuple of mixed strategies.

3.4 DOMINANT STRATEGIES

Dominant strategy equilibrium is the strongest noncooperative equilibrium concept that has been widely studied in game theory and social science. In the strict sense, it means that each player has a dominant strategy. This will be best for him no matter what the others do. It does not even require that a player know the payoffs to the other players.

DEFINITION 3.4.1. The strategy x is *dominant* for player i if for all $a_1, \ldots, a_n \in A_1 \times \ldots \times A_n$ and $b_1, \ldots, b_n \in A_1 \times \ldots \times A_n$ if $a_i = x$ then $F(a_1, \ldots, a_n)\ R_i\ F(b_1, \ldots, b_n)$.

EXAMPLE 3.4.1. In the prisoner's dilemma every player has a dominant strategy. This shows the outcome need not be Pareto optimal.

EXAMPLE 3.4.2. *Dominant cooperation.*

$$\begin{bmatrix} (0, 0) & (0, 1) \\ (1, 0) & (2, 2) \end{bmatrix}$$

Here the second strategy of each player is dominant, and the outcome is Pareto optimal.

For noncooperative, simultaneous play, we think dominant strategies are a valid concept of individual (imperfect) ratio-ality. A dominant strategy equilibrium is necessarily a Nash equilibrium.

EXAMPLE 3.4.3. *Bossy game.*

$$\begin{bmatrix} (0,\ 0) & (1,\ -1) \\ (-1,\ 1) & (1,\ 1) \end{bmatrix}$$

Here the first strategy is dominant for each player, yet the second strategies give a Nash equilibrium which it better for both players.

The reason dominant strategies give a dubious result in this case is that it can happen that by changing his strategy a player can affect others' payoffs without affecting his own. Games of this type are called by Satterthwaite and Sonnenschein (1978) "*bossy*." They have no well-defined solution, in general, since a player seeking his own interest will not have a definite strategy. H. Moulin makes an assumption like the following in his work on dominance solvability.

PLAIN ASSUMPTION. If $F(x_1, \ldots, x_n)\ I_i\ F(y_1, \ldots, y_n)$ *and* $x_j = y_j$ *for* $j \neq i$ *then* $F(x_1, \ldots, x_n)\ I_j\ F(y_1, \ldots, y_n)$ *for all* j.

In other words, if player i changes his strategy, he cannot affect the payoffs of others without affecting his own. This property is particularly desirable in an economic or voting setting, but it is highly restrictive in some cases. For instance it more or less implies that for the effective strategy set of each player is 1-dimensional (i.e., is completely reflected in his own utility function), at least for specified strategies of the other players.

EXAMPLE 3.4.4.

$$\begin{bmatrix} (1,\ 3) \\ (1,\ 5) \end{bmatrix}$$

In this "bossy" game there is no definite solution. One can say that the security levels are 1, 3.

For three players the situation becomes even more undefined. This is a problem because in economic or other continuous games only rarely will Moulin's assumption be satisfied. Usually a player's strategy set and the outcomes resulting from his strategy are multidimensional.

EXAMPLE 3.4.5

$$\begin{bmatrix} (1,\ 1,\ 2) \\ \\ (1,\ 2,\ 1) \end{bmatrix}$$

Here the choice is between two distributions for the other players, both Pareto optimal.

Two person zero-sum games are *nonbossy*, since each player's utility completely determines the other player's utility. Three person zero-sum games with mixed strategies are generally bossy however. There is one kind of 3-person zero-sum game whose equilibrium points are nonbossy, and whose solution has properties similar to that of two peroson zero-sum games: one which is equivalent to 3 separate zero-sum games between pairs of players.

Dominant strategies, like Nash equilibrium, have a property of *independence of irrelevant alternatives*: if a subgame contains a solution x, then x is a solution of the subgame. Solutions by dominance solvability do not necessarily have this independence property. Any solution with the property must be some form of Nash equilibrium.

In a dominant strategy equilibrium, the players do not have to know the payoffs to one another for the outcome to be predicted, nor how the other players will reason. However a weakening of the dominant strategy equilibrium is of interest when players do have knowledge of one another's payoffs, called *dominance solvability.* The second game of this chapter is an example of dominance solvability.

In dominance solvability, all dominated strategies of each player are deleted, as unnecessary to consider. Then in the subgame formed by the remaining players all dominated strategies are deleted. The process is continued as long as possible. If all outcomes then give every player the same utility, the game is called *d-solvable*, and it is assumed this is the set of outcomes which can occur.

DEFINITION 3.4.2. Strategy x is *dominated* by strategy y for player if (1) for all $(x_1, \ldots, x_n) \in A_1 \times \ldots \times A_n$, $(y_1, \ldots, y_n) \in A_1 \times \ldots \times A_n$ such that $x_i = x$ and $y_i = y$ and $x_j = y_j$ for $j \neq i$ we have $F(y_1, \ldots, y_n)\ R_i\ F(x_1, \ldots, x_n)$, (2) for some such $x_1, \ldots, x_n, y_1, \ldots, y_n$; $F(x_1, \ldots, x_n)\ P_i\ F(y_1, \ldots, y_n)$, where P_i is strict preference.

In other words, strategy y is always at least as good as x, and is strictly better in at least one case.

DEFINITION 3.4.3. Let D_1 be the set of *undominated strategies* of a game. Let D_i for $i > 1$ be the set of undominated strategies of the subgame formed by restricting the game to strategies in D_{i-1}. If for some n, any two outcomes from strategies in D_n are indifferent for every player, the game is said to be *d-solvable*. If $s \in D_n$, s is called a *d-solution*.

EXAMPLE 3.4.6.

$$\begin{bmatrix} (7,\ 9) & (18,\ 8) & (4,\ 4) \\ (6,\ 7) & (3,\ 13) & (11,\ 1) \\ (5,\ 5) & (1,\ 0) & (9,\ 10) \end{bmatrix}$$

The only dominated row or column is row 3, dominated by row 2. Delete it. Then column 3 is dominated by column 2. Delete it. Next row 2 is dominated. After it is deleted column 2 is dominated. The solution strategies are 1, 1 giving the payoffs (7,9).

As this example illustrates, the solution by d-solvability is always a Nash equilibrium. If equality is allowed, there can exist other Nash equilibria.

EXAMPLE 3.4.7.

$$\begin{bmatrix} (2, 2) & (0, 0) \\ (1, 5) & (4, 4) \\ (0, 0) & (4, 4) \end{bmatrix}$$

Only row 3 is dominated. Delete it. Then column 2 is dominated, then row 2. The solution payoffs are 2, 2. However strategies 3, 2 giving payoffs 4, 4 are a Nash equilibrium.

If the following strengthened form of the *Plain Assumption* holds, the solution according to d-solvability will be the unique Nash equilibrium.

STRONG ASSUMPTION. For any i, if $x \neq y$ in A_i, and $x_1, \ldots, x_n$ and $y_1, \ldots, y_n$ in $A_1 \times \ldots \times A_n$ such that $x_j = y_j$ for $j \neq i$ and $x_i = x$ and $y_i = y$ it is not true that $F(x_1, \ldots, x_n)\ I_i\ F(y_1, \ldots, y_n)$.

In other different strategies of a player give inequivalent outcomes, provided that the other players maintain the same outcome. This assumption is not appropriate to voting theory, unlike the former assumption.

H. Moulin (1979, 1980) has designed d-solvable games which when played by a group of voters, give special methods of group choice. D-solvability causes there to be a unique solution with specified properties, provided the voters are informed about each other's true preference.

EXAMPLE 3.4.8. *Kingmaker.* Suppose in a group of three people, social choice is as follows. One specified person is the kingmaker. He must choose one of the other two. Then that person makes the choice for the group. This has an effect similar to majority rule: if any two players agree, their choice is adopted. Yet power is not equally distributed.

EXAMPLE 3.4.9. *Voting by veto.* The n voters in fixed sequence alternately vote against any alternatives they choose r times. There are m alternatives. Let $s = (nr + 1)m^{-1}$. Any alternative is removed from consideration as soon as there are s votes against it. There will be at the end exactly one alternative left which is chosen. Moulin showed this method for n prime, $n > m$, r large gives equal power to every voter, and is Pareto efficient.

The reason that these games are d-solvable is essentially the same as the argument for existence of perfect equilibrium: consider the last stage of the game. Here everything depends on one player's move, and every strategy not best for him is dominated. Delete them. Every strategy which is left is equivalent for him. By Plain Assumption it is equivalent for every player. Then for the next to last player all strategies except certain dominated ones will be equivalent, given that last player' strategy. Delete them.

In order for this argument to be strictly valid something must be shown that the order of deleting dominated strategies does not matter. This is not hard to prove under the Strong Assumption, but is more subtle under Plain Assumption.

DEFINITION 3.4.4. Two strategies x, y of the ith player are *equivalent* if for all $x_1, \dots, x_n$ and $y_1, \dots, y_n$ in $A_1 \times \dots \times A_n$ such that $x_i = x$, $y_i = y$, $x_j = y_j$ for $j \neq i$, $F(x_1, \dots, x_n) = F(y_1, \dots, y_n)$ for every j.

EXAMPLE 3.4.10.

$$\begin{bmatrix} (1, 2) & (2, 0) \\ (1, 2) & (2, 0) \end{bmatrix}$$

In this game the two strategies of player 1 are equivalent.

If a strategy equivalent to another is deleted, the structure of a game, including d-solvability, is unchanged.

The following result was proved by Gretlein (1980a, 1980b). Rochet (1980). Moulin (1981) and Kim and Roush (1982) proved extensions of it.

LEMMA 3.4.1. *Let G be a finite game and let H be a subgame obtained by deleting certain dominated strategies of G. Then G is d-solvable if and only if H is, and their d-solutions have the same payoffs.*

Proof. We make the induction assumption that the lemma is true for all games having strictly fewer strategies than G. If G has only strategy or has no dominated strategies or G = H the result must be true. Let G^i, H^i denote the games obtained from G, H by successively deleting all dominated strategies i times. Let $B = H^1 \cup G^2$. Then $H^1 \subset B \subset H$. By the induction assumption B is d-solvable if and only if H is, and the d-solutions have the same payoffs.

Let $C = (H^1 \cap G^1) \cup G^2$. Then $B \subset C$. We will show that C can be obtained from B by deleting strategies which are equivalent to other strategies. Let x be a strategy of player i in B but not C. Then x belongs in H^1 but not G^1. Thus there exists y in G which dominates x in G. By taking y maximal under the quasiorder of domination in G, y in G^1. However y does not dominate x in H. Thus restricted to the strategies of H; y, x must be equivalent. Therefore in B the two are equivalent. Moreover y is in G^1 and is therefore in H. Suppose it were dominated in H. Then x would be, since the two are equivalent in H. Thus $y \in G^1 \cap H^1$. This proves C is obtained from B by deleting strategies equivalent to other strategies. This means B is d-solvable if and only if C is, and the d-solution of both have the same payoffs. Finally $G^2 \subset C \subset G^1$ so by induction C is d-solvable if and only if G^1 is, and the d-solutions have the same payoffs. Finally G^1 is by definition d-solvable if and only if G is, and the d-solutions have the same payoffs. This completes the proof. □

It readily follows from this by induction that if a game can be reduced to a subgame all of whose outcomes are equivalent by repeatedly deleting dominated strategies in any order, it is d-solvable, and its outcomes give the same payoffs.

EXAMPLE 3.4.11.

$$G = \begin{bmatrix} (4,\ 4) & (1,\ 2) & (2,\ 1) \\ (4,\ 4) & (2,\ 1) & (1,\ 2) \end{bmatrix}$$

$$H = \begin{bmatrix} (4,\ 4) & (1,\ 2) \\ (4,\ 4) & (2,\ 1) \end{bmatrix}$$

This shows the solutions are not necessarily identical as sets, since

$$G^1 = \begin{bmatrix} (4,\ 4) \\ (4,\ 4) \end{bmatrix}$$

$$H^1 = [(4,\ 4)]$$

This also implies that *perfect equilibrium of a game with perfect information depends only on the normal form, not the extensive form.*

The principal advantage of d-solvability being the uniqueness and strong reasons for a particular solution, it may be of interest to consider whether there are other classes of games with this property. Two person zero-sum games with mixed strategies do, as do multi-person games made up of separate two person zero-sum games between pairs of players.

Uniqueness of Nash equilibrium has been proved under various conditions by Rosen (1965), Karamadian (1969), and Gabay and Moulin (1980).

PROPOSITION 3.4.2. *Let G be a finite game in mixed strategies. If every Nash equilibrium of G in mixed strategies involves every pure strategy of every player, then G has a unique Nash equilibrium.*

Proof. All Nash equilibrium in the interior of the simplex of mixed strategies must satisfy the equations

$$\frac{\partial u_i}{\partial p_{ik}} = \lambda_i$$

where u_i is the utility of player i and p_{ik} is the probability he uses strategy k, and λ_i is a constant corresponding to the relation $\Sigma\, p_{ik} = 1$. These equations are linear with respect to the over all product lottery. So if there exists more than one solution, there will exist a solution on the boundary. This will be a Nash equilibrium since u_i will be independent of the strategy of player i. The boundary consists of mixed strategies not involving every pure strategy of every player. □

PROPOSITION 3.4.3. *Supposed a mixed strategy is a Nash equilibrium for a finite game. Then the set of pure strategies of each player which occur nonzero coefficient form an equilibrium subset.*

Proof. Suppose player i uses the mixed strategy (p_{ik}) in a Nash equilibrium, but that $p_{is} > 0$ and strategy r where $p_{ir} < 0$ gives him a higher payoff than strategy s. Then he would do better to set $p_{is} = 0$, p_{ir} = former value of p_{is}. This contradicts the definition of Nash equilibrium. □

PROPOSITION 3.4.4. *If a finite game has no equilibrium subset in pure strategies, then it has a unique Nash equilibrium in mixed strategies.*

Proof. This follows immediately from the two propositions above. □

3.5 SUPERGAMES, METAGAMES, AND COOPERATION

The question of how to motivate people to play games cooperatively instead of noncooperatively is of importance, for instance in international affairs. Prisoner's dilemma games have better outcomes for all concerned under cooperative behavior. Three main methods have been proposed: (1) *repetition of the game*, (2) *communication*, (3) *binding contracts*.

If the prisoner's dilemma is repeated a fixed, finite number of times, the noncooperative strategy remains the unique Nash equilibrium. This can be proved by considering the last game where a player does not play the second strategy. It would be better for him at that point to change to the first strategy. In actual play, this frequently does not happen. In stead players try the strategy of playing cooperatively as long as the other player cooperates, but if he fails to cooperate, playing the noncooperative strategy for a while to punish him and then returning to the cooperative strategy.

Nigel Howard has made precise a notion something like this in his theory of metagames. Strategies involve "if," as "if you play x, I'll play y." In order for these to give a determinate outcome, one person's strategy must be imagined as of higher order in "if" than the other.

Consider a 2-person game. The first order metagame has one player play his usual strategies and the other play strategies of the form "if you play x I'll play y." The second order metagame has the former player now play all strategies of the form "if you play a given conditional strategy, I'll play y."

EXAMPLE 3.5.1. For the prisoner's dilemma, the first order metagame is

	never confess	always confess	do likewise	do the opposite
not confess	(-1, -1)	(-10, 0)	(-1, -1)	(-10, 0)
confess	(0, -10)	(-5, -5)	(-5, -5)	(0, -10)

The second order metagame is lengthy to write down since the second player has the same 4 strategies but the first player has now 16 strategies. One strategy, for instance, is "if you do likewise, I will not confess, else I will confess." This turns out to give a Nash equilibrium in the second order metagame which Pareto dominates all others. Payoffs are -1, -1 if the other player plays "do likewise," and he cannot improve on this. If the second player plays the "likewise" strategy, the first cannot do better than -1 either.

Thus the metagame is somewhat like actual behavior, and makes cooperation reasonable. The second order metagame was proved by Nigel Howard to coincide with higher orders.

PROPOSITION 3.5.1. *For a 2-person game, every Nash equilibrium gives a corresponding Nash equilibrium in each metagame. If* x_1, x_2 *gives an outcome which both players prefer to a Nash equilibrium* y_1, y_2, *there is a Nash equilibrium in the second order metagame as follows:*

Player 2: if you play x_1 *I play* x_2*; else I play* y_2

Player 1: if you play the strategy above, I play x_1*,*
else I play y_1.

Proof. For the first statement, let both players play the strategies which are always the Nash equilibrium. Then neither has a better reply.

For the second, if either player departs the other will play for the Nash equilibrium, for which he cannot do as well as for x_1, x_2. □

If the game is repeated a fixed number of times, the ordinary Nash equilibrium still seems convincing. But if the number of repetitions is not known, metagames may have validity.

Another way of looking at repetitions is by the idea of a supergame. A supergame with discount rate α can be regarded as a game repeated a number of times depending on chance, such that if the game has been played n times, the probability is α that it will be played an $(n + 1)^{st}$ time. An alternative view, convenient for mathematical treatment, is that the supergame is always repeated an infinite number of times, but a payoff x of the nth repetition is counted as having a present value of $\alpha^n x$. Supergames are of special interest in economic competition, in particular oligopoly. See J. W. Friedman (1977). They may explain why competing companies in the same business (assuming they cannot take one another over, or any have a monopoly) do not engage in price wars until equilibrium prices are reached. Binding contracts with the second viewpoint, different players may have different discount rates.

PROPOSITION 3.5.2. *Every Nash equilibrium in a game G remains a Nash equilibrium if it is played as a supergame. Let* $x_1, \ldots, x_n$ *give payoffs* $(u_1, \ldots, u_n)$ *which all players prefer to a Nash equilibrium* $y_1, \ldots, y_n$ *of G with payoffs* $(v_1, \ldots, v_n)$. *Let* α_i *be the discount rate of player i. Let* a_i *be the payoff to player i from his best response to* $x_1, \ldots, x_n$. *Then if* $1 > \alpha_i \geq (a_i - u_i)(a_i - v_i)^{-1}$ *the following strategy is a supergame Nash equilibrium: play* x_i *until any player departs from* $x_1, \ldots, x_n$, *if this happens play* y_i *afterwards.*

Proof. If all players play the given strategy the payoff to player i is

$$u_i(1 + \alpha_i + \alpha_i^2 + \ldots)$$

If player i departs at time i, his total payoff is at most

$$u_i(1 + \alpha_i + \alpha_i^2 + \ldots + \alpha_i^{i-1}) + \alpha^i a_i + v_i(\alpha^{i+1} + \ldots)$$

The difference is

$$\frac{u_i\alpha_i^i}{1 - \alpha_i} - \alpha_i^i a_i - \frac{v_i\alpha_i^{i+1}}{1 - \alpha_i}$$

$$= \frac{\alpha_i^{\,i}}{1 - \alpha_i}\left(u_i - (1 - \alpha_i)a_i - \alpha_i v_i\right)$$

which will be nonnegative. □

Thus for a sufficiently long-range viewpoint (sufficiently large α_i), new outcomes preferable to the players can result.

EXAMPLE 3.5.2. To have a Pareto optimal outcome in the prisoner's dilemma

$$\begin{bmatrix} (-1, -1) & (-10, 0) \\ (0, -10) & (-5, -5) \end{bmatrix}$$

it is enough that $\alpha_i \geq (0 + 1)(0 + 5)^{-1} = \frac{1}{5}$.

Therefore if the prisoners consider that there is at least a $\frac{1}{5}$ probability that they will again be in a similar situation, they may not confess.

The last proposition allows many solutions, none distinguished from the rest. Friedman made the following definition to single out solutions.

DEFINITION 3.5.1. An n-tuple $x_1, \ldots, x_n$ gives a *balanced temptation equilibrium* in the situation of the last proposition if the payoffs are Pareto optimal and the quantities

$$\frac{(a_i - u_i)}{(a_i - v_i)}$$

$i = 1, \ldots, n$ are equal to one another

The minimum discount rate

$$\frac{(a_i - u_i)}{(a_i - v_i)}$$

can be regarded as a measure of the temptation to player i not to play the cooperative strategy.

So repetition of a game an unknown number of times can in some cases induce cooperative behavior instead of wasteful competition. This is a positive effect in international affairs, though not in oligopoly.

Communication with no guarantee that the communication is true seems ineffective with a few possible exceptions. If a person has an incentive to not to play a strategy he communicates, it is reasonable to assume he will break his word, in noncooperative game theory. A possible exception is that if there are several Nash equilibria, communication may serve to isolate one of them. However the result depends on which player talks first.

EXAMPLE 3.5.3.

$$\begin{bmatrix} (0, 0) & (1, 2) \\ (2, 1) & (0, 0) \end{bmatrix}$$

If either player tells the other first that he will play one of the two Nash equilibria, he has an incentive to actually do it. So one-way communication may work here. Moreover for 2-way communication it is possible to a players could coordinate their moves to arrive at a fair solution of playing for (2, 1) with probability 50% and (1, 2) with probability 50%.

Bargaining games may have this nature. They will be studied in the next chapter.

Then we consider games in which agreements are binding, briefly. These are the cooperative games. In cooperative games it is frequently postulated that a solution must be Pareto optimal and individually rational, that is each player receives at least as much as he could be sure of having by playing a maximin strategy.

This means that in the prisoner's dilemma, in any cooperative solution both players should not confess. So Nash equilibrium is no longer viable in general, not even dominant strategies in the 2-person case.

Cooperative game theory could be reduced to noncooperative game theory if a definite mechanism could be found for reaching an agreement. Few such results have been obtained.

For one, Ehud Kalai has proposed a solution to the prisoner's dilemma. In this method, players play sequentially a game of perfect information. The first player proposes a pair of moves for both. The next player can either accept, in which case these are played, or propose. The number of such moves is pre-specified and finite. If agreement is not reached by the last such move, the game is played non-cooperatively. Then it is an optimal strategy for the last player before noncooperative play to propose the cooperation (-1, -1) outcome.

J. Nash earlier proposed a less compelling but more symmetrical procedure. In each, to play a 2-person game cooperatively, each player chooses a threat strategy, which he would play theoretically if agreement were not reached. The game is then arbitrated by a procedure to be described later.

E. Thompson and R. Faith (1980) have proposed a highly asymmetrical procedure which gives a Pareto optimal outcome, as a model in some cases. The players are arranged in a definite hierarchy, or sequence. The first player in the sequence does not play, but tells what his response will be to any plays by the other (n - 1) players. In turn, the ith player tells what his response will be to any sequence of plays by players i + 1, ... , n. Finally the last player plays. This is a game of perfect information, so that except for problems of "bossiness," in which Plain Assumption of Section 3.3 does not hold, the resulting payoffs are unique. This is called *the solution according to truly perfect information.*

EXAMPLE 3.5.4. For the game

$$A \quad \overset{B}{\begin{bmatrix} (0,\ 0) & (3,\ 3) \\ (2,\ 2) & (4,\ 1) \end{bmatrix}}$$

Suppose player A is first. He says I will play my second strategy if and only if you play your second. Player B must play his second strategy to avoid a zero payoff. The outcome is (4, 1). Suppose Player B is first. Then he says "I will play strategy 2 if and only if you play strategy 1." Then player A plays strategy 1 to receive a payoff of 3 instead of 2. The outcome is (2, 2).

This concept is not the same as Stackelberg equilibrium.

EXAMPLE 3.5.5. For the prisoner's dilemma the solution according to truly perfect information is for neither to confess.

EXAMPLE 3.5.6. For the battle of the sexes, the payoffs will be (2, 1) by this concept.

EXAMPLE 3.5.7. If two players' interests are strictly opposed, and there is a Nash equilibrium, this will be the solution according to truly perfect information.

It is advantageous to be the first player for truly perfect information.

Getting people to act cooperatively in prisoner's dilemma game is perhaps the main goal of *conflict resolution*, from international down to interpersonal relations. It is also crucial in questions of public goods such as pollution. It could be said that the purpose of government is to solve the prisoner's dilemma paradox. Yet such solutions may leave a question unanswered: *distributive justice*. We are not aware of a mechanism of the foregoing type, except in voting theory (Moulin 1980) which for more than 2 players gives Pareto optimality and also equality of power among the different players and does not artificially favor certain outcomes.

3.6 CONCLUSION

A number of typical human situations can be modelled by simple games. The prisoner's dilemma reflects situations where if people pursue *self-interest*, everyone is harmed. Brinksmanship depicts a situation of bluff and counter-bluff. Competition is frequently a zero-sum game. If people share common interests but differ in their view of the best goal, it is like the battle of the sexes. If people respond to one another's actions in sequence, it may be a game of perfect information.

Games of perfect information, excpet for bossiness, in which a player can affect his opponent without affecting himself have a unique solution called *perfect equilibrium*. This concept is a special case of both d-solvability and Nash equilibrium.

Nash equilibrium is the most important solution concept in noncooperative game theory. It means a point such that no player would wish to change his strategy, given the others do not. Every n-person game has at least one Nash equilibrium point, in mixed (randomized) strategies.

If the Nash equilibrium is not unique, maximin solutions may be of use. In these each player chooses that strategy for which the worst possible outcome is as good as possible. This is a policy of *risk-avoidance*.

Nash equilibrium and maximin strategies can be combined in a *hybrid solution*. If the interests of the players are strictly opposed any two Nash equilibrium are equivalent and coincides with maximin strategies.

Dominant strategy equilibria are stronger than Nash equilibria, but do not usually exist except for specially constructed games. If repreated deletion of dominanted strategies lead to unique payoffs, a game is said to be d-solvable. Dominant strategy equilibria do not require knowledge of the opponents' strategies or payoffs. D-solvability, important in voting theory, does require a knowledge of the opponents' payoffs. For instance if the people of a country know roughly how other voters rank various issues, but this knowledge is not precise enough that the government can officially use it, a d-solvable game might be appropriate in principle.

In noncooperative games the players neither communicate nor make agreements with one another. If the players can communicate, but there is no guarantee of truth in communication, this makes a difference essentially only in games with multiple Nash equilibria, in which a particular one may be selected. In cooperative games the players can bargain and make binding contracts. Cooperative behavior is generally Pareto optimal, and avoids problem with the prisoner's dilemma and battle of sexes games.

Diplomacy is an attempt to cause games to be played cooperatively even though contracts are not fully binding. If a game is repeated an unknown number of times, such behavior is reasonable, according to either the theory of metagames or supergames. If binding agreements are possible, there are specific mechanisms for achieving cooperative behavior in the prisoner's dilemma. Such mechanisms seem to be rather one-sided for some games. Thompson and Faith have proposed a strictly hierarchical solution concept. Cooperative game theory could be reduced to noncooperative game theory, as Nash partly did for 2-person games, if a bargaining mechanism could be explicitly described.

CHAPTER 4

COOPERATIVE GAME THEORY

4.1 INTRODUCTION

In cooperative game theory any subset of the players (coalition) can make binding agreements as to how they will play. For overlapping coalitions, this greatly complicates the analysis of the best strategies. However it is frequently assumed that of two overlapping coalitions, that one will prevail which offers most to the players who are in the overlap. This is to some degree the basis of the $M_1^{(i)}$ family of solutions. These fit best games in which utility is transferable and side payments are permitted, that is, a coalition may redistribute payoffs among its members in any way it chooses. An outcome is in $M_1^{(i)}$ if it is Pareto optimal, individually rational (each individual receives at least his security level), and whenever player i proposes a change that would exclude j, player j can propose a change that would exclude i, and is at least as good for players in the overlap. The *kernel* is a subset of $M_1^{(i)}$ and the *nucleolus* is a subset of the kernel.

Bargaining games are games in which every player must agree, or the end result will be the initial position. The Nash bargaining solution is that outcome which maximizes the product of the utility gains of the different players. It is the unique solution following from axioms of symmetry, invariance, independence, and Pareto efficiency. Yet two other bargaining solutions, the RCGKS and the Kalai, have other arguments in their favor.

For general cooperative games a multitude of solution concepts have been discovered. Some can be listed as follows:

I. THREAT EQUILIBRIA

1. Nash cooperative solution
2. Harsanyi weighted equilibrium
3. Myerson's modification

II. VALUES OF GAMES

1. Shapley value
2. Owen's value
3. Shapley λ-transfer value

III. BARGAINING SET SOLUTIONS

1. Ordinal bargaining set
2. Cardinal bargaining set
3. $M_1^{(im)}$

IV. COALITION DOMINATION CONCEPTS

A. Deterministic Solutions
1. Unmajorized outcomes
2. Top cycle
3. Pareto set

B. Group-Dependent Solutions
1. von Neumann-Morgenstern stable set (NM)
2. Competitive solution

C. Approximate Solutions
1. Minimax set
2. Least vulnerable set
3. Least objectionable set

D. Probabilistic Solutions
1. Markov chain solution
2. Ecological solution

V. COALITION FORMATION THEOREIS

1. Theories for triads
2. ψ-stability

Some of these are less widely used now, such as NM but a number are the subject of ongoing research. Luce and Raiffa (1957) discuss a number of concepts related to NM which are rarely seen now and which we do not take up. In addition some concepts relevant to social choice theory will be taken up in Chapter 6.

The core and strong equilibrim are related but distinct concepts in which it is assumed that no coalition can force a better position for all its members. For many games, neither exists, but in the 1960's and 1970's strong results were proved giving a condition, balancedness, for their existence. Let x be an n-tuple of numbers. To be *balanced*, we must have that if any coalition in a suitable family can guarantee its members their shares in x, then the whole group can achieve x as an n-tuple of payoff. In other words the coalition of all players is strong relative to smaller coalitions. For games presented in strategy-outcome (normal) form there exists two distinct concepts, α and β core. The core has applications to many types of trading games.

There are two different approaches to noncooperative game theory, which can be called *strategic* and *normative*, although all game theory is in a sense strategic. The strategic approaches provide a "strategic scenario" leading to the given solution, usually in terms of stability of a coalition against attempts by other coalitions to break it up. This includes most of group III, IV, V.

Normative cooperative solutions make certain postulates which are assumed to be behaviorally valid, such as an equiprobable distribution on coalitions that form, or an *invariance property*, or an *additivity assumption*. Group II is normative, and to a lesser extent Group I and Group IV; C, D.

In some cases both normative and strategic justifications can be found for the same solution concept, for example bargaining solutions. Presumably the justification of normative solutions is behavioral: psychological and cultural, while that of strategic solutions should be a kind of rationality independent of culture. It has been found that people from different social and cultural groups bargain somewhat differently. Normative solution may also be considered as "*linearizations*," approximations which have convenient mathematical properties.

4.2 GAMES WITH SIDE PAYMENTS

Cooperative game theory is a considerably less settled area than noncooperative game theory. There is tremendous variety of different solution concepts, most of which have serious drawbacks.

There are even at least two basically different ideas of what a cooperative game is, *normal form* and *characteristic function form*. Normal form means we have a game of the type considered in the last section of Chapter 3 except that any coalition of players may make binding agreements as to what moves they will play before the game is played. Characteristic function form means that for each coalition we specify what distributions of utility that coalition can guarantee to its members.

EXAMPLE 4.2.1. In majority rule committee games, a majority coalition can guarantee any action possible for the committee.

EXAMPLE 4.2.2. In 2-person games, any single player can guarantee himself his security level. Both players can guarantee themselves any outcome of the game.

The solution concept analogous to Nash equilibrium is called for *normal form, strong (Nash) equilibrium* and for games in characteristic function form, the core. A *coalition* is any subset of the set of players.

DEFINITION 4.2.1. An n-tuple of strategies $x_1, \ldots, x_n$ forms a *strong Nash equilibrium* if for all coalitions C, n-tuples $y_1, \ldots, y_n$ such that $x_i = y_i$ for $i \notin C$ for some member $j \in C$; $F(x_1, \ldots, x_n)\ R_j\ F(y_1, \ldots, y_n)$.

That is, no coalition by changing its strategies can guarantee better payoffs to all its members than $x_1, \ldots, x_n$.

EXAMPLE 4.2.3. A Nash equilibrium in a 2-person game is strong if and only if it is Pareto optimal. This will be true, for example for two person zero-sum games. Both Nash equilibria of the game of brinksmanship are strong.

A strong equilibrium must be a Nash equilibrium, be Pareto optimal, and be individually rational (give each player at least as much as his security level).

It is somewhat exceptional for a game to have a strong equilibrium. Nonexistence is the main drawback, although brinksmanship indicates that non-uniqueness can also be a problem (negotiation might lead to -1, -1).

DEFINITION 4.2.2. An outcome is in the *core* for a game in characteristic function form if it can be realized by the coalition of all players, and no subcoalition can guarantee all its members move.

EXAMPLE 4.2.4. The core of an economy is a special case of this, in which any coalition can guarantee to its members any redistribution of their initial holdings.

The core does always exist for a variety of trading games similar to the last example but for more general games it frequently does not exist.

To illustrate this, we will turn to the special topic of this section. A game with side payments is one which utility is comparable and transferable among different people. Thus a coalition may distribute a certain total wealth among its members in any way it pleases.

Such a game is specified in characteristic function form by specifying the total wealth each coalition can guarantee itself. For a coalition C, this is denoted v(C).

The reason for considering this special case first is that more satisfactory solution concepts have been determined for games with side payments than for more general games. We first consider a family of strategic solutions.

EXAMPLE 4.2.5. Consider the three person game with side payments such that v(1) = v(2) = v(3) = 0, v(1, 2) = 3, v(1, 3) = 3, v(2, 3) = 2, v(1, 2, 3) = 7. Then there are an infinite number of core allocations: (2, 2, 3), (4, 3, 0), (3, 0, 4), (0, 4, 3) and so on.

DEFINITION 4.2.3. A game with side paymetns in characteristic function form is *superadditive* if $v(C) \geq v(A) + v(B)$ whenever $A \cup B = C$, $A \cap B = \emptyset$. It is *strictly superadditive* if $v(C) > v(A) + v(B)$ for $A \cup B = C$, $A \cap B = \emptyset$, $A \neq \emptyset$, $B \neq \emptyset$.

EXAMPLE 4.2.6. The last game was superadditive.

Superadditivity is reasonable, since any action which can be taken by separate sub-coalitions should be a possible action of the total coalition. Many superadditive games have no core. We assume all games with side payments are superadditive.

EXAMPLE 4.2.7. Let $v(1) = v(2) = v(3) = 0$, $v(1, 2) = v(2, 3) = v(1, 3) = 3$, $v(1, 2, 3) = 4$. Let the payoffs be (x, y, z). To be in the core $x + y \geq 3$, $y + z \geq 3$, $x + z \geq 3$, $x + y + z = 4$. This is not possible.

What is the solution to such a game ? For any distribution of utility, some coalition will receive less than the total it could secure by itself. Thus two players would find it advantageous to act as a coalition by themselves.

But then the third player could say, "if we all join together you could have a larger total than 3, and my total would be nonzero."

The $M_1^{(i)}$, kernel, nucleolus, and related solutions consider the possibility of retaliation: if one coalition could break up a solution, another could break up the first, and would reasonably do so.

Of these $M_1^{(i)}$ is the most general. It can be defined for both normal and characteristic function form. Let $N = \{1, \ldots, n\}$ denote the coalition of all players. For a partition of the players into coalitions, we assume that a distribution of payoffs is feasible if (1) it is individually rational, that is each player i receives at least $v(i)$, (2) it is Pareto efficient for each coalition, that is in the partition there is no way a coalition in the partition could give all its players more.

When not otherwise specified, we assume the coalition structure, or partition into coalitions, consists of the unique coalition E.

DEFINITION 4.2.4. Let a distribution of utilities $(u_1, \ldots, u_n)$ be feasible for a coalition structure. An *objection* of player i against j consists of a coalition C and a distribution $(u_k)_{k \varepsilon C}$ of utilities to its members which it can secure such that $v_k \geq u_k$ for all $k \varepsilon C$, $i \varepsilon C$, $v_i > u_i$, $j \notin C$. A *counter-objection* of j against i is a coalition D_j, $i \notin D$, $j \varepsilon D$ and a distribution $(w_k)_{k\ C}$ of utilities it can secure such that for $k \varepsilon D$, $w_k \geq u_k$ and for $k \varepsilon C \cap D$, $w_k \geq v_k$.

The $M_1^{(i)}$ bargaining set consists of those vectors $(u_1, \ldots, u_n)$ such that for every objection of i against j there is a counterobjection of j against i, if i, j belong to the same coalition of the given partition.

EXAMPLE 4.2.8. For a game with side payments, every element of the core is a solution for $M_1^{(i)}$, since no objections will exist.

EXAMPLE 4.2.9. Consider a 3-person game with $v(1) = v(2) = v(3) = 0$, and empty core. Then we assert that (x_1, x_2, x_3) is an $M_1^{(i)}$ solution for the coalition E, where

$$\begin{cases} x_1 = \frac{1}{3}(v(1,2,3) + v(1,2) + v(1,3) - 2v(2,3)) \\ x_2 = \frac{1}{3}(v(1,2,3) + v(1,2) + v(2,3) - 2v(1,3)) \\ x_3 = \frac{1}{3}(v(1,2,3) + v(1,3) + v(2,3) - 2v(1,2)) \end{cases}$$

Note that this is symmetric, that $x_i \geq 0$ by superadditivity, $\Sigma x_i = v(1,2,3)$. Suppose there exists, by symmetry, an objection of 1 against 2. Let this be y_1, y_3 where $y_1 + y_3 = v(1,3)$ $y_1 > x_1$, and $x_3 \leq y_3$. Then there exists a counterobjection z_2, z_3 where $z_3 = y_3$, $z_2 = v(2,3) - y_3$. To check this, it must be shown $z_2 \geq x_2 \geq 0$.

$$z_2 = v(2,3) - y_3 = v(2,3) - v(1,3) + y_1 > v(2,3) - v(1,3) + x_1 = v(2,3) - v(1,3) + \frac{1}{3}v(1,2,3) + \frac{1}{3}v(1,2) + \frac{1}{3}v(1,3) - \frac{2}{3}v(2,3) = x_2$$

In fact this will be the only element of $M_1^{(i)}$ for partition $\{E\}$.

DEFINITION 4.2.5. The *kernel* of a game with side payments is the set of distributions $(v_1, \ldots, v_n)$ which are feasible for a given coalition structure such that for any i, j the maximum m_{ij} of $v_i - u_i$ over all objections of i against j equals the maximum m_{ji} of $v_j - u_j$ over all objections of j against i, if i, j belong to the same coalition of the partition, if u_i, v_j exceed $v(i)$, $v(j)$, and if $u_i > v(i)$, $u_j = v(j)$ then $m_{ij} > m_{ji}$. Here $v(i)$ is the security level of player i, and $(v_1, \ldots, v_n)$ is an objection.

EXAMPLE 4.2.10. Any core element is in the kernel.

EXAMPLE 4.2.11. The preceding example for a 3-person game is also in the kernel. The maximum m_{12} of $y_1 - x_1$ over objections of x_1 against x_2 is attained when $y_3 = x_3$, assuming x_1, $x_3 < v(1,3)$ so an objection exists.

$$m_{12} = y_1 - x_1 = v(1,3) - x_3 - x_1 = -\frac{2}{3}v(1,2,3) + \frac{1}{3}(v_{12} + v_{23} + v_{13})$$

In general m_{12} is the maximum of 0 and this expression. This expression is symmetric in 1, 2, 3 so it equals m_{21}.

The kernel reflects the idea that for any i, j, the power of i against j equals the power of j against i. The kernel is always a subset of $M_1^{(i)}$. The reason is for any objection of i against j, m_{ij} is the maximum amount that can be distributed to the members of C in excess of the u_i. Consider an objection of j against i with value m_{ji}. To make this into a counterobjection, redistribute the excess m_{ji} to the members of $C \cap D$ so that it equals or exceeds their portion of m_{ij}. This takes care of the case $m_{ij} \geq m_{ji}$. If player i receives v(i) then the singleton coalition {i} gives a counterobjection.

Thus to every objection there will be a counterobjection.

The definitions and basic results on the bargaining set and kernel are due to R. J. Aumann, M. Davis, and M. Maschler. For the coalition of all players and strictly superadditive games the conditions about the security levels may be deleted, and we can define the kernel by $m_{ij} = m_{ji}$ for all i, j. See Rosenmuller (1981), p. 309.

DEFINITION 4.2.6. The *excess* of coalition C for $(v_1, \ldots, v_n)$ is

$$\sum_{i \in C} u_i - v(C)$$

EXAMPLE 4.2.12. An outcome is in the core if and only if every coalition has nonnegative excess.

EXAMPLE 4.2.13. In the $M_1^{(i)}$ bargaining example the excess are as follows:

1	x_1	12	$\frac{2}{3}v(1,2,3) - \frac{1}{3}(v(1,2) + v(1,3) + v(2,3))$
2	x_2	13	"
3	x_3	23	"
	123	0	

The lowest of these, the 2-person coalition excesses are all equal.

DEFINITION 4.2.7. A utility distribution $(u_1, \ldots, u_n)$ is in the *nucleolus* if and only if the vector (e_c) of coalition excesses is leximin, that is, for any other vector (f_c) of coalition excesses, rearrange (e_c) and (f_c) in nondecreasing order. Then in the first component where (e_c) and (f_c) differ, (e_c) is greater.

One consequence of this is that the lowest coalition excess is as large as possible. Among all vectors with this property, the second lowest coalition is a maximum, and so on.

This can be phrased that the maximum dissatisfaction of any coalition is as little as possible.

EXAMPLE 4.2.14. For 3-person games with $v(1) = v(2) = v(3) = 0$, the formulas in previous examples give the nucleolus, provided that the equal 2-person coalition excesses are the lowest, except for the constant zero excess of $\{1, 2, 3\}$. It suffices that for all i,

$$x_i \geq x_i + x_j - v(i,j)$$

$$v(i,j) \geq x_j$$

$$2v(i,j) + 2v(i,k) \geq v(1,2,3) + v(j,k)$$

$$x_i \geq 0$$

$$2v(j,k) \leq v(1,2,3) + v(i,j) + v(i,k)$$

This will always hold if the core is empty, since $x_i + x_j - v(i,j) < 0$.

If $v(1,2,3) \geq 3 \max v(i,j)$ then the nucleolus is the equal division solution

$$\frac{v(1,2,3)}{3}, \quad \frac{v(1,2,3)}{3}, \quad \frac{v(1,2,3)}{3}$$

EXAMPLE 4.2.15. Consider the special case $v(1,2,3) = 1$, $v(1,2) = a > v(1,3) = v(2,3) = b$. Then the following cases are some what reasonable. In the first two cases the core exists. If $a > 2b$ then coalitions 1, 3; 2, 3 cannot form since coalition 12 will offer both 1, 2 more than they could otherwise gain. So the solution should depend on a only. If $a \leq \frac{1}{3}$ all subcoalitions are illogical, so equal division is reasonable.

Region	Nucleolus
$a \le \frac{1}{3}$	$\frac{1}{3}, \frac{1}{3}, \frac{1}{3}$
$a \ge \frac{1}{3}$, $4b \le 1 + a$	$\frac{1+a}{4}, \frac{1+a}{4}, \frac{1-a}{2}$
$4b \ge 1 + a$	$\frac{1}{3} + \frac{a-b}{3}, \frac{1}{3} + \frac{a-b}{3}, \frac{1}{3} + \frac{2b-2a}{3}$

The concept of nucleolus and the next theorem are due to D. Schmeidler (1969). He also proved uniqueness (see Rosenmuller 1981).

THEOREM 4.2.1. *For superadditive games with side payments, and coalition structure E,* $M_1^{(i)} \supset$ *kernel* $\supset$ *nucleolus. If the game is strictly superadditive all players receive payoffs in the nucleolus more than their security levels.*

Proof. We have already noted the first inclusion. Suppose $(u_1, \ldots, u_n)$ does not belong to the kernel but is in the nucleolus. Then for some i, j; $m_{ij} < m_{ji}$ but $u_i > v(i)$. For a given coalition C, m_{ij} will be

$$v(C) - \sum_{i \varepsilon C} u_i$$

since player i gets the most if he gives himself this and gives all others zero. So the lowest surplus for coalitions C containing j but not i is less than the lowest surplus for coalitions D containing i but not j. Then we can transfer a small amount of utility from j to i. This will increase the excesses for coalitions containing i but not j, slightly reduce the excesses for coalitions containing j but not i, and not affect other coalitions. This contradicts the leximin property. This proves the containment. We prove the last statement. Suppose $u_j = v(j)$. Then every coalition having a minimum excess contains j since if $j \not\in C$, $B = C \cup \{j\}$

$$\sum_C x_k - v(C) > \sum_B x_k - v(B)$$

by strict superadditivity. Thus by transferring a small amount of utility from other players to j we increase the excess of the coalitions with least excess. This contradicts the leximin property. □

It is always nonempty since the leximin ordering will have a maximum element on any compact set. Therefore also the kernel and $M_1^{(i)}$ are nonempty for games with side payments (for some other types of games such as committee games, $M_1^{(i)}$ can be empty).

THEOREM 4.2.2. *Suppose for all 3-person games without core, a solution formula is given which is symmetric in the players, individually rational, Pareto optimal, linear in the v(C), and approaches the core as v approaches a game with unique core. Then the solution formula coincides with the nucleolus.*

Proof. Fix the v(i). We can normalize the game so that v(i) = 0 by subtracting

$$\sum_{i \in C} v(i)$$

from v(C). By symmetry, and linearity, the solution formula must have the form

$$x_i = av(1,2,3) + bv(i,j) + bv(i,k) - cv(j,k)$$

By Pareto optimality, $\Sigma x_i = v(1,2,3)$, so $a = \frac{1}{3}$, $c = 2b$. These games have a unique core if and only if

$$v(1,2,3) = \frac{1}{2}(v(1,2) + v(1,3) + v(2,3))$$

Therefore

$$\frac{1}{6}(v(1,2) + v(1,3) + v(2,3)) + b(v(i,j) + v(i,k) - 2v(j, k)$$

must equal the formula for the core,

$$\frac{1}{2}(v(i,j) + v(i,k) - v(j,k))$$

So $b = \frac{1}{3}$. This proves the theorem. □

The same formulas for the nucleolus hold if security levels are nonzero.

In an ordering of the players it is said that the *value contributed* by player i is the $v(C \cup \{i\}) - v(C)$ where C is the coalition formed by all previous players in the ordering. The Shapley value is the average of this quantity over all orderings.

EXAMPLE 4.2.16. For a 3-person game with $v(1) = v(2) = v(3) = 0$.

Ordering	Value added by player 1
123	0
132	0
213	$v(2,1)$
312	$v(1,3)$
231	$v(1,2,3) - v(2,3)$
321	$v(1,2,3) - v(3,2)$

The average of these is

$$\frac{1}{2}v(1, 2, 3) + \frac{1}{6}(v(1, 2) + v(1, 3) - 2v(2, 3))$$

The Shapley value is characterized by symmetry, additivity (i.e., linearity in the quantities $v(C)$), Pareto optimality, and the fact that a player whose contribution is zero for any ordering, does not affect the payoff. It does not always lie in the core, even if the core is unique.

EXAMPLE 4.2.17. Let $v(1,2) = 5$, $v(1,3) = 6$, $v(2,3) = 7$, $v(1,2,3) = 12$. The core is (3, 4, 5). The Shapley value is $(3\frac{1}{2}, 4, 4\frac{1}{2})$.

$M_1^{(im)}$ is a modification of $M_1^{(i)}$ which lacks some of the theoretical properties of the latter but has found experimental support. Fix any partition of the players into coalitions.

Choose a "*standard of fairness*" which assigns to each coalition in the partition a value w depending on the characteristic values v. For instance if the sum of the v's of coalitions in the partition is less than v(N), the excess could be distributed equally to all players.

Then payoffs are required to be such in $M_1^{(i)}$ except that w(C) is used in place of v(C).

Thus for any partition into coalitions there exists a set of payoffs. For games in normal form, this definition is somewhat more complicated.

The bargaining set theories were partly formulated by a study of experimental results, and have been supported fairly well by it except in certain cases. Consider the game in which v(1,2,3) = v(1,2) = v(1,3) = 50, v(2,3) = v(1) = v(2) = v(3) = 0. The unique element of the core is 50, 0, 0. This also is given by $M_1^{(i)}$. Yet this does not occur in practice often, because players 2, 3 can in combination deny 50 to player 1. Thus they can bargain with him to receive a total of say 25, in order that one of them join with him. Thus the actual payoffs will be like 25, 12.5, 12.5.

Such bargaining behavior motivated the definition of $M_1^{(im)}$.

EXAMPLE 4.2.18. Choose the standard of fairness w(1,2) = w(1,3) = 50, w(2,3) = 25, w(1) = 25, w(2) = w(3) = 0. Then 50, 0, 0 is not in $M_1^{(im)}$ since player 2 has the objection 0, 12.5, 12.5 to which player 1 has no counterobjection. We can use the formulas of preceding examples with these w values to obtain the element 33.3, 8.3, 8.3 of $M_1^{(im)}$.

Kahan and Rapaport (1980) found however that no fixed standard of fairness worked uniformly experimentally. They used a sort of variable standard of fairness having a parameter α which fit well. The core did not fit well at all.

For 3-person games and the coalition E, the "cooperative" standard of fairness and $M_1^{(im)}$ yield results identical to the Shapley value. In this standard of fairness, all coalitions in the partition share the excess equally.

That is

$$w(i,j) = v(i,j) + \frac{1}{2}(v(1,2,3) - v(i,j))$$

$$= \frac{1}{2}(v(i,j) + v(1,2,3))$$

$$w(k) = \frac{1}{2}(v(1,2,3) - v(i,j))$$

Now apply the $M_1^{(i)}$ formulas

$$x_i = \frac{1}{3}(v(1, 2, 3) + v(i, j) + v(i, k) - 2v(j, k))$$

with w substituted for v. This gives for $M_1^{(im)}$

$$x_i = \frac{1}{3}v(1,2,3) + \frac{1}{6}(v(i,j) + v(i,k) - 2v(j,k))$$

the same formula as for Shapley value.

If we assumed that players instead of coalitions gained equally, so that in bargaining between $\{i, j\}$ and $\{k\}$, the former receives $\frac{2}{3}$ of the gain, then

$$w(i,j) = v(i,j) + \frac{2}{3}(v(1,2,3) - v(i,j))$$

which yields

$$x_i = \frac{1}{3}v(1,2,3) + \frac{1}{9}(v(i,j) + v(i,k) - 2v(j,k))$$

4.3 BARGAINING GAMES

Bargaining games represent negotiations of two or more parties when there are two possibilities *(1) agree on some point in a set R or (2) disagree and receive the disagreement point d.* Examples include haggling over the price of an item, diplomatic negotiations, labor management disputes, swapping goods, committee decisions where unanimity is required. If utility were transferable, or things had the same value to different people it would simply be a matter of giving all parties equal increases in utility. And this is one bargaining solution (Kalai 1977).

However for other uses it seems desirable to have a solution which depends only on preferences rather than numerical utility, and so will be unchanged if anyone's utility u is replaced by $au + b$, $a > 0$.

In strictly game theoretic terms, a bargaining game can be represented in characteristic function as a game in which the coalition of all players can assure its members any outcome of the set R, but any smaller coalition can only guarantee its members the values of d. Here we assume R is a compact, convex set of n-tuples of utilities such that every point of R gives each player at least as much utility as in d, and some point gives all players strictly more. A solution will be a function from F(R, d) to R whose value is the agreement reached by the players. At present we will mainly consider the question "*what might the players actually do ?*" instead of the question "*what is the fairest arbitration method ?*" However as game theory solutions, bargaining solutions are most often presented as *normative*, derived from postulates.

DEFINITION 4.3.1. The *Nash bargaining solution* consists of that point $(x_1, \ldots, x_n)$ of R such that $(x_1 - d_1) \ldots (x_n - d_n)$ is a maximum, where $d = (d_1, \ldots, d_n)$.

This point will exist and be unique.

EXAMPLE 4.3.1. Let $d = (0, 0)$ and R be the triangle with vertices $(a, 0)$, $(0, b)$, $(0, 0)$. By elementary calculus, the Nash bargaining solution is $(\frac{a}{2}, \frac{b}{2})$. Each person attains half of what he could.

DEFINITION 4.3.2. A bargaining solution is *symmetric* if for any permutation π of the coordinates of n-dimensional space, $F(\pi(R), \pi(d)) = \pi F(R, d)$.

This means that one player is not favored over another.

EXAMPLE 4.3.2. This implies that for a symmetrical region, each player must have the same increase in utility.

DEFINITION 4.3.3. A bargaining solution is *invariant under utility transformations* if $T(F(R, d)) = F(T(R), T(d))$ for any transformation $T(x_1, \ldots, x_i, \ldots, x_n) = (a_1x_1, \ldots, a_ix_i, \ldots, a_nx_n) + (b_1, \ldots, b_i, \ldots, b_n)$.

EXAMPLE 4.3.3. Such transformations can firstly, reduce any bargaining problem to the case $d = (0, 0, \ldots, 0)$. Then any triangle (0, 0), (a, 0), (0, b) can be reduced to a symmetrical triangle (0, 0), (1, 0), (0, 1).

DEFINITION 4.3.4. A bargaining solution is *Pareto efficient* if there is no $x > R$ such that $x_i > F(R, d)_i$ for all i.

This means that the solution is such that no other point is better for everyone. It will lie on the boundary of R.

EXAMPLE 4.3.4. This property and symmetry imply that for any symmetrical R with $d = (0, \ldots, 0)$ the bargaining solution is $(x, x, \ldots, x)$ for the largest x such that this point is in R.

The Nash bargaining solution has all these properties but is not uniquely characterized unless another is added.

DEFINITION 4.3.5. That a bargaining solution is *independent of irrelevant alternatives* means, if $S \subset R$ and $F(R, d) \in S$ then $F(R, d) = F(S, d)$.

EXAMPLE 4.3.5. If a point of S maximizes $\Pi (x_i - d_i)$ in R it will maximize it in S. So the Nash bargaining solution has this property.

EXAMPLE 4.3.6. Consider a triangle R with vertices (a, b), (c, d), (0, 0) where $a > b$, $c < d$. This lies in the triangle with vertices

$$(0, 0),\ (a + \frac{bc - ba}{d - b}, 0),\ (0, b + \frac{ad - ab}{c - a})$$

So if its solution

$$\left(\frac{a}{2} + \frac{bc - ba}{2d - 2b}, \frac{b}{2} + \frac{ad - ab}{2c - 2a}\right)$$

lies between (a, b) and (c, d) it will also be the solution of R.

This means that a bargaining solution in a given range of possibilities will also remain the solution if the possibilities are restricted but so as to include it.

THEOREM 4.3.1. *The Nash bargaining solution is the unique bargaining solution having the properties independent of irrelevant alternatives, Pareto efficiency, invariance under utility transformations, and symmetry.*

We will not prove this theorem, but give another argument, more strategic, for the Nash bargaining solution in the 2-person case, following Harsanyi (1977).

ZEUTHEN'S PRINCIPLE. In bargaining, whichever party can tolerate the least risk of disagreement makes the next concession.

For instance if disagreement would be very serious for one side but involve only a slight loss for the other, the former may be expected to concede. Conceding means replacing one's current proposal by one more favorable to the other.

Consider in particular the case when two players bargain at a time, alternately making proposals. Suppose player 1 has proposed (x_1, x_2). Then player 2 must choose (y_1, y_2) better for him such that player 1 will concede, i.e., player 1's risk limit must be less than player 2's. For player 1 be the loss under disagreement is $x_1 - d_1$ and under the other's solution $x_1 - y_1$. Thus if p is the probability of disagreement, as long as

$$p(x_1 - d_1) > x_1 - y_1$$

it may be better to yield. Thus the risk limit is:

$$p = \frac{x_1 - y_1}{x_1 - d_1}$$

the maximum risk player 1 can tolerate. Likewise the maximum risk player 2 can tolerate is

$$\frac{y_2 - x_2}{y_2 - d_2}$$

For player 1 to concede

$$\frac{x_1 - y_1}{x_1 - d_1} < \frac{y_2 - x_2}{y_2 - d_2}$$

$$1 - \frac{y_1 - d_1}{x_1 - d_1} < 1 - \frac{x_2 - d_2}{y_2 - d_2}$$

$$\frac{y_1 - d_1}{x_1 - d_1} > \frac{x_2 - d_2}{y_2 - d_2}$$

$$(y_1 - d_1)(y_2 - d_2) > (x_1 - d_1)(x_2 - d_2)$$

This means the product defining the Nash solution will increase. Thus it is reasonable to expect the final agreement to be the maximum of this product.

Other arguments can be found in a recent book of A. Roth (1979). M. Kaneko (1981) has showed that the Nash bargaining solution in the 2-person case is the solution of a certain 2-person case is the solution of a certain 2-person noncooperative game. Others have showed that the competitive equilibrium is a solution of a noncooperative game in which players choose concave utility functions and then the Nash or other bargaining solution is used to arbitrate a solution. Independence of irrelevant alternatives will be a necessary assumption later when we turn to social arbitration functions.

On the other hand, another solution has advantages in some respects.

DEFINITION 4.3.6. The *ideal value* $x_i{}^*$ of player i is $\sup\{x_i : x_1, \ldots, x_n \in R\}$. That is, it is the best possible outcome for him. The *Raiffa-Crott-Germeier-Kalai-Smorodinsky* (*RCGKS*) *solution* to the bargaining problem for R, d is the point of R of the form $(d_1 + \lambda(x_1{}^* - d_1), \ldots, d_n + \lambda(x_n{}^* - d_n))$ such that λ is a maximum.

Thus the utility increases of the players are proportional to their increases for the best possibilities.

EXAMPLE 4.3.7. For the triangle with vertices (0, 0), (1, 1), (2, 0) the RCGKS solution is $(\frac{4}{3}, \frac{2}{3})$ in proportion to $x_1{}^* = 2$, $x_2{}^* = 1$. The Nash solution is (1, 1).

DEFINITION 4.3.7. A bargaining solution is *monotone* if whenever $R \subset S$ and the ideal values are the same then $f(R, d)_i \leq f(S, d)_i$ for each i.

EXAMPLE 4.3.8. Let R be the triangle with vertices (0, 0), (1, 1), (2, 0) and S be the trapezoid which is the convex hull of R and (2, 0.9). Then the Nash solution for R is (1, 1) but for S, (2, 0.9). So the Nash solution is not monotone.

The RCGKS solution is characterized by monotonicity, invariance under utility transformations, Pareto efficiency, and symmetry. An alternative solution of Kalai (1977) involves interpersonal comparison of utilities, but has additional properties such as a stronger monotonicity, and a property that the outcome is unchanged if negation takes place in stages.

Bargaining solutions are among the most precise cooperative solution concepts. For example, every Pareto efficient point of R will be in the core, and therefore in $M_1{}^{(i)}$ and other solutions.

Some experiments have supported RCGKS more than the Nash solution. Recent experimental work of A. E. Roth and M. W. K. Malouf (1981) supports the Kalai solution when the bargainers know the true value of each outcome to the other players.

4.4 A SURVEY OF SOLUTIONS

Here we discuss some of the better known solutions for games not having transferable utility. We will not be encyclopedic, since there are a very great number of solutions, and many variations on those presented here.

First we consider *TYPE I*. The bargaining process is taken to consist of two stages (1) each player or coalition chooses a threat, (2) with the utilities from these threats as disagreement point, the players compromise according to some bargaining solution. Some experts object to this procedure as being an unnatural combination of two different types of solution: a strategic, noncooperative choice of threats and a normative, cooperative bargaining or arbitration method.

J. Nash provided a solution of this kind for 2-person games. For stage 2 he used the Nash bargaining solution previously discussed. For stage 1 he used Nash equilibrium, which he proved exists. Since all outcomes are Pareto optimal for a bargaining solution, the interests of the players are strictly opposed, so the Nash equilibrium points are exchangeable and in fact perfectly rational as defined in the last chapter. For the prisoner's dilemma, battle of the sexes, and brinksmanship games the Nash cooperative solution by symmetry and Pareto optimality gives the largest payoffs of the form (x, x).

Harsanyi (1977) has given a complicated generalization to n-person games. See also Friedman (1977). For games with side payments, Harsanyi's solution is equal to the Shapley value (see Rosenmuller 1981). There is an initially unknown set of weights used in dividing payoffs among the players, and in assigning a total value to the payoffs to the members of each coalition. There is one initially unknown threat strategy for each coalition other than the whole group E. To these are associated a marginal value of each player to each coalition containing him. The sum of such marginal payoffs gives a threat payoff for the player. Stage 2 is Nash bargaining using the threat payoffs as disagreement point. Stage 1, determination of threats involves a 2-person zero-sum game between each coalition ($\neq$ E) and the coalition of all players not in it, using differences of the weighted sum of payoffs.

R. Myerson proposed a modification of this for games with transferable utility but not in characteristic function form.

The $M_1^{(i)}$ solution applies directly to games without side payments, however it is generally empty for games with more than 3 players, and even for some 3 player games. However Asscher's ordinal bargaining set M^0 is generally nonempty. For a fixed outcome, we say that i is stronger than j if i has an objection against j for which j has no counterobjection. Such an objection is said to be justified.

The condition for the bargaining set is then that if i is stronger than j, there exist $k_1, \ldots, k_r$ such that k_1 is stronger than i, k_2 than $k_1, \ldots$, j than k_r. This reduces to $M_1^{(i)}$ for games with side payments.

In committee games under an assumption that if x is a possible outcome in terms of utilities and $y \leq x$ then y is possible, Asscher proved every winning coalition has at least one outcome it can guarantee, in the ordinal bargaining set.

Asscher has also developed a subset of M^0 called the *cardinal bargaining set*. Moulin and Laffont developed a weaker bargaining set notion in which counterobjections need only be better for the players in the intersection with the coalition giving the objection, regardless of how players not in the intersection of the 2 coalitions fare. Pattanaik has formulated related ideas, to be discussed later.

To a game without side payments we can associate a game with side payments.

DEFINITION 4.4.1. The *characteristic value* v(C) of a coalition C is the maximum total payoff the members of C can assure themselves.

The Shapley value is defined as before for such a game, the average member that a player will contribute under coalitions formed in a random order.

DEFINITION 4.4.2. For weights $w_1, \ldots, w_n$, $w_i \geq 0$, $\Sigma w_i = 1$, the *rescaling* of a game G is the game which is identical except that player i's utilities are multiplied by w_i.

This does not affect the structure of a game without side payments for $w_i > 0$, since it gives each utility a new expected utility function equivalent to his old one. However it would affect transferability of utility since the "*rate of exchange*" might not be one.

DEFINITION 4.4.3. An n-tuple $(x_1, \ldots, x_n)$ of utilities which the coalition E can guarantee itself is a Shapley λ-*transfer value* if there exists a rescaling $w_1, \ldots, w_n$ such that $w_1x_1, \ldots, w_nx_n$ is the Shapley value of the corresponding game with side payments.

EXAMPLE 4.4.1. For games with side payments, ordinary Shapley value is a λ-transfer value.

EXAMPLE 4.4.2. For bargaining games, the Shapley λ-transfer value is the Nash bargaining solution.

EXAMPLE 4.4.3. For 2-person cooperative games the Shapley λ-transfer value is the Nash bargaining solution applied to the security levels of the players as disagreement point (by subtracting the security levels from all payoffs, we can reduce this example to the preceding example).

EXAMPLE 4.4.4. (Rosenmuller 1981). Suppose the coalition 1, 2, 3 can guarantee its members any payoffs $x_i \geq 0$ with $\Sigma x_i = 100$ and coalition 1, 2 can guarantee its members any payoffs such that $x_1 + 4x_2 \leq 1$. The characteristic value of other coalitions is zero. The Shapley value of the corresponding game with side payments is 50, 50, 0, and this can be realized by the coalition 1, 2, 3. Thus it is the λ-transfer value (it is unique). In contrast Harsanyi's solution is 40, 40, 20.

Thus the utility scales are changed until the Shapley value is a possible outcome of the game, and this gives λ-transfer value. Shapley proved that the λ-transfer value exists in general, although some weights may be zero. It is unique if the set of payoff n-tuples can be defined by a single linear inequality, but otherwise may be non-unique (Rosenmuller 1981).

Owen's value is a generalization of the Shapley value making use of differential equations. All players start with probabilities $y_i = 0$ of participating. The probabilities are then continuously increased to 1. The differential equation specifies that if any player increased his probability of playing alone, and received the excess value of the increase, the result would be Pareto optimal for the given probabilities y_i.

Next we consider a special class of games for which solutions are particularly unlikely to exist: committee games.

DEFINITION 4.4.4. A *majority rule committee game* is a game such that any majority coalition can secure any outcome in a set U.

EXAMPLE 4.4.5. Consider n people where the U is the set of points in the plane and each player has an ideal point p_i such that he prefers x to y if and only if $|x - p_i| < |y - p_i|$.

This type of game is called a *spatial game*. It is frequently used in political models.

EXAMPLE 4.4.6. Consider S to be a game with side payments, where $v(1) = v(2) = v(3) = 0$, $v(1,2) = v(1,3) = v(2,3) = v(1,2,3)=$

EXAMPLE 4.4.7. Consider S to be a finite set {a, b, c} where the preference orderings of 3 voters are abc, bca, cab. Such games are of interest in voting theory.

EXAMPLE 4.4.8. Consider S to be a finite set formed by all subsets of these three proposals:

	Utility to player		
Proposal	1	2	3
a	1	-.11	-.12
b	-.11	1	-.13
c	-.12	-.13	1

For a subset containing more than one proposal, utilities are obtained by addition. This is known as a *log-rolling game*. The idea is that each member has a favorite proposal which has slight negative value for the others.

One common feature of these games is that the core is generally empty. For the last two, $M_1^{(i)}$ is empty. For 3-person spatial games, $M_1^{(i)}$ exists, but it appears that this is generally false for more than 3 players.

For committee games it is frequently convenient to indicate an action as a pair (u, C) called a *proposal* where u is an outcome and C is the majority coalition which causes the outcome.

DEFINITION 4.4.5. A pair (u, C) *invalidates* (*dominates*) another (v, D) if every member of $C \cap D$ (of C) prefers u to v.

EXAMPLE 4.4.9. In the fourth game above ({a, b}, {1, 2}) is dominated and invalidated by ({b}, {2, 3}).

Several solutions use the binary relations of domination and invalidation. The core is the set of non-dominated outcomes.

DEFINITION 4.4.6. A *competitive solution* is a family S of proposals such that (1) each coalition makes at most one proposal, (2) if $x, y \in S$ then x does not invalidate y, (3) if $x \in S$ and $y \notin S$ invalidates x then $z \in S$ invalidates y for some z.

EXAMPLE 4.4.10. If the core is nonempty, any of its elements will be a competitive solution.

The idea is that the group, though negotiation, will limit its consideration to a certain family of proposals. These are unknown but will satisfy Definition 4.4.6, (1)-(3). Eventually one of the proposals of S will be the outcome.

The competitive solution is defined for any characteristic function game. McKelvey, Ordeshook, and Winer have supported it with experimental data (1978a, 1978b).

The main unsolved problems are existence and uniqueness.

EXAMPLE 4.4.11. For a three person spatial game with A, B, C being the three ideal points of the players, there exists a competitive solution with three points P, Q, R on the sides of the triangle such that any two of P, Q, R are equidistant from the vertex joining the sides they lie on.

EXAMPLE 4.4.12. For three person noncommittee games, the competitive solution may not exist. This is the case for a game with side payments where $v(1,2,3) = 4$, $v(1,2) = v(1,3) = v(2,3) = 3$, and $v(i) = 0$.

For three person committee games with convex payoff set there is generally a competitive solution which if the core is empty involves the three coalitions 12, 13, 23. For each coalition a Pareto optimal (for the coalition) outcome is found such that the payoffs to player i in the proposals for coalitions ij and k are equal.

For the four person committee game where the outcome set $\{(x_1, x_2, x_3, x_4): \Sigma x_i = 1\}$ we do not know whether a competitive solution exists.

DEFINITION 4.4.7. For $x, y \in S$, x *majorizes* y if x dominates y, and every z that dominates x also dominates y.

The unmajorized elements form a solution concept of Gillies (1963).

EXAMPLE 4.4.13. For the log-rolling example above, the relation of domination gives this matrix among the 8 subsets of the set of proposals. Let a 1 entry in row x and column y means x dominates y, that is, at least two players receive higher utilities from x than y. The set of outcomes dominating a given outcome is represented by the column under it. From the table, $\emptyset$ is majorized by abc and c is majorized by ab. All other outcomes are unmajorized.

	abc	bc	ac	ab	a	b	c	∅
abc	0	0	0	0	1	1	1	1
bc	1	0	0	0	1	0	0	1
ac	1	1	0	0	0	1	0	1
ab	1	1	1	0	0	0	1	1
a	0	0	1	1	0	1	1	0
b	0	1	0	1	0	0	1	0
c	0	1	1	0	0	0	0	0
∅	0	0	0	0	1	1	1	0

DEFINITION 4.4.8. For binary relation R, S the *composition* $R \circ S$ is $\{(x, y)$: for some z, $(x, z) \in R$ and $(z, y) \in S\}$.

EXAMPLE 4.4.14. If R, S are functions f(x), g(x) this would give the composition g(f(x)). For instance if $R = \sqrt{x}$ and y is log x, the composition is log $(\sqrt{x})$.

If R is "taller than" and S is "oldest son of" then $R \circ S$ is the binary relation "x is taller than the eldest son of y."

Composition can be used to obtain a transitive binary relation from any binary relation.

DEFINITION 4.4.9. The *transitive closure* $\overline{R}$ of a binary relation R is the union of all binary relations R, $R \circ R$, $R \circ R \circ R$, ...

EXAMPLE 4.4.15. The transitive closure of $x + 1 = y$ on the set of integers is the union of $x + 1 = y$, $x + 2 = y$, $x + 3 = y$, ... which is $x < y$.

In fact $\overline{R}$ is always the smallest (in the sense of set containment) transitive binary relation containing R.

Transitive binary relations are like order relations generally, and have a set of highest elements.

DEFINITION 4.4.9. That an element x is *maximal* for a transitive binary relation R means if $(y, x) \in R$ then $(x, y) \in R$.

The *top cycle set* of an arbitrary binary relation R is the set of maximal elements of its transitive closure.

EXAMPLE 4.4.16. For the transitive relation of containment for a family of sets, the maximal sets are those which are not proper subsets of other sets in the family.

The top cycle set for the relation of domination, also called the *admissible set*, or, sometimes *Gocha*, gives another cooperative game solution concept. For many games, however, it will be the entire set of possible outcomes.

DEFINITION 4.4.10. The *identity binary relation* on a set S is $\{(x, x): x \in S\}$. The empty relation is $\emptyset$. The *universal relation* is $\{(x, y): x, y \in S\}$.

Thus the universal relation consists of all possible ordered pairs on S.

EXAMPLE 4.4.17. For the log-rolling example and the three examples preceding it, the transitive closure will be the universal relation, and the top cycle set consists of every element.

These examples are fairly typical.

The ordinal bargaining set can be defined by saying that the transitive closure of the relation "is stronger than" is symmetric.

EXAMPLE 4.4.18. For the log-rolling game, {a, b, c} does not belong in the ordinal bargaining set. There are three outcomes which can be objections against it, {a, b}, {b, c}, {a, c}. Player 1 is stronger than player 3 by {a, b} and than player 2 by {a, c}. Yet neither of these player is stronger than player 1, since they would have to use {b, c} to which {a, b} or {a, c} will be a counterobjection. Therefore in the transitive closure player 1 is not symmetric with the others.

The von Neumann-Morgenstern cooperative solutions are not generally used today because they are so non-unique they can be almost arbitrary. However variations on them do keep coming up, such as a recent noncooperative concept of M. Kaneko which involves the information available to the players in a special way.

The idea behind them is that a solution concept is something evolved by each group separately, in the course of its play, a sort of anthropological construct or element of culture. It must satisfy the rationality properties of individual rationality and Pareto optimality but otherwise must only have these properties; *(1) consistency: no solution outcome dominates another, (2) completeness: if an outcome is not a solution, it is dominated by a solution.*

EXAMPLE 4.4.19. Consider the three person zero-sum game with side payments v(1) = v(2) = v(3) = 0, v(1,2) = v(1,3) = v(2,3) = 1, v(1,2,3) = 1. Then one solution consists of the three outcomes $(\frac{1}{2}, \frac{1}{2}, 0)$, $(\frac{1}{2}, 0, \frac{1}{2})$, $(0, \frac{1}{2}, \frac{1}{2})$. There are three other classes of solutions, each uncountably infinite. Choose $c < \frac{1}{2}$, and a player, say player 1. Then $\{(c, t, 1- c - t)\}$ where t ranges from 0 to 1 - c forms a solution. It follows that every possible outcome is a member of some solution.

Every von Neumann-Morgenstern solution must contain the core of a game. For most 3-person games, not every outcome can be in a von Neumann-Morgenstern solution, but infinitely many can.

EXAMPLE 4.4.20. Let v(1) = v(2) = v(3) = 0, v(1,2) = v(1,3) = v(2,3) = 3, v(1,2,3) = 4. There is no core. A von Neumann-Morgenstern solution consists of the points $(\frac{3}{2}, \frac{3}{2}, 1)$, $(\frac{3}{2}, 1, \frac{3}{2})$, $(1, \frac{3}{2}, \frac{3}{2})$, together with 3 some what arbitrary curves from these points to the boundary of the triangle whose vertices are (4, 0, 0), (0, 4, 0), (4, 0, 0). These curves must continually increase the two largest variables. Thus (x_1, x_2, x_3) where $x_i \geq 0$, $\Sigma x_i = 1$, is in some solution if and only if at least two $x_i \geq \frac{3}{2}$.

Von Neumann-Morgenstern solutions always exist for small numbers of players (see the discussion in Luce and Raiffa 1957), but W. F. Lucas found a 10-person game with no solution.

J. Harsanyi (1974) has formulated a bargaining process among coalitions in such a way that von Neumann-Morgenstern solutions are Nash equilibrium points. At each stage of bargaining there is a vector $x<k>$ under consideration as a payoff vector. This changes to y at the next stage if all members of a coalition S all propose y as the next payoff vector, and y dominates $x<k>$ for coalition S. There exists an extra player, a chairman, to decide cases when two or more coalitions both are able to change to the vector $x<k>$ to different vectors. He is considered a *personification* of the factors which lead one coalition to make the first effective counterproposal y.

Then $x<k + 1> = y$ if y exists, else $x<k + 1> = x$. For a fixed large number k the game ends at stage k if $x<k> = x<k - 1>$ else payoffs are considered zero. The chairman's payoff is

$$a_k = \begin{cases} 2^{-k} & \text{if } x<k + 1> \neq x<k> \\ 0 & \text{otherwise} \end{cases}$$

Strategies of the players are choices of coalitions and proposed payoff vectors given the past history of play. This method works for a class of games with side payments in characteristic function form including 3-person games and committee games. A more general method involving retaliation against indirect dominance works for other side payment games.

Several solution concepts of an approximate character have been formulated in which the criterion involves the number of players or coalitions who prefer x to y, or the number of alternatives preferred to x. See R. D. McKelvey and P. C. Ordeshook (1978). Ferejohn, Fiorina, and Packel (1978) developed a *Markov chain* concept of this nature. Let c(x, y) be the number of coalitions preferring x to y. Then let the *transition matrix* of this Markov chain be

$$m(x, y) = \frac{c(x, y)}{\sum_{y} c(x, y)}$$

The limiting probabilities give the probabilities that various outcomes will occur.

Kim and Roush (1982) proposed a modification of this which is *quadratic*, more like the equations for an *ecosystem* than a Markov chain. The dynamic equations are

$$\frac{dp_x}{dt} = p_x \Sigma (c(x, y) - c(y, x))p_y$$

Equilibrium points which are stable in a certain sense turn out to be the same as vectors p of probabilities satisfying

$$(C - C^T)p \le 0$$

Kim and Roush (1982) have defined a concept of *partially cooperative game* in which each coalitions is allowed to make binding agreements only regarding certain types of actions. For instance politics and economics are interrelated, yet political games are usually cooperative and economic ones noncooperative. Certain types of contracts are banned by law. R. D. Luce had earlier considered situations in which the set of coalitions which could form is restricted. Frequently mixed cooperative-noncooperative situations can be modelled as games in which the cooperative play precedes the noncooperative play. Such 2-stage games can be analyzed with existing concepts.

Kim and Roush used a generalization of $M_1^{(im)}$ in their work.

Shubik (1975) and Kahan and Rapaport (1980) contain references on other solution concepts.

4.5 CORE AND STRONG EQUILIBRIUM

The core and strong equilibrium both express the idea that no coalition can do better for all its members than the given solution. For many games they do not exist and in many cases they exist but are not unique. For example for bargaining games, all Pareto optimal outcomes are in the core.

Some experimental studies have supported the core but others have not for special types of games. An example of the latter was Aumann's experiment cited earlier where v(1,2,3) = v(1,2) =

$v(1,3) = 50$, $v(C) = 0$ for other coalitions. The core is (50, 0, 0) but in fact players 2, 3 realized they could together deny 50 to 1, and thus bargain with him.

However in actual economic situations it is questionable whether such implicit bargaining by the have-nots occurs, and the core is usually assumed to be valid. The core does exist for many types of trading games.

Recall that formally, the core is the set of all n-tuples $(x_1, \ldots, x_n)$ such that for any coalition C,

$$\sum_{i \varepsilon C} x_i \geq v(C)$$

and

$$\sum_{i=1}^{n} x_i = v(N)$$

The core will exist if v(N) is sufficiently large compared to v(C) for proper subcoalition C. For three players there is the condition

$$v(1,2) + v(1,3) + v(2,3) \leq x_1 + x_2 + x_1 + x_3 + x_2 + x_3$$
$$= 2\, v(1,2,3)$$

DEFINITION 4.5.1. A game with side payments is *balanced* if and only if for every collection of proper nonnegative real numbers r_C such that for all $j \varepsilon N$,

$$\sum_{j \varepsilon C} r_C = 1$$

we have

$$\sum r_C\, v(C) \leq v(N)$$

The treatment in this section will follow Hildenbrand and Kirman (1976) in some places. See also Friedman (1977).

EXAMPLE 4.5.1. Let $n = 3$, $r_{12} = r_{13} = r_{23} = \frac{1}{2}$, $r_C = 0$ otherwise. Then we have

$$r_{12} + r_{13} = 1, \quad r_{12} + r_{23} = 1, \quad r_{13} + r_{23} = 1$$

$$\frac{1}{2}(v(1,2) + v(1,3) + v(2,3)) \leq v(1,2,3)$$

This is the preceding condition.

If a game has a core, it must be balanced, since

$$\Sigma\, r_C\, v(C) \leq \Sigma\, r_C \sum_{j \varepsilon C} x_j = \sum_j x_j \sum_{j \varepsilon C} r_C = \Sigma\, x_j = v(N)$$

We will show the converse.

In studying convex sets, the following hyperplane separation theorem is useful.

THEOREM 4.5.1. *Let C_1, C_2 be compact, convex sets with no point in common. Then there exists a hyperplane separating C_1 from C_2. In vector terms, this means there exists a vector w and a number b such that for all $x \varepsilon C_1$, $w \cdot x > b$ and for all $y \varepsilon C_2$, $w \cdot x < b$.*

More generally, if $C_1 \cap C_2$ lies in a hyperplane of lower dimension, there exists a hyperplane separating $C_1 \setminus C_1 \cap C_2$ from $C_2 \setminus C_1 \cap C_2$ containing $C_1 \cap C_2$.

THEOREM 4.5.2. *If a game with side payments is balanced, its core is nonempty.*

Proof. Suppose the game is balanced. Take a vector $(x_1, \ldots, x_n)$ in the nucleolus, so that the lowest coalition excess is a great as possible. Since it is not in the core, this excess is negative. Let $\{C_k\}$, $k = 1$ to r be the set of coalitions with negative or zero excesses. Let the first s be zero. We represent each C_k be a 0-1 vector $w\langle k\rangle$ where $w\langle k\rangle_i = 1$ if $i \varepsilon C_k$ and $w\langle k\rangle_i = 0$ if $i \not\varepsilon C_k$. Suppose first that

$$\Sigma\, r_k\, w\langle k\rangle = (1, \ldots, 1)$$

where $r_k \geq 0$ and $r_k > 0$ for some $k > s$. This contradicts the condition of being balanced, since

$$\Sigma\, r_k\, v(C_k) > \Sigma\, r_k \sum_{i \varepsilon C_k} x_i = \sum_i x_i \sum_{i \varepsilon C_k} r_k = \Sigma\, x_i = v(N)$$

Thus (1, 1, ... , 1) cannot be represented in this way.

This means there exists a vector v such that $v \cdot (1, 1, \ldots, 1) = 0$ and $v \cdot w<k> \geq 0$ for all k and $v \cdot w<k> > 0$ for some $k > s$, by the hyperplane separation theorem (increase v if necessary).

Now replace the element x by $x + \lambda v$ for λ small. Then this will not decrease the excess of any coalition with nonpositive excess, since $v \cdot w<k> = 0$. It will increase at least one. We can choose λ small enough that no positive excess becomes non-positive. Then in the lexicographic ordering, $x + \lambda v$ has larger excesses than x. This contradicts the definition of nucleolus. □

For games without side payments, the core must be defined differently. There are two standard definitions.

DEFINITION 4.5.2. A collection of proper coalitions $\{C_k\}$ is *balanced* if there exist nonnegative numbers r_k such that

$$\Sigma\, r_k\, w<k> = (1, 1, \ldots, 1)$$

where $w<k>_i = 1$ if $i \varepsilon C_k$ and $w<k>_i = 0$ otherwise.

EXAMPLE 4.5.2. The family {1, 2, 3}, {1, 4}, {2, 4}, {3, 4} is balanced but not {1, 2, 3}, {1, 3, 4}, {1, 4, 2}, {1, 2}.

Geometrically balancedness means that the line through the origin containing (1, 1, ... , 1) is in the convex hull of the lines through the origin and the vectors $w<k>$. An unbalanced family is generally one in which certain members occur "more often" than others, in a weighted sense. This can made more precise as follows.

THEOREM 4.5.3. *If $\{C_k\}$ is an unbalanced family then there exist disjoint nonempty subsets S and T and positive integers a_i, $i \in S$ and b_j, $j \in T$ which are determinants of $(n - 1) \times (n - 1)$ 0-1 matrices such that for every k,*

$$\sum_{i \in C_k} a_i \geq \sum_{j \in C_k} b_j$$

but

$$\sum_S a_i = \sum_T b_j$$

and strict inequality holds in at least one case. Conversely, if this condition holds then $\{C_k\}$ is not a minimal balanced family.

Proof. A family is balanced if and only if the vector $(1, 1, \ldots, 1)$ does not lie in the cone generated by the $w<k>$. This means that in the cone generated by $(1, 1, \ldots, 1)$ and $w<k>$ there is a face containing $(1, 1, \ldots, 1)$. It will be generated by $(1, 1, \ldots, 1)$ and certain $w<k(i)>$. A hyperplane containing this face can be expressed as $z \cdot x = 0$ where z is any vector perpendicular to $(1, 1, \ldots, 1)$ and all the $w<k(i)>$.

Take this face. It will have dimension 1 less than the cone. Add a vector $w<k(0)>$ which with it spans the cone. If there are now less than n vectors, add enough 0-1 vectors with exactly 1 one to make a basis B for the entire space.

Now in the dual basis to this, the dual of $w<k(0)>$ will give a vector z such that $z \cdot (1, 1, \ldots, 1) = 0$, $z \cdot w<k> \geq 0$ for all k, and $z \cdot w<k(0)> > 0$. This dual basis vector up to a multiple, is the vector of minors of the matrix whose rows are all members of B except $w<k(0)>$.

Then let $S = \{i: z_i > 0\}$, $T = \{j: z_j < 0\}$ and a_i and b_j be the absolute values of the corresponding entries of z. The inequalities hold.

If $\{C_k\}$ is a minimal balanced family then

$$\sum v_k w<k> = (1, 1, \ldots, 1)$$

where all $r_k > 0$.

This contradicts the stated inequalities. This completes the proof. □

EXAMPLE 4.5.3. For $n = 3$, all 2×2 0-1 matrices have determinant 0, ±1 so all a_i and b_i are 1. Therefore $|S| = |T| = 1$. If a family is unbalanced then for some i, j; $j \in C_k$ whenever $i \in C_k$ and some C_k contains i but not j.

The determinant of an $n \times n$ 0-1 matrix is less than $(\sqrt{n})^n$, the product of the lengths of its rows. But better inequalitiies are known.

Consider a game without side payments but in characteristic function form. Let $V(S)$ be the set of utility k-tuples u such that a coalition of size k can guarantee to its members some $y \geq x$.

DEFINITION 4.5.3. That a game in characteristic function form without side payments is balanced means for every balanced family $\{C_k\}$ and n-vector w, if w restricted to each C_k is in $V(C_k)$ then w is in $V(N)$.

EXAMPLE 4.5.4. If a game with side payments is balanced in the previous sense, it is balanced in this sense also, since we have

$$\sum_{i=1}^{n} w_i = \sum r_k \sum_{i \in C_k} w_i \leq \sum r_k \, v(C_k) \leq v(N)$$

where the middle inequality follows from w restricted to C_k being in $V(C_k)$.

DEFINITION 4.5.4. The core of a game in characteristic function form without side payments consists of those vectors w in $V(N)$ such that for any coalition C there does not exist y in $V(C)$ with $y_i > w_i$ for all $i \in C$.

EXAMPLE 4.5.5. For a game with side payments, this coincides with the previous definition. For an exchange economy this coincides with the concept considered in Section 2.4.

The core is the set of possible outcomes such that no coalition can do better for all its members.

DEFINITION 4.5.5. That a game in characteristic function form without side payments is *strongly balanced* means that for every system of nonnegative weights $\lambda_1, \ldots, \lambda_n$ the corresponding game with side payments whose characteristic values are

$$v(C) = \max_{w \in V(C)} \sum_{i \in C} \lambda_i w_i$$

is balanced.

EXAMPLE 4.5.6. We will show that the game associated with an exchange economy is strongly balanced. Suppose not. Then there exists C_k, r_k, λ_i such that $\Sigma\, r_k w\langle k\rangle = (1, 1, \ldots, 1)$;

$$\Sigma\, r_k\, v(C_k) > v(N)$$

Thus there exist vectors $z\langle k\rangle$ such that $z\langle k\rangle_i = 0$ for $i \notin C_k$ and C_k can guarantee its members at least their payoffs in $z\langle k\rangle$, and

$$\Sigma\, r_k\, \Sigma\, \lambda_i\, z\langle k\rangle_i > v(N)$$

Thus $\Sigma\, r_k\, z\langle k\rangle$ is not less than or equal to an utility vector which the whole coalition can obtain by redistribution. Yet let $y(k, i)$, $i \in C_k$ be a set of commodity bundles for C_k which is zero outside of C_k and redistributes the goods of the members of C_k among themselves to obtain at least $z\langle k\rangle$ on utilities. Then consider the distribution in which agent i receives

$$\sum_{C_k \supset \{i\}} r_k\, y(k, i)$$

By convexity of preferences, his utility is at least $\Sigma\, r_k\, z\langle k\rangle_i$, since

$$\sum_{C_k \supset \{i\}} r_k = 1$$

To obtain a contradiction, it will suffice to show this distribution is feasible. The total quantity of good j involved is

$$\sum_i \sum_{C_k \supset \{i\}} r_k\, y(k, i)_j = \sum_{C_k} r_k \sum_{i \varepsilon C_k} y(k, i)_j = \sum_{C_k} r_k \sum_{i \varepsilon C_k} b\langle i\rangle_j$$

$$= \sum_i \sum_{C_k \supset \{i\}} r_k\, b\langle i\rangle_j = \sum_i b\langle i\rangle_j$$

where b<k> is the initial commodity bundle of trade k. This proves feasibility.

The condition of being strongly balanced is equivalent to $\sum r_k\, w\langle k\rangle \;\varepsilon\; v(N)$ where w<k> is a vector such that $w\langle k\rangle_i = 0$ for $i \not\in C_k$ and C_k can guarantee its members at least their utilities in w<k>.

A strongly balanced game is necessarily balanced. Many trading games in which goods can only be traded in whole number quantities are strongly balanced (Shapley and Shubik 1969, Shapley and Scarf 1972).

Every balanced game has nonempty core under an assumptions of free disposal and a compactness assumption. *Free disposal* means that if coalition K can guarantee its members a utility vector x and $y \leq x$ then they can also guarantee y. The compactness assumption is that for any coalition K the set of utilities in V(K) which give each player at least his security level is compact. This means the v(K) are closed, the security levels are finite, and the elements of v(K) are bounded above. For a proof, consult Friedman (1977) or Hildenbrand and Kirman (1976).

For games in normal form, there are two concepts of core, α-core and β-core. The *α-core* is the more usual concept. The difference is in V(C). For the α-core, V(C) is the set of vectors x such that C has a strategy which yields its members utilities of at least x for all strategies of the complementary coalition. For the *β-core*, V(C) is the set of all vectors x such for every strategy of the complementary coalition, C has a strategy which yields its members payoffs of at least α. Thus in the β-core case, strategies of C may vary. Since V(C) for α-core $\subset$ V(C) for β-core, but V(N) is the same, we have β-core $\subset$ α-core.

EXAMPLE 4.5.7. For the 2-person game

$$\begin{bmatrix} (1, 2) & (2, 1) & (0, 0) \\ (0, 0) & (1, 2) & (2, 1) \\ (2, 1) & (0, 0) & (1, 2) \end{bmatrix}$$

the α-core consists of (1, 2) and (2, 1) but the β-core is empty.

Although the core as a concept is analogous to strong equilibrium, the set of payoffs from strong equilibrium points may differ from both the α and β-cores. The strong equilibrium payoffs are a subset of the β-core.

EXAMPLE 4.5.8. For the 2-person game

$$\begin{bmatrix} (1, 1) & (0, 2) \\ (0, 0) & (0, 0) \end{bmatrix}$$

Here (1, 1) is in the β-core but is not a strong Nash equilibrium.

R. J. Aumann (1959, 1960, 1961) proved that the strong equilibria of a supergame correspond to the β-core of the game. A *supergame* is a game repeated infinitely often with future payoffs discounted at a given interest rate.

H. Scarf (1971) proved that the α-core of a game in normal form is nonempty if its payoffs are quasi-concave as a function of all strategy n-tuples. If they were only quasi-concave in each person's strategy separately, a Nash equilibrium could be guaranteed.

THEOREM 4.5.4. *Consider a cooperative n-person game in which each player's strategy set* A_i *is compact and convex. Suppose that the utility* u_i *to player i satisfies*

$$u_i(\frac{x+y}{2}) \geq \min \{u_i(x), u_i(y)\}$$

(quasi-concavity) for all strategy n-tuples x, y and is continuous. Then the α*-core is nonempty.*

The proof will not be given in detail. It reduces to showing the game in characteristic function form is balanced. Let $(v_1, \ldots, v_n) \in V(C)$ for all C in a balanced family. Let s_{iC} be strategies for members of C guaranteeing payoffs at least this large. Then it is shown the strategy n-tuple

$$s_i^* = \Sigma\, r_k\, s_{iC_k}$$

will give payoffs of at least v_i, by writing this a different way and using quasi-convexity. For a complete proof, see Friedman (1977)

4.6 CONCLUSION

The solutions based mainly on strategic considerations include $M_1^{(i)}$, kernel, nucleolus, core, strong equilibirum, ordinal and cardinal bargaining sets, competitive solution, von Neumann-Morgenstern solution, unmajorized set, Pareto set, top cycle set. Of those the first seven form a single family which more or less agree with one another on suitable side payment games. This family seems to have the strongest mathematical justification, although experimentally the modification $M_1^{(im)}$ has been found more successful. Von Neumann-Morgenstern solutions offer less definite predictions since usually a wide range of outcomes can belong to a solution. Existence and uniqueness properties of the competitive solution are largely unknown for games with more than three players. The last three are mainly appropriate to special committee games.

A second major class of solutions is the value-type solutions including bargaining solutions, Shapley value, λ-transfer value, Owen's value, Myerson's value and Harsanyi value. Although strategic models have been constructed for some of them, they are more normative in character, several being axiomatically derived. Shapley has argued that his value might not be approximately true for a single play of a game, but might approximately equal the average over many plays. These solutions have some what the character of arbitration procedures, and all equal the Shapley value for games with side payments when defined.

The $M_1^{(im)}$ solution is in some respects a bridge between the two classes, in that it utilizes the bargaining set idea but also a normative standard of fairness. It has been confirmed experimentally to some degree, but no single standard of fairness seems to work.

Then there are the probabilistic or approximate solutions based on the number of coalitions preferring one proposal to another, or the number of proposals favored to a given proposal. These have applications to the otherwise difficult to study log-rolling games.

For side payment games there exists a necessary and sufficient condition, balancedness, for the core to exist, which generalizes to a sufficient condition for arbitrary characteristic function games. It means that if we have a balanced family of coalitions and a payoff n-tuple such that each coalition can guarantee its part of the payoff n-tuple, then the set of all players can achieve the payoff n-tuple. A strong equilibrium exists for a convex game in normal form.

As exercises the reader might try working out the nucleolus for certain 3-person games with side payments having a core, writing formulas for $M_1^{(im)}$ for a partition into more than one coalition, proving that the axioms characterize the Nash bargaining solution, computing the various values for the 3-person game characteristic function form without side payments such that $v(1,2,3) = (x_1, x_2, x_3): x_i \geq 0$ and $\Sigma x_i = 100\}$, $v(1,2) = \{(x_1, x_2): x_i \geq 0, x_1 + 4x_2 \leq 100\}$, writing out in full the proof that convex games have a strong equilibrium point.

A different type of core theorem was established by Kenjiro Nakamura (1975). A simple game consists of a set of players and a set of coalitions called *winning coalitions*. One alternative x dominates another, y, if all members of some winning coalition prefer x to y. The core is the set of undominated alternatives. Let k (*Nakamura's number*) be the least number of winning coalitions with empty intersection if this is possible. Then Nakamura's theorem states, a simple game has nonempty core for all n-tuples of preferences if and only if either some player is in every winning coalition (veto player) or k exceeds the number of alternatives. This result is used in social choice theory.

We are sorry that this author died at such an early age. He might have contributed a lot more to game theory.

CHAPTER 5

NONCOOPERATIVE EQUILIBRIUM AND DISEQUILIBRIUM

5.1 INTRODUCTION

The general equilibrium theory assumes perfect competition, in that all traders accept the market prices and do not use strategy and monopoly power to set their own prices at a level yielding greater profits. For many buyers and sellers this assumption is consistent with self-interest. However for few sellers or buyers setting prices other than at equilibrium is realistic. Choice of prices (or quantities) by n competing sellers with many buyers becomes an n-person game. For one seller we have monopoly, for more than one, oligopoly.

A. Cournot devised a model of oligopoly in which n sellers choose quantities they sell to maximize profits. Prices are intermediate between monopoly and perfect competition, approaching the latter as n increases. Economies with such oligopoly will be Pareto-inefficient. J. Bertrand noted that the model is completely different if prices are set instead of quantities. E. H. Chamberlin constructed a theory in which competition is on the basis of quality, or product differentiation.

Monopolistic competition (noncooperative equilibrium) can also be defined for an entire economy divided into firms and consumers, in which the consumers maximize utility without trying to influence prices, but the firms set prices as a strategy to maximize profits. As the number of sellers tends to infinity this equilibrium has been shown to converge to the competitive equilibrium. However a key problem is that for few sellers, it may not exist.

Disequilibrium may thus result. It is also frequently taken as an explanation of unemployment, such as in depressions.

Treatment of disequilibrium usually involves a rationing mechanism, a way of allocating goods for which demand exceeds supply. J. H. Dreze and J. P. Benassy have provided such models. We argue that in trading in which each agent is a monopolist (no two products identical) every trader has an incentive to raise prices, even under the most pessimistic assumption that the other traders receive all they want of each rationed good. This could explain cost-push inflation. Monetary policy does not seem to help in this case.

Another type of disequilibrium is caused by unexpected shortages or surpluses of goods. It can be assumed that prices change at a rate dependent on the excess or lack of demand in relation to supply, or for a different theory, the difference between the prices calculated on the basis of supply and the actual (demand) price. The cobweb model assume supply adjusts over a fixed time only, but demand adjusts instantaneously.

Temporary general equilibrium is a succession of equilibria of expectations about the future, at different time periods. We take up the question, *does the market system favor immediate exploitation over conservation ?*

5.2 COURNOT'S AND RELATED MODELS

In trading there are about nine situations according to whether each of the buyers and sellers consist of one, few, or many agents. By the case of many agents is meant the situation of a large number of traders, each of whom can have only an insignificant effect on prices. Each of these individuals has no market power. The many-many case is a case of competitive equilibrium (in one industry), treated in Chapter 2. The one-one case can be treated as a bargaining game, for instance by the Nash bargaining solution, as M. Kaneko has done. The few-few case is a problem in game theory. The core will exist, and can be used to study this case, as M. Kaneko has done. Concepts such as λ-transfer value, the Harsanyi solution, or ordinal bargaining set can be used instead. The same is more or less true of the one-few case, which is a little simpler.

The one-many case is *monopoly*.

Since the situation of buyers and sellers is essentially symmetric, there is only one more case, few sellers and many buyers, called *oligopoly*. It may be mentioned that if there are many small sellers which together make up a significant part of the market, and a few large ones which also are significant, the situation depends on whether the game is considered cooperative or noncooperative (Friedman 1977). In the noncooperative case, where the small sellers do form large-scale coalitions the large firms have market power. In the cooperative case Farrell (1970) proved the competitive equilibrium is the only core element.

At least under the noncooperative hypothesis much of American industry is oligopolistic: grain companies, automobile, airlines, agricultural equipment, steel, computers, television networks, electronics, food processing, paper, chemicals, defense manufacturers, and so on. The areas of food production, clothing, housing, and retail trade are fairly competitive. J. K. Galbraith has held the market power implied by oligopoly responsible for some current economic problems. Unions also have market power, in a sense.

Arguments can be made both ways. As we will show later in this chapter, oligopoly can lead to persistent inflation, otherwise hard to explain. The ethical standards of giant corporations have frequently been low. Oligopolistic competition seems frequently to depend on expensive, irritating advertising in order to create a distinctive image, rather than differences in quality. Oligopolistic markets can be manipulated.

On the other hand, many giant corporations have been efficient and innovative. The competitive agricultural sector is a constant problem area, and there are some problems also with housing. The *supply-side theories* favored by some would seek the solution by strengthening corporations. Uncertainty, especially about the actions of government, but also with regard to energy, may be a major contributor to stagnation. During most of the 70's Japan and Germany, which are much more oligopolistic than the United States, did not have nearly as much trouble with stagflation. In these countries government was a more dependable ally of business.

First consider the case studied by Cournot in 1838. Suppose we have a single commodity without differences in quality, and n sellers. Since binding agreements are illegal, the Nash equilibrium is a natural solution concept, although if the game is considered a supergame, cooperative behavior might occur. Competition can in principle be either on the basis of price. However price competition for Nash equilibrium would mean prices cannot rise above the equilibrium level, since by lowering prices slightly, if they are above cost, a producer could take all the business from his competitors. This paradox is due to J. Bertrand (1883).

Instead Cournot assumed that producers compete in terms of quantity x_i. The total quantity then determines price by the demand relation. Let price be a function $f(\Sigma x_i)$ of quantity. In the simplest case, let cost of production be a constant, c. Then the profit of producer i is

$$f(\Sigma x_n)x_i - cx_i$$

Thus for each i

$$f'(\Sigma x_n)x_i + f(\Sigma x_n) - c = 0$$

So all x_i are equal, say to $\frac{x}{n}$ where x is the total quantity.

$$f'(x)\frac{x}{n} + f(x) - c = 0$$

This equation determines quantity, and thus price f(x). Since $f'(x) < 0$, the price will always be greater than the equilibrium level c, but will tend to approach it as n tends to infinity. If f is only refused to be decreasing and continuously differentiable, and to be zero for sufficiently high prices then solutions may not be unique, even for monopoly.

EXAMPLE 5.2.1. Consider f(x) to be the polygon with vertices $(0, 2 + \varepsilon)$, $(1, 2)$, $(1 + \varepsilon, 1 + \varepsilon)$, $(2, 1)$, $(2 + \varepsilon, 0)$. By comparison with the graph for $\varepsilon = 0$ it can be seen that xf(x) has two maxima, at $x = 1$ and $x = 2$.

If the maximum is unique in a strong sense, that

$$\frac{x}{n}(f(x) - c)$$

increases to a maximum and then decreases, the price necessarily decreases with n. The reason is that if $m < n$,

$$f'(x)\frac{x}{m} + f(x) - c = 0$$

then

$$f'(x)\frac{x}{n} + f(x) - c > 0$$

so the latter is still increasing. So x must be increased and therefore the price must be reduced.

If f is linear, $f = a - bx$, as in the linear expenditure system, then the solution is

$$\begin{cases} x = \dfrac{n}{n+1} \dfrac{a-c}{b} \\ \\ p = a - \dfrac{n}{n+1}(a - c) \end{cases}$$

Here p denotes the price.

If cost is not constant, things can be more complicated. For instance if cost has the form

$$d + c\frac{x}{n}$$

so that each firm has a fixed set-up cost there is only a limited number of firms which can profitably enter the market.

For finite n, this oligopoly model is not Pareto efficient in general, since efficiency requires that price equals marginal cost c.

The proportion of an added cost that is passed to consumers is $\frac{dp}{dc} = \frac{n}{n+1}$. Thus the more competitive the market, the more such increases in cost will be borne by the consumer.

Suppose a certain share of the market is occupied by small, perfectly competitive firms, at price c_1, the demand function is simply altered for the few large firms. Such an alteration depends on the rationing assumption made. If each consumer buys a mixture of the goods, his marginal utility should be the price c_2, so that the total demand is still $f(p)$ if p is the price of the large firms. So if s_o is the total competitive supply then $f(p) - s_o$ is the adjusted demand for the oligopolistic firms.

Suppose next that each consumer either buys all at price c_1 or all at price p. Let x be the fraction of consumers who buy at price c_1. Then $xf(c_1) = s_o$ and $(1 - x)f(p)$ is the adjusted demand for the oligopolistic firms. This is somewhat larger.

Which method gives higher total utility to consumers ? Under the equal plan each consumer buys the same amount x_1, he would at the higher price, and pays c_1 for the amount

$$\frac{s_o x_1}{f(p)}$$

and p for the rest of x_1. Under the separated plan the consumer has probability

$$\frac{s_o}{f(c_1)}$$

of buying at c_1 the amount x_o he would naturally buy at that price and otherwise he will buy x_1 at price p. Those expressions are linear in s_o, so it suffices to consider the extreme cases $s_o - f(p)$ and $s_o = 0$. The latter gives no difference. Assume $s_o - f(p)$. Then the equal plan gives a purchase of amount x_1 at c_1. The separate plan gives a

$$\frac{s_o}{f(c_1)}$$

chance of buying x_o at price c_1, and a

$$1 - \frac{s_o}{f(c_1)}$$

chance of buying x_1 at price p. The monetary difference, where u(y) is the utility in dollars to a consumer of quantity y, is

$$(u(x_1) - c_1x_1) - (\frac{f(p)}{f(c_1)})(u(x_o) - c_1x_o)$$

$$- (1 - \frac{f(p)}{f(c_1)})(u(x_1) - px_1)$$

We have

$$\frac{f(p)}{f(c_1)} = \frac{x_1}{x_o}, \quad u'(x_o) = c_1, \quad u'(x_1) = p$$

This gives

$$\frac{f(p)}{f(c_1)} (u(x_1) - c_1x_1 - u(x_o) + c_1x_o)$$

$$+ (1 - \frac{f(p)}{f(c_1)})(p - c_1)x_1$$

or

$$\frac{x_1}{x_o}(u(x_1) - u(x_o) + u'(x_o)(x_o - x_1))$$

$$+ (1 - \frac{x_1}{x_o})(u'(x_1) - u'(x_o))x_1$$

$$= x_1(u(x_1) - u(x_0) - (x_1 - x_0)u'(x_0))x_0{}^{-1} < 0$$

Thus consumers should prefer the *equal rationing plan*. Without government intervention, perhaps the other plan is more likely, of *first-come, first served*.

Cournot's model is a case of Nash equilibrium, and in fact Cournot may be considered the discoverer of Nash equilibrium.

This model does yield the expected sort of behavior with respect to n. However it is puzzling in that sellers frequently choose their price and not the quantity they wish to sell. Both alternatives happen. If the price is right, a seller may decide to increase or restrict production at that price. On the other hand, a seller cannot set both price and quantity sold, unless he reduces production below the demand at that price, which is never worthwhile. So perhaps we can consider a game in which the players' strategies are the union of {set price at p} and {set quantity at x}. Under suitable hypothesis about what happens if one sets price and the other quantity, to eliminate this event, there are two Nash equilibria: (1) *both set quantities at the oligopoly point*, (2) *both set prices at the competitive equilibrium*. Since both players prefer (1), it appears that this will result, for instance it seems to be the *hybrid solution*.

Several other models have been proposed as an explanation for oligopolistic prices being above competitive ones, that competition should be viewed as a supergame, that oligopolistic competition depends on perceived qualitative differences in product, and that we have some type of Stackelberg equilibrium. We will not consider the last. Viewing competition as a supergame yields as solution the same prices and total production as in monopoly if fixed costs are negligible, otherwise the same solution as a hypothtical monopoly whose fixed costs are the sum of the fixed costs of all firms. Whether this is true may be a question that can only be decided empirically. Are prices for oligopoly strictly between what they would be for monopoly and for perfect competition ?

R. E. Cave (1980) states figures of less than 1% have typically been obtained as the inefficiency costs of monopoly in the American economy.

One measure of the degree of market power is corporate profits, in relation to the interest rate. Under competition the return on capital should be its price, that is, the interest rate plus some allowance for risk. Monopoly should have the effect of raising profits above this level. This is very roughly indicated by the increase in stock prices, approximately, since these are proportional to profits, that is the average profits on the capital value represented by stock should equal the interest times its price.

Over long periods average stock prices have somewhat declined relative to inflation. Cave (1980) gives average American postwar profits as 5.8%.

Next we turn to a model of *qualitative competition.* The basic idea is each producer makes a slightly different product. The different brands are not indifferent to one another in the same quantities. Each consumer has a favorite brand. But they are all gross substitutes, in that if his favorite brand is raised in price sufficiently, a consumer will substitute another brand.

This makes a model possible in which competition on the basis of prce is possible, developed by Chamberlin (1956). In Chamberlin's model each firm's demand function is given, as a function of the price of its good and the prices of all other goods.

Such demand functions can be derived from utility functions provided they can be expressed in the form $u\,(f(x_1, \ldots, x_n, y_1, \ldots, y_n)$ where $x_1, \ldots, x_n$ are the products of the firms in question, and $y_1, \ldots, y_n$ are other goods, and a total demand function for the quantity $f(x_1, \ldots, x_n)$.

A very simple model of such a market could be considered as follows. Suppose for each brand i there is a fraction r_i of the market who have it as favorite. However they will change to another brand if the other is cheaper by amount δ_i. Then prices will typically be at least $\delta_i + c$. If δ_i are equal and the r_i are equal, prices should not exceed $2\delta_i + c$ since at this price any firm could reduce its prices to $\delta_i + c$ and attract the business of the others, more than doubling its business with least half the profit.

In qualitative competition, advertising in order to create the image of qualitative distinction seems to be of crucial importance in areas in which little difference exists.

Which of the above theories are correct for Western economies is as far as we know, not settled. There must be some truth in the qualitative competition model, at least role for industries with large advertising budgets.

W. J. Baumol has a theory in which firms maximize a combination of sales and profits, rather than profits only.

5.3 GLOBAL MODELS

There is a problem in trying to obtain global models of oligopoly. In extending Cournot's model, *how will the entire economy change if one producer changes his price or quantity* ? And in modifying general equilibrium, if equilibrium does not exist, there will be an oversupply of some goods but a shortage of others. *How will the short goods be rationed* ? If some people get their most desired bundles but others do not, it may be just chance who gets what.

In what is usually called *noncooperative equilibrium*, *producers*, i.e., *firms* are distinguished from consumers. Regarding consumers there is equilibrium: they obtain their most preferred consumption bundles. But producers act in a more sophisticated way than in general equilibrium. In general equilibrium they maximize profits, taking prices as fixed. In noncooperative equilibrium, they maximize prices, taking into account the effect of their own actions on prices. That is, if they choose to produce certain quantities this determines a set of prices at which equilibrium occurs, by equality of supply and demand. Then they maximize profits for these profits which depend on their own actions. Cournot's model is a special case of this. Competition here is on the basis of quantity, as in Cournot's model.

EXAMPLE 5.3.1. If there are no firms, noncooperative equilibrium coincides with general equilibrium. If there is a single firm, noncooperative equilibrium treats it as a monopolist, while general equilibrium treats it as if there were perfect competition.

Noncooperative equilibrium may not exist under realistic conditions, unlike general equilibrium. This discovery is due to Roberts and Sonnenschein (1977). It is known that if a certain concavity assumption holds, then noncooperative equilibrium exists, but it is not known how generally that assumption is true.

We will discuss their example in general terms.

EXAMPLE 5.3.2. There are two monopolistic firms (producing different products) and a single consumer (representing the entire public). The consumer owns both firms. The firms produce their goods without cost. The consumer owns a third good (money) whose price is set equal to 1. The firms choose the amounts they produce of their own goods. They price them at the highest price at which they will sell, the consumer's marginal substitution rate in terms of his own good. The production amounts are chosen so as to maximize profits.

To complete the specification of the example, we need only give the consumer utility function $u(x_1, x_2, x_3)$. The prices will be

$$p_1 = \frac{\frac{\partial u}{\partial x_1}}{\frac{\partial u}{\partial x_3}}, \qquad p_2 = \frac{\frac{\partial u}{\partial x_2}}{\frac{\partial u}{\partial x_3}}$$

The profits resulting from production of x_1, x_2 are x_1p_1, x_2p_2.

The maximization conditions are

$$\max_{x_1} (x_1p_1), \qquad \max_{x_2} (x_2p_2)$$

These conditions give what is called the *reaction curve* of each firm, that is, how it will respond to the other's prices. A noncooperative equilibrium will be an intersection point of the reaction curves.

In the construction, one reaction curve will be discontinuous, and specifically we will have the curves below. These curves do not intersect, so noncooperative equilibrium will not exist.

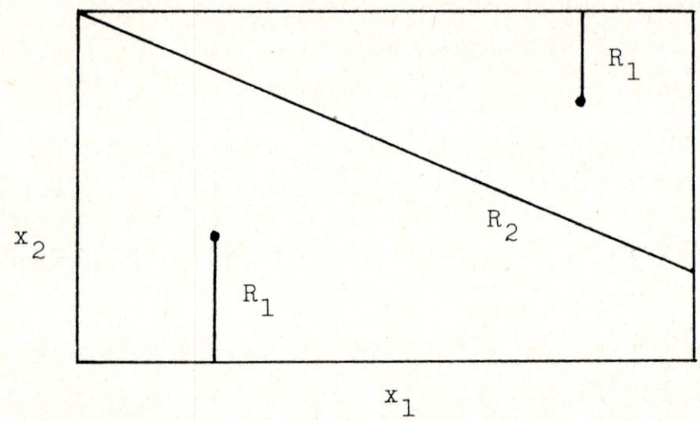

In order to do this, we choose functions a, b such that x_1a and x_2b are maximized on the two indicated curves. Let $a = 3$, $b = 2$ for $x_1 = 0.1$, $x_2 \leq 0.75$, $a = \frac{1}{3}$, $b = 1$ for $x \geq 0.75$, $x_2 = 0.9$, and for $x_2 = 1 - 0.5x_1$, $a = -3.42 + 0.45x_1 + (3)1.49^{1-x_1}$, $b = 3$. Off the two curves, a and b are simply required to be very low, so these values will not be a maximum.

Finally Roberts and Sonnenschein proved that general lemma that for any $\frac{a}{b}$ which arises as

$$\frac{\frac{\partial u}{\partial x_1}}{\frac{\partial u}{\partial x_2}}$$

for a utility function on the plane $x_3 = 1$, and for essentially any a, b having this ratio, we can find a utility function defined on a neighborhood of the plane, such that

$$a = \frac{\frac{\partial u}{\partial x_1}}{\frac{\partial u}{\partial x_3}}, \quad b = \frac{\frac{\partial u}{\partial x_2}}{\frac{\partial u}{\partial x_3}}$$

They did this by constructing level surfaces for the function u. If one is not concerned about matters such as quasi-concavity, this could be achieved by simply replacing u by a function u + (1 - z)v.

This utility function will give the reaction curves in question, which have no intersection.

A key point in this example is that the profit functions $x_i p_i$ are not quasi-concave else the maximum would be achieved on a convex set, and the curves could not be disconnected as they are.

Roberts and Sonnenschein felt that the reaction function, that is how much each firm will produce given the other's production, have the fundamental place in noncooperative equilibrium, just as demand functions are fundamental for competitive equilibrium.

In the case of a monopolists, it seems that noncooperative equilibrium is a better representation of an economy than general equilibrium. For oligopoly there is the same question as with Cournot: *is competition on the basis on quantity realistic ?*

If this model is correct, what can be done about non-existence ? Roberts and Sonnenschein mention as possibilities, *(1) the convexity assumption (i.e., the function giving profits is concave, which implies that R_1, its maximizing set, is continuous), (2) other game theoretic solution concepts, (3) a study of disequilibrium.*

Nearly the only solution concept which would avoid the problem of nonequilibrium here would be mixed strategies, that is randomization by corporate planners. Roberts and Sonnenschein feel this is unrealistic, and instead recommend alternative (3).

Other work on noncooperative equilibrium has established the plausible result that as the number of firms tends to infinity, if the size of each tends to zero as function of the whole, noncooperative equilibrium exists and approaches the (Pareto efficient) competitive equilibrium.

According to the reaction curves, what should actually happen for the previous example:

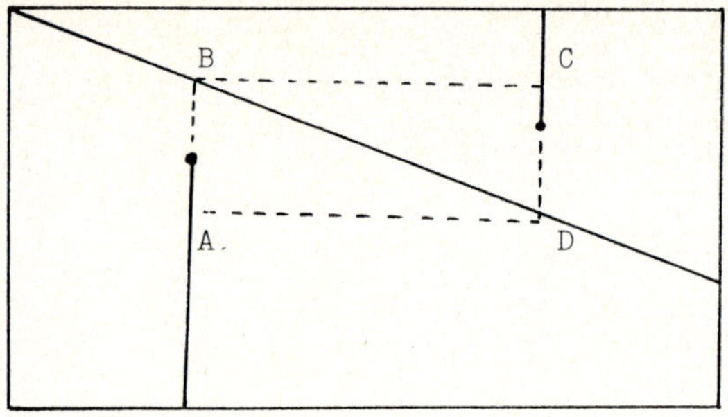

is an oscillation between the 4 points A, B, C, D in that order where B = (0.1, 0.95) and D = (0.9, 0.55). Starting at any points of the diagram, the reaction functions will lead to this cycle.

Whether this type of instability plays a role in actual economic problems as perhaps a question for empirical research, as is the same question for the different instability in the competitive equilibrium when goods are not gross substitutes and multiple equilibria can occur.

5.4 DISEQUILIBRIUM

Disequilibrium is inequality of supply and demand. It was invoked by J. M. Keynes as an explanation of the Great Depression, when the supply of labor deceed demand, and today is still involved in most theories of recession and unemployment. Inflation also generally involves disequilibrium, since at equilibrium, price ratios are unique. The only sort of inflation that could occur then would be a proportional increase in all prices. This may be true of inflation caused by people's expectations of inflation, or perhaps expansion of the money supply, but not other types. Inefficiency in an economy also implies disequilibrium.

Disequilibrium can arise, as in the last section, by strategies of traders based on their ability to influence prices. It can arise from "supply shocks," sudden changes in the supply function. The demand function is less likely to change suddenly, but if the public realizes that the object of some speculation or bubble is worthless, a demand shock might occur, or if many individuals lose their source of income or suffer other financial calamity. Equilibrium can also be prevented by many types of artificial constraints on an economy, such as regulations or price controls. Constraints of this kind can sometimes also result in a Nash equilibrium which is not Pareto efficient.

The main alternative to disequilibrium as a theory of unemployment is that the marginal product of someone's labor is not enough to pay him a wage he can live on. Conceivably this could occur for instance in heavily populated agricultural countries or when drought or war occurs, or in other societies for individuals who lack discipline and the "work ethic."

Since Pareto efficiency is optimal up to distribution and under assumptions of private goods, perfect information and equilibrium, the competitive equilibrium is Pareto optimal a market economy can only have a few types of problems: (1) *distributional inequity*, (2) *inefficient allocation of public goods*, (3) *disequilibrium, including monopoly, excessive regulation, unfair competition, inflation*, (4) *imperfect information such as fraud, unexpected disturbances to the system, difficulty in forecasting the future.*

Inequality of supply and demand is at the center of Keynes's theory and some modern mathematical disequilibrium models are attempts to find a *global mathematical setting* for his work, that is, one which takes in an entire economy. His theory was that people with money tend to save it at a certain rate, either by productive investment or unproductive investment in fixed property such as land or gold. If the interest rate is below a certain level, they will do the latter, since the ability to have one's assets in such a form that they can be converted into cash at any time is useful.

We can model the situation as consisting of one trader who has only his labor to offer and another who the capital needed to make that labor productive. The capital and labor are complementary goods, not gross substitutes. The capitalist prefers not to trade if the return to him is below a certain rate. Actually this appears closer to the situation of the workers whose marginal product is not enough for him to live on, judged by the capitalist's standard, since the capitalist would lose the advantage to him of liquidity on his goods, which to him is more than the worker can offer in return.

There is some complication in that an explanation must also be found, as to why the interest, or profit rate is low. Since labor is in effect competing for capital, just as capital is for labor, the rate of return on capital should be raised to a point where labor can be hired.

In the case of the depression and possibly other panics, this may have been due to prior speculation which caused excessive investment, so that capital had too much competition, immediately before the depression. Perhaps due to the complementary goods, capital and labor, there are multiple equilibria, and a catastrophic shift from one to the other. Labor requires capital to be productive, and without employed labor capital has no market for its goods.

At the lower equilibrium the interest rate is still low because now their is no market for the goods.

Can Keynesian ideas be used in a multiple equilibrium explanation of depressions, instead of a disequilibrium explanation ? With this theory, a cure would involve going from the low equilibrium to a high equilibrium perhaps by some how giving labor an adequate income, either by government spending or possibly transfer payments.

To return to disequilibrium, there are two types of models: *static*, or *steady-state*, which we consider in this section, and dynamic models, taken up later. The former are appropriate to diequilibrium caused by either market power due to oligopoly or due to artificial restrictions on the economy. The latter are appropriate to problems caused by to monetary or supply shocks.

The problem in dealing with disequilibrium is the uncertainty as to who will get goods in too much demand and the question of how agents will plan their strategies, with uncertainty.

In the *rationing equilibrium* of J. H. Dreze, part of the equilibrium is a specific rationing scheme, which must be such that within it all agents can simultaneously maximize their utilities. The rationing scheme has the general form of upper and lower limits on how much of each good an individual can buy or sell.

The individuals choose their consumption bundles within their budget sets but so as to be within the rationing limits for each good. Their is said to be equilibrium if then supply equals or exceeds demand for each good. Prices are fixed beforehand.

Dreze proved that rationing limits always exist such that there is equilibrium. This is true even with various restrictions on the form of rationing. For instance, it can be assumed that short goods are rationed equally among the consumers.

To be more specificy for a pure exchange economy we can formulate the idea of *Dreze rationing equilibrium*.

Given are a set of m goods, a set of n agents, an initial allocation $w<i>$ and utility function u_i for each agent, a price p_j for each good. A rationing equilibrium for each good consists of upper and lower limits $m<i>$ and $M<i>$ for each agent's final allocation, and a final allocation $x<i>$ for the agent, such that

(1) $\sum_i x<i> = \sum_i w<i>$

(2) $\sum_j p_j x<i>_j = \sum_j p_j w<i>_j$

(3) $m<i> \le x<i> \le M<i>$

and (4) subject to (2) and (3), $x<i>$ maximizes u_i.

There are also a number of other models of fixed-price disequilibrium. Benassy (1975) developed a second main class of models. These require a given rationing scheme which gives allotments Z as a function F of total demand Z^*, and is required to give the proper total of each good, to give each person at least as much utility as his initial allocation, and to agree with demand on the short side, i.e., if supply is short, suppliers sell the amounts they bid to sell. Total demand Z^* is the sum of bids by each trader.

Each agent has estimates or perceived limits $\overline{G}_i^{\,j}$ and $\underline{G}_i^{\,j}$ of the maximum and minimum amounts of each good j he can sell. The demand of a trader for good j is based on his estimated limits for all commodities other than j.

Traders have information about the demand of other agents.

Perceived constraints are modified according to past experience. If a trader is not able to make what he bid, his perceived constraint (upper or lower as appropriate) becomes equal to his bid. But if he is able to trade the amount bid, then his perceived constraint is raised or lowered beyond this.

This method is dependent on the particular rationing scheme used, and for many types of scheme is manipulable. That is, traders have an incentive to overbid.

Models related to these have been developed, in which prices are not fixed. Benassy (1976) has developed a monopolistic equilibrium in which the outcome for any given set of prices uses his fixed-price equilibrium considered above. The agents then choose their prices so as to maximize their own profits, that is there is a Nash equilibrium.

Hahn (1978) has a concept of conjectural equilibrium. Each agent has a conjecture as to what the demand function is for the goods he wishes to sell. There are rationing constraints, and there is no possibility of exceeding them at the market prices. However he can possibly sell excesses over these constraints by offering a price sufficiently much above the market price, according to his conjecture.

Each agent chooses price and quantity given his conjecture, so as to maximize his utility. The total amount sold of each good must equal the total amount bought. The condition on the conjecture functions is that they correctly predict the actual trades that occur.

This is a very weak restriction on the conjecture functions. Hahn introduced a modification, the infinitesimally rational conjectural equilibrium.

This is a conjectural equilibrium for which price behavior is not only maximizing according to the conjectured demand functions but is also a local maximum according to the actual demand functions.

Grandmont and Laroque (1976) use a Dreze model in which firms choose quantities so as to maximize prices, where the prices are such that there is a Dreze equilibrium for those quantities.

These ideas can be summarized as follows: In the Dreze model there is rationing by a system of upper and lower limits. These limits can be chosen so that there is equilibrium. In the Benassy model there is a rationing scheme which is variable in that it depends on the demand expressed by bids of traders. Traders bid on the basis of their own perception of what the market will bear. This perception is modified by experience.

Next we will consider a type of model in which there is no definite rationing method, but in the presence of uncertainty each agent uses a maximin strategy. Suppose we have a finite exchange economy, in which each agent is a monopolist, that is, sells a different good. (Qualitatively different goods or goods offered at locations differing in convenience, are considered different as in the models of qualitative competition. If two sellers offered identical goods, Bertrand's paradox for price competition, mentioned in Section 5.2, would show prices must be the equilibrium price). The model of noncooperative equilibrium given in Section 5.3 is similar to this except that firms are not distinguished from individuals.

If prices are within certain range of equilibrium, but not necessarily equal to it, it will be possible for any (n - 1) persons to realize their desired consumption bundles. That is, the other person simply takes what is left. In general this is the worst outcome that person can reasonably expect, so it will be the basis for his maximin strategy.

Suppose we consider more particularly the case of two traders and two goods. As monopolistic competition, this could be dealt with by the Nash bargaining solution, as Kaneko (1981) has done. However it has been shown that for Nash arbitration, strategic playing (choice of utility functions) results in the competitive equilibrium. Moreover we want to consider the 2-player case not for itself but only as a simplified illustration of the situation with a number of traders and goods.

Here bargaining may not really be what takes place. So we will consider it as monopolistic competition.

We review markets with two traders and two goods, represented by diagrams called *Edgeworth boxes*. Units are chosen so that the total amount of good of each kind is 1 unit. Then if trader A has quantities (x_1, x_2) of the two goods, trader B must have $(1 - x_1, 1 - x_2)$. There are two coordinate systems. Trader A's coordinates are centered at (0, 0) and go upward and to the right. Trader B's coordinates are centered at (1, 1) and go downward and to the left. Then a point (x_1, x_2) in trader A's coordinates will be precisely $(1 - x_1, 1 - x_2)$ in trader B's coordinates. In trader B's coordinate system, it represents 0.7 units of grain and 0.6 units of wheat.

Assume both traders have strictly quasi-concave and monotone utility functions, which have continuous second derivatives. A necessary and sufficient condition that an allocation be Pareto optimal is that the ratios of marginal utilities be equal:

$$\frac{\dfrac{\partial u_1}{\partial x_1}}{\dfrac{\partial u_1}{\partial x_2}} = \frac{\dfrac{\partial u_2}{\partial x_1}}{\dfrac{\partial u_2}{\partial x_2}}$$

The set of Pareto optimal points will form a continuous curve from (0, 0) to (1, 1), increasing in both variables. This is called the *contract curve*. There will be exactly one point on the curve for each utility level of trader A between his highest and least possible utilities. As his utility decreases, that of player B will increase. The contract curve is the set of possible equilibrium outcomes from trading, according to competitive equilibrium.

EXAMPLE 5.4.1. Let traders A, B have respective utility functions $x_1^{a_1} x_2^{a_2}$, $x_1^{b_1} x_2^{b_2}$ where $a_i, b_i > 0$. The contract curve is given by

$$\frac{a_1 x_2}{a_2 x_1} = \frac{b_1(1 - x_2)}{b_2(1 - x_1)}$$

This will be a portion of a hyperbola passing through (0, 0) and (1, 1) and having it axis parallel to $y = x$. For instance if

$$\frac{a_1}{a_2} = \frac{b_1}{b_2}$$

the contract curve is the line segment $y = x$.

On the contract curve the tangent lines to the indifference curves u_1 and u_2 coincide. For an initial allocation (w_1, w_2) of player 1 a point (x, y) on the contract curve is a competitive equilibrium if and only if (w_1, w_2) lies on the tangent to u_i at (x, y).

Suppose trader 1 initially has all of good 2 and trader 2 has all of good 1. Suppose trader 1 raises his prices above the equilibrium level, but trader 2 does not. Then in general some trade will still occur. Trader 2 will exchange at the new rates until he achieves an optimum. He will purchase less than before, and trader 1 will be glad to have him purchase this much, in fact would prefer that he purchase more. The new point as indicated B below, will not be Pareto optimal. For what prices p will it be better for player 1 than the equilibrium A ?

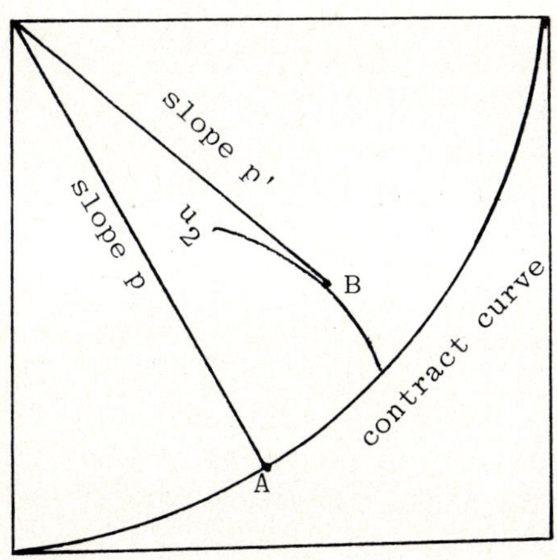

The curve described by points B is given by

$$\frac{x_1}{1 - x_2} = \frac{\frac{\partial u_2}{\partial x_2}}{\frac{\partial u_2}{\partial x_1}}$$

For $u_2 = x_1^{b_1} x_2^{b_2}$ this gives

$$\frac{x_1}{1 - x_2} = \frac{b_2(1 - x_1)}{b_1(1 - x_2)}$$

a vertical straight line

$$x_1 = \frac{b_2}{b_1 + b_2}$$

Along this line the utility of trader 1 will constantly increase. Thus the higher trader 1's prices are in relation to trader 2 the more he gains.

However the same is true for trader 2. So each trader tries to outdo the other in price increases. This is a model of runaway inflation.

Suppose that a monetarist policy is adopted, so that the total monetary value of trade cannot exceed a bound c.

Here if both prices increase, the price of trader 1 is higher, the amount traded of good 1 will be

$$\min \left\{\frac{b_2}{b_1 + b_2}, \frac{c}{p_2}\right\}$$

For any given p_2, we again have a vertical line, and it is in trader 1's interest to raise his prices as high as possible. Trader 2 will do likewise. But now the volume of trade will tend to zero, that is, there is a depression in addition to inflation.

In this model, since it is a prisoner's dilemma game, the only way to eliminate the problem is to make the game cooperative. This means there must be an agreement enforced from the outside, that is government regulation. Breaking the companies into many smaller companies would theoretically solve this problem, but in industries such as the manufacture of transportation systems or computers, this would be inefficient. J. K. Galbraith has proposed that in industries in which there are a few large corporations there is usually a largest corporation, and that this firm should be regulated. It is standard to regulate monopolies (in the model above, both firms are actually monopolists).

In the case of n traders and n goods, we will assume a trader will raise prices, provided it is to his advantage even in the case when everyone else realizes his most preferred consumption bundle, and he himself must take what is left.

Let the initial bundle of trader i be an amount w_i of good i only, p an equilibrium price vector, $x\langle i\rangle$ the consumption bundle of trader i at equilibrium. Let trader 1 raise his price to $p_1 + \varepsilon$. Let $y\langle i\rangle$ be the consumption bundles at these prices, where for $i > 1$, $y\langle i\rangle$ is the most preferred bundle trader i can purchase and $\Sigma\, y\langle i\rangle = \Sigma\, w\langle i\rangle$. Then we have

$$w_j = \Sigma\, x_j\langle i\rangle = \Sigma\, y_j\langle i\rangle$$

$$p_i w_i = p \cdot x\langle i\rangle$$

$$p_i w_i = p \cdot y\langle i\rangle + \varepsilon y_1\langle i\rangle, \quad i > 1$$

$$p_1 w_1 + \varepsilon w_1 = p \cdot y\langle 1\rangle + \varepsilon y_1\langle 1\rangle$$

The marginal utilities of trader 1 at $x\langle 1\rangle$ are proportional to the prices, since $x\langle i\rangle$ is Pareto optimal. Thus the change in trader 1's utility from $x\langle 1\rangle$ to $y\langle 1\rangle$ is proportional to $p \cdot (y\langle 1\rangle - x\langle 1\rangle)$, to terms of first order in ε. This equals

$$(p + \varepsilon)w_1 - \varepsilon g_1\langle 1\rangle - p_1 w_1 = \varepsilon w_1 - \varepsilon y_1\langle 1\rangle$$

by the equations for trader 1. But

$$\varepsilon(w_1 - y_1\langle 1\rangle) = \varepsilon \sum_{i>1} y_i\langle 1\rangle$$

which to first order is

$$\varepsilon \sum_{i>1} x_i\langle 1\rangle$$

Thus the only case in which it will not be profitable for a trader to raise prices is when at equilibrium no one would purchase his good.

This indicates that *in monopolistic competition, each monopolist raises his prices, i.e., there is inflation.*

5.5 DYNAMIC MODELS

The equations of equilibrium have been generalized in several ways to the case when demand does not equal supply. *Tatonnement processes* have previously been mentioned. These are basically theoretical mechanisms leading from an out of equilibrium point to an equilibrium. It is assumed that in a tatonnement process trading does not actually take place until equilibrium.

One general class of tatonnement processes can be represented by

$$\frac{dp}{dt} = g(z)$$

where z is excess of demand over supply. For instance $g(z) = kz$ can be chosen. There always exist tatonnement processes of this form which converge to an equilibrium.

Here we are not so much interested in tatonnement as the process by which an out of equilibrium economy reaches equilibrium. In such processes transactions will occur during the convergence process. One of the simplest methods for studying this is called the *cobweb model*. The cobweb model assumes that demand adjusts to price immediately, but supply adjusts one time period later, since adjusting supply requires considerable time. For instance, it takes farmers a year to adjust crop production to price since a larger crop must be planted. So the cobweb model can be described by saying that supply at time t is the supply corresponding to profit maximization for prices p_{t-1} at time t - 1. This supply will then sell at the price p_t such that the demand at price p_t equals the given price. Prices and supply can oscillate instead of converging to equilibrium.

Two general *models of convergence* are due to Walras and Marshall.

(*Walras*) $$\frac{dp}{dt} = \lambda z$$

(*Marshall*) $$\frac{dp}{dt} = \lambda(p_s - p_b)$$

where p_s, p_b are seller's price and buyers' price, respectively, for the given quantity of goods produced. These two models give opposite predictions about stability (convergence to equilibrium from points near equilibrium). Walras's model is stable if supply is more price-elastic than demand, while Marshall's model is stable if demand is more price-elastic (see R. G. Allen 1959).

A general matrix differential system

$$\frac{dx}{dt} = Ax$$

is stable if and only if eigenvalues of A have negative real parts. For this to hold it is sufficient that $DA + (DA)^T$ have negative eigenvalues for some diagonal matrix D with positive main diagonal entries. The reason is, that if $Ax = \lambda x$, then

$$0 > (x^*)^T(DA + (DA)^T)x = \lambda(x^*)^T Dx + \lambda^*(x^*)^T Dx$$

so $\lambda + \lambda^* < 0$. Here $(x^*)^T$ is the transposed complex conjugate. Most stability conditions in economics follow from this *D-stability condition*. For example all eigenvalues of a symmetric matrix are negative if and only the determinants of the submatrices formed by the first r rows and columns, $r = 1$ to n are the sign of $(-1)^r$.

One thing that can be done with dynamic models of this kind is to predict the increase in prices resulting from a supply shortage. For the Walras and Marshall models, there are two problems: *first, which of the two fits the situation, and second, evaluating the constant* λ. In the former case this constant has the unlikely dimensions of

$$\frac{\text{money}}{(\text{time})(\text{quantity})^2}$$

and in both cases there does not seem to be any theoretical reason why it should equal a particular number. The cobweb model does not have these problems, although the supply lag may be different for different commodities.

EXAMPLE 5.5.1. For a single commodity, let demand be given by $(a - bp)$ and let supply be $(c + dp)$ where p is price. Then prices obey the law, where p_t is price at time t

$$a - bp_t = c + dp_{t-1}$$

since demand at price p_t equals supply calculated from price p_{t-1}. Thus

$$p_t = \frac{a - c}{b} - \frac{d}{b}p_{t-1}$$

If $b > d$ we have convergence to the equilibrium price $\frac{a - c}{b + d}$. But if $d \geq b$ then convergence will not occur. For instance let $a = 1$, $c = 0$, $b = d = 1$. Let $p_{-1} = 0.25$. Then we have

t	Supply	Price
0	0.25	0.75
1	0.75	0.25
0	0.25	0.75

Thus low production and high price are followed by high production and low price, followed by low production and high price.

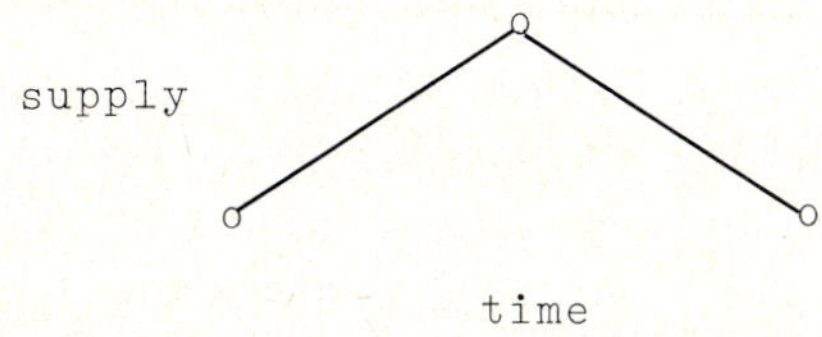

What happens to the market system if there is uncertainty about the future ? Arrow and Hahn provide two models, one of a futures market with contracts for future delivery being traded at the present time, as if they were present goods having a definite utility, and a market involving several time periods but in which economic aspects of the future can be predicted with certainty at the initial time period. These have the usual esistence and optimality properties.

Temporary general equilibria, as formulated by Grandmont (1977) combines the two ideas, but no longer has strong Pareto optimality features. Each agent has his own expectations about the future, and chooses his best strategy according to those expectations. Both present goods and contracts on future delivery are traded. When the future arrives, it may be different than the agents expect. However prices adjust themselves to the conditions that occur quickly, before trading occurs. At each separate time period, supply equals demand, and there is a subjective Pareto optimum in which all contracts are given utilities according to the anticipations of the agents purchasing them.

A paradox occurs in intertemporal expected utility theory, that the rule

$$u(px + (1 - p)y) = p\,u(x) + (1 - p)u(y)$$

may not be consistent, if the agent has to make a decision affecting the values of x, y. For example suppose x and y are business ventures of equal expected return. Then it may be better to choose 1 than a 50-50 lottery between x, y if the certainty of knowing x is chosen enables a person to make a better decision.

It was mentioned earlier than uncertainty about the future is one way basic problems can arise with the market system (or any other system). Uncertainty in effect gives a sort of limited rationality to traders. Future goods do not have as high utility now as present goods, although once the future comes they will. So traders must concentrating more on doing as well as possible at present than planning for the highest total utility over time.

For instance this gives an incentive to rapidly use up resources. However if the discount rate for future goods were given, and all agents evaluated things the same way, there would still be Pareto optimality, as with the Arrow-Hahn model. Thus in this case the market system behaves rationally with regard to uncertainty, as well as a non-competitive system might be expected to. Any system may have a tendency to exhibit cyclic behavior under uncertainty, since the discounted payoffs from a cycle

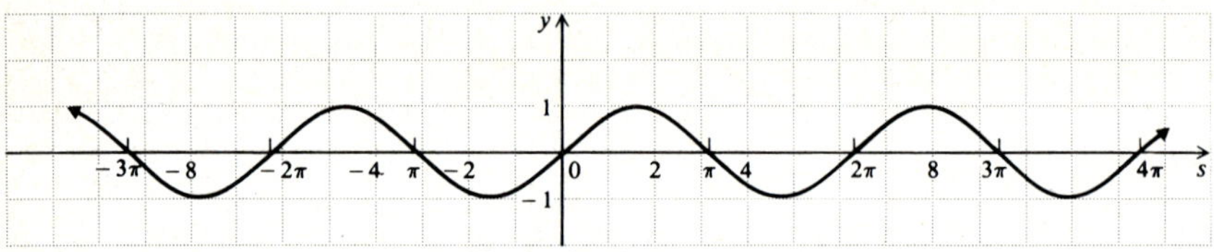

The sine function

may exceed those from a straight line equal to the average

provided one starts on the upper half of the curve, ascending.

Are there special drowbacks to the market system under uncertainty as opposed to others ? To some extent, the absence of centralized planning may itself cause additional uncertainty, an increase in the interest rate.

In addition monopoly profits are frequently a short run phenomenon, for instance due to a process no one has yet succeeded in copying or a fad which will end. Eventually competitors will reduce the profitability of such an operation.

Moreover individuals, the movers of a market system, have an earthly life span much shorter than that of nations, which may increase the rate at which future payoffs are discounted.

5.6 CONCLUSION

Trading involving few traders or few sellers must be analyzed by game theory. The case of few sellers and a set of buyers which is large enough to be considered perfectly competitive is oligopoly, and is analyzed by Nash equilibrium. The question is what variables do the sellers choose in competition: *price*, *quantity*, or *quality* ? This give basically different models.

Noncooperative equilibrium is a model of oligopoly involving the entire economy, divided into firms and consumers. Firms maximize profits and set prices or quantities consumers accept the given prices and maximize utility. Firms calculate the equilibrium resulting from their choice of prices or quantities, and make this choice to maximize utility, given that other firms keep their choices fixed. The result is a Nash equilibrium, a model of monopolistic competition. However equilibrium may not exist in this model. Roberts and Sonnenschein suggest a study of disequilibrium as the best response to this problem.

The problem is that in disequilibrium there is no general way to tell which buyer will get goods in short supply. Dreze, Benassy, and others have proposed models in which a rationing method is given, and agents make their best choices subject to the constraints it gives. We show that if each agent is a monopolist, it will generally be profitable for each to raise prices at the competitive equilibrium. This could cause cost-push inflation. Moreover a limitation on the money supply may cause a recession without curing inflation.

Temporary disequilibrium caused by supply shocks, related to deman-pull inflation, can be handled in several ways. The simple cobweb model assumes supply is determined by prices in the past, and prices are such that demand equals this given supply. Two other models, associated with Leon Walras and

Alfred Marshall assume prices change proportionally to a difference between supply and demand or a difference between prices. This models give contradictory predictions about stability. Under uncertainty about the future represented by a fixed discount rate on future payoffs, the market system gives Pareto optimal expectations under appropriate assumptions. Such uncertainty may help cause cyclic behavior and resource exhaustion. It is possible however that the market system adds to the uncertainty by short-term monopoly profits, by its dependence on the actions of individuals with limited life-spans, and by its unplanned nature, dependent on the actions of millions of unpredictable humans.

CHAPTER 6

SOCIAL WELFARE FUNCTIONS AND SOCIAL ARBITRATION

6.1 INTRODUCTION

In this chapter we discuss the problem of determining a group preference from the possibly conflicting preferences of individuals within the group. If the group is to choose among three or more alternatives, there may be no alternative which wins a majority over all others. There are two aspects: *the practical one of making a group decision and the theoretical one of what is in some sense best for the group.*

In Section 6.2 we discuss the mathematical representation of individual and group preferences by means of binary relations, in particular the set of ordered pairs (a, b) such that a is considered as good as, or better than, b. For consistency, these relations should be transitive or at least acyclic. Individuals for simplicity are usually assumed to rank the alternatives in a definite orders as best, second best, etc. A social welfare function gives a rule for forming a group preference relation from the preference relations of the individuals. For example we can add up points for each alternative, take the alternatives in the order of the numbers of first place votes, or repeatedly delete alternatives with most last place votes. A social welfare function is said to be dictatorial if whenever a certain individual strictly prefers a to b, the group does. It is independent of irrelevant alternatives if the group choice between a, b does not depend on the relative position of alternatives other than a, b in the individuals' preference orderings. Other properties sometimes considered are symmetry in the alternatives (neutrality), symmetry in the individuals (anonymity), and monotonicity: if all individuals raise the position of an alternative, keeping the relative order of the others fixed, the group cannot lower the position of that alternative.

It was observed by Condorcet that majority voting among pairs of alternatives need not be transitive. K. Arrow proved more generally there does not exist any social welfare function defined on all combinations of weak orders which is (1) *nondictatorial*, (2) *independent of irrelevant alternatives*, (3) *transitive*, (4) *complete*, (5) *Pareto efficient* for at least three alternatives

We give a proof of this result using Boolean matrices.

A social choice function gives a single alternative as group choice, instead of a ranking of all alternatives. It is called *manipulable* if some individual would ever find it advantageous to mistate his preferences, given that the other individuals are honest. Otherwise it is called *strategyproof* or *nonmanipulable*. A. Gibbard and M. Satterthwaite showed that every strategyproof social choice function onto a set of at least three alternatives is dictatorial.

A. K. Sen showed that minimal individual liberty cannot alway be reconciled with Pareto efficiency.

R. D. McKelvey showed that in parliamentary voting, by suitably arranging the order in which votes are taken, any outcome can generally be obtained from a given starting point.

Despite these five paradoxes of voting, some positive results are known. If preferences are restricted to a kind of 1-dimensional scale, there do exist strategyproof social choice functions and Arrow social welfare functions. Strategyproof social choice functions also exist for other equilibrium concepts than Nash equilibrium.

If Arrow's theorem is viewed as a question of what is best in some normative sense for the group, social welfare functiona can be defined in terms of numerical, interpersonally comparable utility instead of only preferences. In this way it can be taken into account how much a choice affects any individual.

A number of social welfare functions exist in this setting. J. Harsanyi characterized a function obtained by ranking alternatives according to the sum of their utilities, the utilitarian social welfare function, in terms of consistency over lotteries. The leximin social welfare function considers only the worst-off individual affected by a change. We propose, as have others, a social welfare function based on the Nash bargaining solution, and call it a *social arbitration function.*

6.2 BOOLEAN MATRICES AND BINARY RELATIONS

We first outline the mathematical framework for presenting the preferences of a group or individual. We have a set of alternatives which will frequently be called X.

EXAMPLE 6.2.1. The alternatives may be different candidates among which a voter must choose.

EXAMPLE 6.2.2. The alternatives may be different ways a consumer can spend his money.

EXAMPLE 6.2.3. The alternatives may be different versions of a bill in Congress.

The simplest way to describe the preferences of an individual is to say exactly which alternatives he prefers to which others. This can be done by listing all ordered pairs (x, y) such that the person prefers x to y. For instance if he prefers Mr. Hong to Mr. Brennan, we include (Hong, Brennan). Such a list of pairs in parentheses is called a *binary relation.*

DEFINITION 6.2.1. The *Cartesian product* $A \times B$ is the set of all ordered pairs (a, b), $a \in A$, $b \in B$. A *binary relation* on a set S is a subset of $S \times S$.

EXAMPLE 6.2.4. If a is preferred to b and b to c we have this binary relation: $\{(a, b), (b, c), (a, c)\}$.

It can be noted that all mathematical properties of a relationship can be described in terms of the corresponding set of ordered pairs.

DEFINITION 6.2.2. A binary relation R such that if $(x, y) \in R$ and $(y, z) \in R$ then $(x, z) \in R$ is called *transitive*.

A binary relation R such that if $(x, y) \in R$ then $(y, x) \in R$ is called *symmetric*. A binary relation R such that if $(x, y) \in R$ and $(y, x) \in R$ then $x = y$ is called *antisymmetric*. A binary relation R such that $(x, x) \in R$ for all R ($(x, x) \notin R$ for all R) is called *reflexive* (*irreflexive*). A binary relation R such that for all x, y either $(x, y) \in R$ or $(y, x) \in R$ is called *complete*.

EXAMPLE 6.2.5. The relations $x = y$, $x > y$, $x \geq y$ are transitive, as in the logical relation if x then y and the set inclusion $A \subset B$. The relation $|x - y| < 2$ and $x = y$ are symmetric. The relations $x > y$, $x \geq y$ and $A \subset B$ are antisymmetric. The relations $x > y$, $x \geq y$ are respectively irreflexive and reflexive. The binary relation $x \geq y$ is complete.

As remarked earlier, the preferences of an individual who is perfectly rational and has perfect powers of discrimination should be complete and transitive. *This mathematical formulation of rationality may be considered the fundamental postulate of micro-economics, although a number of results hold under individual preferences which are not be rational in this sense.*

If an individual is rational his preferences should be *transitive*: if he prefers Hong to Brennan and Brennan to Smith, he should also prefer Hong to Smith. If he has adequate information, they should be *complete*: either he prefers Hong to Brennan, or Brennan to Hong, or considers both equally good. We will usually assume individual preferences have these two properties. A complete, transitive binary relation is called a *weak order*. Every weak order on a finite set can be regarded as a *ranking*: some alternatives are best, some others second best, others third best, and so on.

For mathematical purposes it is frequently desirable to assume that no two alternatives are equally good. Since there are usually slight differences between any two alternatives, this is a fairly realistic assumption. A weak order in which no two alternatives are considered equally good is called a *linear* or *total order*. Every linear order on a finite set can be specified by telling which alternative is best, which is second best, which third best, and so on. That is we write the alternatives in order of the person's preference.

EXAMPLE 6.2.6. The previous example is the linear order abc.

DEFINITION 6.2.3. A complete, transitive relation is a *weak order*. An antisymmetric weak order is a *linear order*. A transitive, antisymmetric, reflexive relation is a *partial order*. A transitive, symmetric reflexive relation is an *equivalence relation*. A transitive, irreflexive relation is a *strict partial order*. A transitive, reflexive relation is a *quasi-order*.

EXAMPLE 6.2.7. The relation between line segments that x is at least as long as y, is a weak order. The relation $x \geq y$ on real numbers is a linear order. The relation $A \subset B$ is a partial order. The relation $x > y$ is a strict partial order. The relation that two triangles are similar is an equivalence relation. Any partial order, weak order, or equivalence relation, is also a quasi-order.

For each individual we have a weak or linear order giving his preferences among different alternatives. This binary relation should enable us to predict his behavior. (In some cases it may be necessary to consider random mixtures of alternatives, as well as the alternatives themselves. This leads the idea of expected utility, discussed in Section 6.4).

What about the group ? There are several ways to specify the group preferences, having slightly different names. We may specify the preference relation of the group. If this preference relation is complete and transitive, it is called a *social welfare function*. If there exist no cycles of the form (a is preferred to b, b to c, c to d, and d to a) it is called a *social decision function*. This is a weaker condition.

EXAMPLE 6.2.8. If we say that a group prefer x to y if and only if every member prefers x to y this is a social decision function, but not a social welfare function. The reason is that if some people prefer x to y and some people prefer y to x, it is not complete. Neither x nor y is preferred unanimously to the other.

EXAMPLE 6.2.9. If we have only two alternatives, there is a social welfare function defined by voting between the two. We say that x is preferred to y if more people prefer x to y than prefer y to x.

The name "*social welfare function*" indicates that such a group preference relation tells what is best for the welfare of society. For reasons discussed in Section 6.4, we do not adopt this viewpoint, but simply regard social welfare functions as method of *group choice* or *group decision*. Such functions are also called *voting procedures*.

A more general type of social choice can be indicated which alternative or alternatives the group will choose from the set of alternatives (or from various subsets). Specifying the group choice from various subsets of the set of alternatives is said to give a *social choice function*.

EXAMPLE 6.2.10. Suppose for each alternative we give one point for every one whose first choice it is, two points for every one whose second choice it is, and so on. Then we select those alternatives having the lowest total number of points. This gives the *Borda social choice function*.

EXAMPLE 6.2.11. A social choice function called *simple plurality* means we select those alternatives having the largest number of first place votes.

EXAMPLE 6.2.12. We can select those alternatives which would defeat the maximum number of other alternatives in voting between those two only. This is called *Copeland's social choice method*.

EXAMPLE 6.2.13. We can take those alternatives which would require the fewest changes in the individual preferences to defeat every other alternative by a majority in voting between those two only. This gives *Dodgson's social choice method*.

EXAMPLE 6.2.14. For three alternatives, delete all alternatives such that more than $\frac{1}{3}$ of the voters rank them last. Then if only two alternatives are left, decide between them by majority vote.

EXAMPLE 6.2.15. Take the two alternatives having the most first-place votes and decide between the two by majority vote.

As this list indicates, for more than two alternatives, there are many somewhat plausible methods of social choice. No two of the methods above will give the same choice for every assortment of individual preferences.

A convenient way to represent binary relations such as individual preferences or social welfare functions is the use of Boolean matrices. We number the alternatives 1, 2, ... , m. Then we form an n × m rectangle of numbers, a matrix. Horizontal lines in this rectangle are called *rows* and vertical lines *columns*. Rows are numbered from the top and columns from the left. The numbers within the matrix are calculated by entering a 1 in the location in row i and column j if and only if alternative i has the relationship in question to alternative j. A zero is entered if this relationship does not hold for alternatives i, j. The entry in row i and column j is called the *(i, j)-entry*.

EXAMPLE 5.2.16. Consider the preference ordering cab. Let a, b, c be numbered 1, 2, 3. The ordered pairs are (c, a), (c, b), (a, b). Therefore the (3, 1)-entry, the (3, 2)-entry, and the (1, 2)-entry should be 1. All other entries should be 0. This gives

$$\begin{bmatrix} 0 & 1 & 0 \\ 0 & 0 & 0 \\ 1 & 1 & 0 \end{bmatrix}$$

If the entries are to be operated upon by the rules of Boolean algebra, we call such a matrix a *Boolean matrix*.

Social decision and social choice functions are studied primarily in terms of certain attributes.

(A1) *PARETO OPTIMALITY. If everyone strictly prefers y to x, then x is not the group choice.*

(A2) *NONDICTATORIALITY. There is no individual such that if he prefers x to y, the group always prefers x to y.*

(A3) *ANONYMITY. If we relabel the individuals, group choice is unchanged.*

(A4) *NEUTRALITY. If we relabel the alternatives, the same alternative is chosen.*

(A5) *POSITIVE RESPONSIVENESS, or MONOTONICITY. If we have two sets of preferences, which are the same except regarding alternative x, and alternative x is chosen for the first set, and everyone in the second set regards alternative x at least as highly, alternative x is chosen for the second set.*

EXAMPLE 6.2.17. Except that the run-off (last example) is not monotone, all the examples listed have all these properties. We will next show the run-off method is not monotone. Consider these choices

	Number of voters	Ordering
	100	xyz
I	100	yzx
	99	zxy
	102	xyz
II	98	yzx
	99	zxy

The difference is that two voters have changed from yzx to xyz. Yet in the first case x defeats y by a majority yet in the second case z defeats x by a majority.

The most important other attribute is *independence of irrelevant alternatives*. This means that the group choice between alternatives x, y depends only on how the individuals feel about x and y, not on their choices regarding third alternatives.

EXAMPLE 6.2.18. None of the previous social choice methods satisfies an appropriate form of independence of irrelevant alternatives. We consider for example the simple plurality voting methods for two voter profiles

	Number of voters	Voter preference
I	100	xyz
	99	yzx
II	98	xyz
	99	yzx
	2	zxy

In the first case x is chosen, in the second y. Yet the profiles are identical except that two voters changed the location of a third alternative z.

There are many variations on this idea, of which the most important may be *path independence*. See Richelson (1978) and his other papers for a study of many attributes of social choice functions. Sen (1977) is also a good survey.

Next we state and prove Arrow's theorem using Boolean matrices. Matrix addition, multiplication, and transpose are defined by the same formulas as for other matrices, except that operations on individual entries are Boolean.

A *Boolean vector* is an n-tuple of elements from 0, 1, operated upon by the rules of Boolean algebra. Boolean vectors are added or multiplied entry by entry. We write $v \le w$ if $v_i \le w_i$ for each i, where v_i denotes the ith component of v.

EXAMPLE 6.2.19. Let A^T denote the transpose of A.

$$\begin{bmatrix} 1 & 1 \\ 0 & 1 \end{bmatrix}\begin{bmatrix} 1 & 0 \\ 1 & 1 \end{bmatrix} = \begin{bmatrix} 1 \cdot 1 + 1 \cdot 1 & 1 \cdot 0 + 1 \cdot 1 \\ 0 \cdot 1 + 1 \cdot 1 & 0 \cdot 0 + 1 \cdot 1 \end{bmatrix}$$

$$= \begin{bmatrix} 1 & 1 \\ 1 & 1 \end{bmatrix}$$

$$\begin{bmatrix} 1 & 1 \\ 0 & 1 \end{bmatrix}^T = \begin{bmatrix} 1 & 0 \\ 1 & 1 \end{bmatrix}$$

$$(1, 0, 1) \cdot (0, 1, 1) = (1 \cdot 0, 0 \cdot 1, 1 \cdot 1)$$

$$= (0, 0, 1)$$

Two other entrywise operations are defined: *logical product* and *complement*. In the logical product $\odot$, corresponding entries of two or more Boolean matrices are multiplied. To find the complement of a Boolean matrix, take the complement of each entry.

EXAMPLE 6.2.20. Let A^C denote the complement of A.

$$\begin{bmatrix} 1 & 1 \\ 0 & 1 \end{bmatrix} \odot \begin{bmatrix} 0 & 1 \\ 0 & 1 \end{bmatrix} = \begin{bmatrix} 1 \cdot 0 \\ 0 \cdot 0 \end{bmatrix}\begin{bmatrix} 1 \cdot 1 \\ 1 \cdot 1 \end{bmatrix} = \begin{bmatrix} 0 & 1 \\ 0 & 1 \end{bmatrix}$$

$$\begin{bmatrix} 1 & 1 \\ 0 & 1 \end{bmatrix}^C = \begin{bmatrix} 0 & 0 \\ 1 & 0 \end{bmatrix}$$

There is a one-to-one correspondence between binary relations on a labelled set of n elements and $n \times n$ Boolean matrices. Let the set be $\{x_1, x_2, \ldots, x_n\}$. Then to any binary relation R, associate the Boolean matrix A whose (i, j)-entry is 1 if $(x_i, x_j) \in R$ and whose (i, j)-entry is 0 if $(x_i, x_j) \notin R$. Thus there is exactly one 1 entry in the matrix for every ordered pair in the binary relation.

EXAMPLE 6.2.21. To the binary relation $x > y$ on the set $\{1, 2, 3, 4\}$ we have this matrix

$$\begin{bmatrix} 0 & 1 & 1 & 1 \\ 0 & 0 & 1 & 1 \\ 0 & 0 & 0 & 1 \\ 0 & 0 & 0 & 0 \end{bmatrix}$$

The 1 entries are in location (1, 2), (1, 3), (1, 4), (2, 3), (2, 4), (3, 4), which are precisely the ordered pairs in the binary relation.

All properties of binary relations can be stated in Boolean matrix terms. For example, a binary relation is transitive if and only if $A^2 \le A$. It is reflexive if and only if $I \le A$ where I is the identity matrix. It is symmetric if and only if $A = A^T$. It is antisymmetric if and only if $A \odot A^T \le I$. It is complete if and only if $A + A^T = J$, the matrix each of whose entries is 1.

Now we turn to social welfare and social decision functions. We suppose we have a set of n voters and a set X of m numbered alternatives.

First we consider majority voting for an odd number of voters. We use an $m \times m$ matrix M such that $m_{ij} = 1$ if a majority of the voters prefer alternative x to alternative y and $m_{ij} = 0$ otherwise. We assume here no voters are indifferent about any two alternatives. Let $m_{ii} = 1$ for all i. The matrix M is now antisymmetric and complete, that is, it is what is called a *tournament matrix*. Does M have any special properties ? No, in fact it has been proved that any tournament matrix can result from majority rule.

This can be proved as follows. First, for any i, j we can find two voters such that the sum of their preference matrices (regarded as integer preference matrices) has (i, j)-entry 2, (j, i)-entry 0 and all other entries off the main diagonal equal to 1. To do this use the two orderings 12 ... nij and ijn ... 21. Now take three pairs of such voters for every i, j such that the matrix m_{ij} is to be 1. The matrix M will be realized. Now take 1 additional voter to make the number of voters odd. His vote will not change any of the majorities. Thus no remnant of transitivity whatsoever persists.

DEFINITION 6.2.4. Let D be a set of weak orders on X. A *social welfare function* is a function F from D^n (n-tuples of weak orders) to the set of weak orders.

DEFINITION 6.2.5. A binary relation R is *acyclic* if there do not exist any elements $s_1, s_2, \ldots, s_n$ such that $(s_1, s_2) \in R$, $(s_2, s_3) \in R, \ldots, (s_{n-1}, s_n) \in R$, $(s_n, s_1) \in R$.

This is equivalent to saying that

$$A^n = 0$$

in matrix terms.

DEFINITION 6.2.6. A *social decision function* is a function F from D^n to the set of acyclic binary relations.

We may represent a social decision function or social welfare function as a function from n-tuples of Boolean matrices $(M\langle 1\rangle, M\langle 2\rangle, \ldots, M\langle n\rangle)$ of relations in D, to a Boolean matrix F.

DEFINITION 6.2.7. A social decision (welfare) function is *independent of irrelevant alternatives* if and only if whenever (i) $R_1, R_2, \ldots, R_n \in D$, (ii) $S_1, S_2, \ldots, S_n \in D$, (iii) $(x, y) \in R_i$ if and only if $(x, y) \in S_i$, and (iv) $(y, x) \in R_i$ if and only if $(x, y) \in S_i$, then $(x, y) \in F(R_1, \ldots, R_n)$ if and only if $(x, y) \in F(S_1, \ldots, S_n)$.

EXAMPLE 6.2.22. If we have only two alternatives, any social welfare function is independent of irrelevant alternatives

EXAMPLE 6.2.23. Suppose we set $F(R_1, \ldots, R_n) = R_i$. Then this is a social welfare function and a social decision function, and is independent of irrelevant alternatives. However voter i is a dictator.

We will suppose throughout most of this section that the preferences of individuals are linear orders, not merely weak orders. In this case, independence of irrelevant alternatives means that the (i, j)-entry of F(M<1>, ... , M<n>) depends solely on the (i, j)-entries of M<1>, ... , M<n>. If we write the (i, j)-entries of M<1>, ... , M<n> as a Boolean vector (n-tuple) v, we have a function $f_{ij}(v)$ giving the (i, j)-entry.

DEFINITION 6.2.8. A social decision (welfare) function has the *Pareto property* if and only if whenever $(x, y) \in R_k$ and $(y, x) \notin R_k$ for all k, we have $(x, y) \in F(R_1, \ldots, R_n)$ and $(y, x) \notin F(R_1, \ldots, R_n)$.

EXAMPLE 6.2.24. The social welfare function above has the Pareto property. A social welfare function which does not is given by choosing a fixed linear order R_0 and setting $F(R_1, \ldots, R_n) = R_0$ no matter what $R_1, \ldots, R_n$ are.

In Boolean matrix terms, the Pareto property means that $f_{ij}(1, 1, \ldots, 1) = 1$ and $f_{ij}(0, 0, \ldots, 0) = 0$.

DEFINITION 6.2.9. A social welfare function (social decision function) is *dictatorial* if and only if there exists k such that whenever $(x, y) \in R_k$ but $(y, x) \notin R_k$ then $(x, y) \in F(R_1, \ldots, R_n)$ but $(y, x) \notin F(R_1, \ldots, R_n)$.

EXAMPLE 6.2.25. The social welfare function in Example 6.2.8 is dictatorial.

THEOREM 6.2.1. (Arrow). *There does not exist a social welfare function defined on the set D of all linear orders on a set of at least three alternatives, which is independent of irrelevant alternatives, Pareto, and nondictatorial.*

Proof. (Kim and Roush 1980). In Boolean matrix terms the

property of completeness means that f_{ij} or f_{ji} is always 1. Therefore

$$f_{ij}(v) + f_{ji}(v^c) = 1 \tag{6.2.1}$$

Here v^c denotes the complement of a vector v. The property of transitivity means that if $f_{ij} = 1$ and $f_{jk} = 1$ so $f_{ik} = 1$. In other words, $f_{ij}f_{jk} \le f_{ik}$. We claim that for any vectors u, v, w such that $uv \le w \le u + v$ we can find linear orders $M<h>$ such that $(i, j) \in M<h>$ if and only if $u_h = 1$, $(j, k) \in M<h>$ if and only if $v_h = 1$, $(i, k) \in M<h>$ if and only if $w_h = 1$. To do this, use the table below:

u	v	w	M
0	0	0	kji
1	0	0	kij
0	1	0	jki
1	0	1	ikj
0	1	1	jik
1	1	1	ijk

If we use these $M<h>$, we have that f_{ij} is $f_{ij}(u)$, f_{jk} is $f_{jk}(v)$, f_{ik} is $f_{ik}(w)$. Therefore

$$f_{ij}(u)f_{jk}(v) \le f_{ik}(w) \text{ whenever } u + v \le w \le uv \tag{6.2.2}$$

Set $u = (1, 1, \ldots , 1)$, $v = w$. Then we have $f_{jk}(v) \le f_{ik}(v)$. By symmetry $f_{jk}(v) = f_{ik}(v)$. In similar fashion $f_{ij}(u) = f_{ik}(u)$. Therefore for at least three alternatives, all the functions f_{ij} are equal, and we will just write f for any of them. By equation (6.2.2) with $v(1, 1, \ldots , 1)$ we have $f(u) \le f(w)$ whenever $u \le w$. Thus f is monotone. We know by Pareto that $f(0, 0, \ldots , 0) = 0$ and $f(1, 1, \ldots , 1) = 1$. By equation (6.2.2 with $w = uv$ we have $f(u)f(v) \le f(uv)$. By equation (6.2.1) we have $f(u) + f(u^c) = 1$ for all u.

Let u be a vector with fewest ones such that $f(u) = 1$. If u has more than one 1 write $u = x + y$ where x, y have fewer ones and the sets of ones in them are disjoint. Then $f(x) = f(y) = 0$

since u was minimal for $f(u) = 1$. So $f(x) = 0$. So $f(x^c) = 1$ by equation (6.2.1). So $f(ux^c) \geq f(u)f(x^c) = 1$. Yet $ux^c = y$. This is a contradiction. So u has only one 1. Then for any v, if $v \geq u$, $f(v) = 1$ by monotonicity. If $v \not\geq u$ then $vu < u$ and $f(vu) = 0$. And $f(vu) \geq f(v)$. So $f(v) = 0$. This says $f(v) = 1$ if and only if $v \geq u$. The interpretation of this is that the person represented by the 1 entry in u is a dictator. This proves the theorem. □

This Boolean matrix proof first appeared in Kim and Roush (1980), as far as we know. Another simple proof is given in Goldberger (1976).

A more standard version of this theorem uses weak orders, instead of linear orders, and can be deduced from this. Many variations on the theorem exist: see Sen (1977), Kim and Roush (1980), Fishburn (1973). The Pareto assumption is not really essential, see Kim and Roush (1981) although the conclusion is then a little weaker.

In contrast to social welfare functions, social decision functions satisfying these conditions do exist, as noted in earlier.

Much work has been done with domains smaller than the set of all linear orders. See Kalai and Muller (1977), Kim and Roush (1980).

EXAMPLE 6.2.26. The set of single peaked linear orders on 1, 2, ... , m is the set of orders $\pi(1)\pi(2) \ldots \pi(m)$ such that for any i, j, k if $\pi(i) < \pi(j) < \pi(k)$ then $\pi(j)$ is not the right-most of $\pi(i)$, $\pi(j)$, $\pi(k)$ in the sequence.

This means that if the utility of alternatives i is plotted as a function of i, the graph is either monotone, or increase to a maximum and then falls. Singlepeakedness rules out the possibility of three linear orders having 3 alternatives in cyclically rotated order xyz, yzx, zxy since if y is between x, z in 1, 2, ... , m it cannot occur last in any ordering.

THEOREM 6.2.2. (Sen 1970). *Majority voting between pairs of alternatives is transitive for any preferences selected from a domain D of linear orders and any odd number of voters if and only if no triple x, y, z occurs in three cyclically rotated orders xyz, yzx, zxy in D. On such domains majority voting gives an Arrow social welfare function.*

Sen actually proved several more general results. Other domains D have been constructed having the property of this theorem, most having roughly the same number of preferences as the singlepeaked orders. A weaker condition is that there be a winner over all others in majority voting. Singlepeaked preferences have been generalized to tree graphs on 1, 2, ... , m for this condition (Demange 1982). Kalai and Muller (1977) constructed much larger domains on which social welfare functions exist, and characterized them, but the social welfare functions are usually not anonymous or neutral.

Singlepeaked preferences are an idealization of a situation in which voters are ranked along an 1-dimensional scale extreme to moderate to opposite extreme, for instance liberal-conservative

There does not seem to be any way to generalize singlepeaked preferences to 2 dimensions.

A concept which differs in significance, but is mathematically closely related to independence is strategyproofness. (See also Section 4.2). *Strategyproofness* means that no individual could ever gain a group choice more favorable to him by misrepresenting his personal preferences.

EXAMPLE 6.2.27. None of the previous methods are strategyproof.

Number of voters	Voter preference ordering
1	xzy
101	xyz
100	yzx
100	zxy

Here x will be chosen by any of the social choice methods listed. Yet all voters in the last two categories like z better than x. So they might prefer to state their preferences as zyx. Then

Number of voters	Voter preference ordering
1	xzy
101	xyz
200	zyx

and now any of the above methods will select z as group choice. Thus the voters who misstated their preferences have gained. (Here of course a group rather than a individual, was involved, but the two are more less equivalent for strategyproofness).

6.3 PARADOXES OF SOCIAL WELFARE

For two alternatives, the method of majority decision is a reasonably satisfactory social choice function. Is there some equally satisfactory social choice function for three or more alternatives ? The answer seems to be "no," as indicated by a series of paradoxes. See also Brams (1976).

(P1) CONDORCET PARADOX. *Suppose we have this profile for three voters and three alternatives.*

Number of voters	Voters preference ordering
1	xyz
1	yzx
1	zxy

Then two voters prefer x to y, two voters prefer y to z, two voters prefer z to y. So no matter which alternative is selected, a majority of the voters will prefer some other alternative.

This paradox does seem to occur in practice, and can prevent a legislative body from reaching a decision on a complex matter.

On simple questions of overriding importance, it is less likely to occur, for the reason that group members can be arranged in a sort of spectrum as to how strongly they favor or oppose some action. For instance on questions of *socialism* versus *laissez-faire capitalism*, political viewpoints might range from far right to moderate right to middle of the road to liberal to radical left. People will evaluate a proposal according to how much it differs from their own viewpoint. Then as previously described, voters will have single-peaked preferences. The outcome will be that position on the scale such that at least $\frac{1}{2}$ the people oppose positions farther right and at least $\frac{1}{2}$ the people oppose positions farther left, that is, the median, or Condorcet winner. In general a Condorcet winner is an alternative preferred to each other alternative by a majority.

Can this paradox be avoided by a more sophisticated voting method ? Not if we wish to have independence of irrelevant alternatives.

(P2) ARROW'S PARADOX. *There does not exist a social welfare function which is nondictatorial, Pareto optimal, and independent of irrelevant alternatives, on the set of all possible assortments of individual preferences, for more than two alternatives.*

This theorem, first proved by Kenneth Arrow in 1951, has aroused much debate. Several questions can be raised: (1) while independence of irrelevant alternatives is theoretically desirable is it necessary for a practical voting method ? (2) how likely will Arrow's paradox occur in practice ?

Arrow himself has indicated that voting procedures which do not possess independence of irrelevant alternatives would require gathering of an impossible amount of information to administer. For instance, there might always be discovered some new alternative. Preferences regarding it could upset the group regarding all the previously considered alternatives.

Condorcet's paradox will occur with probability approximately 0.0877 for three alternatives randomly arranged in the preferences for a large number of individuals. A. K. Sen's idea of replacing social welfare functions by social decision functions helps only a little.

EXAMPLE 6.3.1. The only social decision function satisfying independence of irrelevant alternatives, nondictatoriality, and Pareto optimality, and in addition anonymity and transitivity for strict preferences is the method of unanimous decision. That is, x is preferred to y by the group if and only if everyone prefers x to y.

EXAMPLE 6.3.2. For three alternatives, the method of $\frac{2}{3}$ majority voting is independent of irrelevant alternatives, Pareto optimal, and nondictatorial, and is a social decision function.

The former example illustrates the importance of Pareto optimality in economics. That is all the group could say about an alternative under this social decision function is that it is, or is not, Pareto optimal. However unanimous decision may not be practical in legislative bodies or general elections.

The second example is more relevant for legislative bodies. The difference between it and the first example is that a $\frac{2}{3}$ majority could prefer x to y and a $\frac{2}{3}$ majority could prefer y to z but yet a $\frac{2}{3}$ majority might not prefer x to z.

EXAMPLE 6.3.3.

Number of voters	Voter preference ordering
101	xyz
101	yzx
100	zxy

Here only 101 voters of the 302 prefer x to z.

An even more important practical problem is strategy-proofness.

(P3) PARADOX OF SATTERTHWAITE AND GIBBARD. *There does not exist a nondictatorial, strategyproof, single-valued social choice function which can choose among three or more alternatives, if each could possibly be chosen.*

Here single-valued means that one alternative rather than several, is selected. Gibbard later replaced this assumption by allowing lotteries among the set of chosen alternatives if more than one is chosen. Recently much work has been done on the multi-valued case.

One possible objection is that strategyproofness does not incorporate the idea of a game theoretic stable solution here. If one individual chooses to misrepresent his preferences the others may retailiate by misrepresenting their preferences.

Dutta and Pattanaik have considered some rather complicated ideas along these lines. One of the simpler is jointly due to them and Peleg.

If we allow the players to state any ordering instead of the true preference ordering they have this will give a game, in which the object is for the social choice to be as high as possible in a player's true preferences. This corresponds to actual voting, in which a person may not vote for the candidate he likes absolutely best, but if that candidate has no chance to win, he might vote for the candidate he likes best who has a chance to win.

Then *strong and exact consistency* means that this game has a strong Nash equilibrium point which is identical to the outcome if everyone stated his true preferences. The idea is that if everyone did go ahead and misrepresent his strategies, we would have a game, whose outcome should be a strong Nash equilibrium. But if this outcome might be the same as the outcome from the sincere strategies, there is little incentive to manipulate.

Peleg (1978) constructed a number of strong and exactly consistent social choice functions, which were studied in more detail by Polishchuk (1978).

Strong equilibrium is a stricter condition than Nash equilibrium so that except on special domains such as single-peaked preferences, a social choice function cannot be nonmanipulable in the sense of strong equilibrium. However it is possible to find multivalued social choice functions, called *social choice correspondences*, and voting methods such that the set of strong equilibrium points of the voting method is precisely the given social choice correspondence. This is known as *strong implementation* of the social choice correspondence.

An effectivity function tells which coalitions C can force the outcome of voting to be in a given subset S of the alternatives.

DEFINITION 6.3.1. An *effectivity function* E for voter set N and alternative set A is a set of pairs (C, S) of coalitions and sets of outcomes such that (1) if $(C, S) \in E$ and $D \supset C$ then $(D, S) \in E$, (2) if $(C, S) \in E$ and $S \subset T$ then $(C, T) \in E$, (3) $(C, A) \in T$ for all $C \neq \emptyset$, (4) $(N, S) \in E$ for all $N \neq \emptyset$.

EXAMPLE 6.3.4. In majority voting between 2 alternatives, any majority coalition is effective for any nonempty subset.

DEFINITION 6.3.2. An effectivity function is *maximal* if and only if for all C, $S \neq \emptyset$, exactly one fo (C, S), $(\tilde{C}, \tilde{S})$ belongs to E.

EXAMPLE 6.3.5. The preceding example is maximal. That is, if coalition C cannot force the outcome to be in S, then the remaining players can force the outcome not to be in S.

EXAMPLE 6.3.6. Suppose $|A|$ and $|N|$ have no common divisor greater than 1. Choose positive x, y such that $1 + x|N| = y|A|$. Define (C, S) to be effective if and only if $x|C| + y|S| \geq y|A|$. This is maximal.

DEFINITION 6.3.3. An effectivity function is *stable* if for any set of voter preferences which are linear orders, there exists at least one alternative a such that for any C it is not true that $(C, S) \in E$ and every member of C prefers each element of S to a. The set of such a is called the *core*.

EXAMPLE 6.3.7. The preceding example is stable.

Moulin and Peleg (1980) proved that a strongly implementable social choice function is contained in the core of a maximal stable effectivity function and that the core of a maximal stable effectivity function is strongly implementable. Moulin (1981) showed that if $|A|$, $|N|$ have no common divisor greater than 1, the above example gives the unique maximal stable effectivity function symmetric in the voters and alternatives.

EXAMPLE 6.3.8. Suppose we have 3k + 1 people for some integer k, and three alternatives. Call an alternative feasible if less than $\frac{1}{3}$ of the voters rank it last and no other alternative defeats it by a $\frac{2}{3}$ majority. Feasible alternatives always exist, and any social choice function whose value is always feasible is strongly and exactly consistent. The set of feasible alternatives is strongly implementable.

Other weak versions of strategyproofness can be considered.

DEFINITION 6.3.4. A social choice function has the *worst alternative property* if no voter can manipulate when the actual outcome is the outcome he least prefers.

The reason for this is that if a voter's worst outcome is chosen, he has no incentive not to manipulate. Another notion is due to Pattanaik (1977).

DEFINITION 6.3.5. A social choice function is *strategyproof (Type III)* if whenever some voter can manipulate to his advantage some other coalition can then manipulate so as to reduce him to no more than his original value, and so that the other coalition is at least as well off as after the first voter's manipulation.

EXAMPLE 6.3.9. For three alternatives and 3k + 1 voters for some integer k, suppose we first delete all alternatives ranked last by more than $\frac{1}{3}$ of the voters and then choose among the (at most two) remaining alternatives by majority vote. This procedure has the worst alternative property and is strategyproof (Type III).

We do not know whether anonymous, neutral, strategyproof (Type III) procedures exist for other numbers of alternatives and voters.

Moulin has studied *d-solvability* in social choice. This means we have a game such that by repeatedly deleting dominated strategies we arrive at essentially a single outcome.

EXAMPLE 6.3.10. Suppose we have three players. Suppose we allow player 1 to choose either of the other two players. Then that one chooses what alternative he most prefers. This game is d-solvable.

Moulin has shown that d-solvable games exist which represent quite reasonable social choice functions. For instance the social choice functions can be neutral, anonymous, and Pareto efficient.

D-solvability guarantees an essentially unique outcome provided that the players know each others' true interests.

Pattanaik (1976) showed that there do not exist social choice functions satisfying certain conditions which are strategyproof using $M_1^{(i)}$ as solution concept. Laffont and Moulin (1980) have proposed a weaker type of bargaining set.

Strong and exact consistency, the weak alternative property, strong implementation, strategyproofness (Type III), and d-solvability all seem to be related to what Moulin (1981) calls the *minority principle*, that a minority of size greater than $\frac{n}{m}$ can veto any alternative, for n voters and m alternatives. This gives a reason for considering social choice functions satisfying this principle the least succeptible to strategy of any social choice functions.

To have a neutral, anonymous, Pareto efficient social choice function the necessary and sufficient conditions are that no prime less than or equal to m divide n.

EXAMPLE 6.3.11. One neutral, anonymous, Pareto efficient social choice function satisfying the minority principle for these n, m first deletes all alternatives which are the worst choice for more than $\frac{n}{m}$ voters. If k alternatives are left, delete all alternatives which are the worst choice for more than $\frac{n}{k}$ voters. Continue this until only one alternative is left.

S. J. Brams has recommended a different voting method called *approval voting* which is strategyproof in case the preferences of each voter are dichotomous (weak orders having precisely two equivalence classes). Each voter votes for a set of candiates and the candidate with largest total wins.

Sen has discovered what is called the *libertarian paradox*. In effect this means that if we give each individual unrestricted rights over something, the result cannot always be Pareto optimal for the group.

EXAMPLE 6.3.12. Suppose we give individual A rights over choice c and individual B rights over choice d. Suppose the interests of the players are strictly opposed. Suppose c is more important to B than to A, and d is more important to A than to B. Thus we give the right most important to any person, to his enemy. This situation will not be optimal.

The paradox in general arises because of the phenomenon of this example, although more complicated things can happen for three persons.

One version of the libertarian paradox can be stated as follows.

THEOREM 6.3.1. *Let F be a social choice function such that the value of F is always Pareto optimal. Then it is impossible to find distinct alternatives x, y, z, w and voters 1, 2 such that voter 1 has the right to rule out whichever of x, y he chooses and voter 2 has the right to rule out whichever of z, w he chooses.*

Proof. Consider the preference orderings

Voter 1	zxyw
Voter 2	ywzx

Then both voters prefer y to w and z to x. Therefore only y or z can be chosen, by Pareto optimality. Let y will be ruled out by voter 1 and z will be ruled out by voter 2. □

McKelvey (1979) has discovered a paradox about legislative bodies which consider issues by successive majority votes against amended version. That is, the current bill is tried against some alternative by majority vote, and the winner is tested against the next alternative. He proved that in general, starting with any possible alternative, we can arrive at any other by a series of majority votes. This shows that the person who sets the order in which the alternative bills are voted on has a great deal of power.

The concept of *fairness* (see Feldman and Kirman 1974) is of some interest in relation to social welfare. A fair allocation of goods is one such that everyone considers his own bundle of goods at least as good as anyone else's, that is, no one envies another. In a pure trading situation, fair and Pareto optimal allocations always exist: imagine that initially the goods are equally divided, and that a *Walras equilibrium* is then reached. The condition that each trader maximizes his final allocation subject to the budget constraint means that no one can prefer someone else's bundle of goods to his own.

6.4 MORE ON UTILITY

So far we have assumed that the value of different alternatives for an individual can be represented by giving his preference relation. However in fact, there is a question, how much does he prefer one good to another ? He may like one brand of car slightly better than other, but much better than a motorcycle.

One way to assign numerical values to preferences is by means of the *theory of expected utility*. What this means is that we consider preferences over gambles, when an individual has a certain probability of obtaining one thing and a certain probability of obtaining another.

EXAMPLE 6.4.1. Suppose we give someone a choice between $1,000 and a 15% chance at $10,000. If he chooses the latter we can say that the expected utility of $1,000 to him is less than 15% of the expected utility of $10,000. (We set the value of $0 as 0). By making experiments of this kind we may set up in principle a complete utility scale for the individual.

With such a scale we may now compare the intensity of preference of two different choices. For instance we may say that someone's preference for one car over another is one-tenth of his preference for a care over a motorcycle.

However two things about the expected utility are still arbitrary, the choice of a zero point and the choice of a unit of measurement. For instance we could define these by saying the utility of $0 is 0 and the utility of $10 is 1. But any other choices could also be made.

What about Arrow's paradox ? With this added information about the intensity of preference, can we construct social welfare functions satisfying the conditions of his theorem ? A. K. Sen (1970) showed the answer is still "no."

But some workers feel that there is still more to utility than comparative intensity of preferences for one individual.

That is, possibly we can compare the value of a house for one individual to the value of a house for another person. This is known as *interpersonal comparison of utilities*.

We ourselves feel that a notion of interpersonal comparison of utilities is involved in many concepts of justice. For instance one man's life, or the well-being of his children, is worth as much as him as another's life, or the well-being of his children is to the other. If we say some people are poor, but others are rich, this implies such a comparison. It could happen that by majority vote between two alternatives, one group of people would choose to commit genocide on a minority, but this does not seem to represent the welfare of society. In this situation the minority must also be considered. Unless we have a belief that others have feelings of joy or pain similar to ours, it is hard to know how we should act towards them.

John Harsanyi (1977) has been a champion of one version of this viewpoint, the *utilitarian view*. This idea in an imprecise statement goes back to Jeremy Bentham, who said that to determine the welfare of society, we should add the utility to each person in society of his present condition. Harsanyi not only gave this precise form but also proved that if we reqire the welfare of society to satisfy axioms analogous to the expected utility axioms for individuals, that his social welfare function is the only one possible.

EXAMPLE 6.4.2. Suppose we three people faced with two choices x, y. Let the utilities of the choices to the people be

Voter	Utility of x	Utility of y
a	3	4
b	3	2
c	3	2

Then x has a total of 9, y a total utility of 8. Thus x is preferable for the group, from a utilitarian standpoint.

One of the axioms is somewhat controversial: if x is better than y, then for any alternative z, a 50-50 lottery between x and z is better than a 50-50 lottery between y and z.

EXAMPLE 6.4.3. Suppose we have two individuals. Let x have utilities (0, 5) for the two persons. Let y have utility (4, 0) for the two persons. Let z have utility (0, 4) for the two persons. Then a lottery between x and z gives expected utilities (0, 4.5) and a lottery between y and z gives expected utilities (2, 2). Some might say the latter is fairer and that in it the group has higher welfare. Harsanyi argues that this view is illusory.

Harsanyi also argues for his viewpoint as follows: consider a person in the imaginary situation of being equally likely to occupy any position in society. Then the utility of such a person is really the welfare of society.

Harsanyi's argument from the axioms in brief, is as follows: the preferences of society over alternatives should depend only on the n-tuples of utilities associated with each, and gives a preference ordering on all such n-tuples, by independence of irrelevant alternatives. The resulting preference relation on utility n-tuples is assumed to the axioms for expected utility (this is a group rationality assumption). Therefore there exists a utility function for it, which is linear over convex combinations $u(px + (1 - p)y) = pu(x) + (1 - p)u(y)$. Set $u(0) = 0$. Then u is actually linear. So $u(x) = \Sigma\, w_i v_i(x)$ where w_i are constant weights and v_i is the utility of individual i. If symmetry in the individuals is assumed, all w_i are equal, so we can take $w_i = 1$.

Many social scientists agree with these arguments and the simplicity of utilitarianism lends itself to mathematical treatment.

John Rawls is associated with another social welfare function, in a roundabout way. Rawls does not strictly believe in interpersonal comparison of utilities and is a philosopher rather than a social scientist. However he argues in effect that society should choose between two states according to the welfare of the poorest individual. His reasoning to imagine a group of people making a social contract or constitution before they know what their situations in society would be, that a person would consider the condition of the worst-off individual because he might be that individual. This in effect replaces Harsanyi's expected utility rule for decision-making under uncertainty with a maximin rule. The general form of Rawls's rule is called *leximin*: consider the lowest utility level at which there is a difference between two states. Whichever state has fewer individuals at this utility level is preferable.

EXAMPLE 6.4.4. Suppose that alternative x has utilities (1, 3, 5, 6) and alternative y has utilities (2, 1, 7, 10) for four people. The lowest utility level at which there is a difference between the states is 2: alternative y has 1 person with a utility of 2 and alternative x has no people at this level. Thus x is preferable by the leximin criterion.

Both the utilitarian and leximin concepts produce social welfare functions satisfying condition's of Arrow's theorem if interpersonal comparison of utilities is allowed. Thus in this case Arrow's paradox can be resolved. Deschamps and Gevers characterized the utilitarian and leximin social welfare functions as being the only ones satisfying six axioms.

AXIOM DG 1. ANONYMITY. *If* $u(i, x) = v(\pi(i), x)$ *for all* i, x *for some permutation* π *of the voters,* $R(u) = R(v)$.

AXIOM DG 2. STRONG PARETO. *If* $u(i, x) \geq u(i, y)$ *for all* i *and* $u(i, x) > u(i, y)$ *for some* i *then not* $y\ R(u)\ x$.

AXIOM DG 3. INDEPENDENCE OF IRRELEVANT ALTERNATIVES. *If* $u(i, x) = v(i, x)$ *for all* i *and* $u(i, y) = v(i, y)$ *for all* i *then* $x\ R(u)\ y$ *if and only if* $x\ R(v)\ y$.

AXIOM DG 4. INDEPENDENCE OF UNCONCERNED VOTERS. *If* $u(i, x) = v(i, x)$ *for* $i \neq k$ *and for all* x, y, $u(k, x) = u(k, y)$ *and* $v(k, x) = v(k, y)$ *then* $R(u) = R(v)$.

AXIOM DG 5. NOT BEING LEXIMAX. *The function* $R(u)$ *does not coincide with the leximax social welfare function.*

AXIOM DG 6. INVARIANCE UNDER JOINT UTILITY TRANSFORMATIONS. *If* $v(i, x) = au(i, x) + b$ *for all* i, x *where* $a > 0$, b *are constants then* $R(u) = R(v)$.

It is also assumed there are at least three voters. Firstly neutrality can be established from these axioms, then independence of irrelevant alternatives allows us to reduce the situation to that of considering pairs of alternatives. We make an assumption to rule out leximax.

The independence of irrelevant alternatives is closely related to the Thomson condition in the theory of additive conjoint measurement, and allows an additive representation. Then invariance under joint utility transformations determines the specific form of this representation to be linear.

A. K. Sen has argued that social welfare functions might be considered *partial orders* instead of weak orders. A strong candidate for such a partial order can be defined from the Lorentz curves associated with utility n-tuples.

DEFINITION 6.4.1. The function $L(\frac{k}{n})$ is the proportion of total utility received by the k members having the lowest utility. The *Lorentz curve* is the graph of L(p). If p is not of the form $\frac{k}{n}$, L(p) is obtained by linear interpolation.

EXAMPLE 6.4.5. Suppose utility is uniformly distributed from 0 to 1. Then L(x) is x^2 since the total utility possessed by the lowest x of the population is

$$\int x \, dx = \frac{1}{2}x^2$$

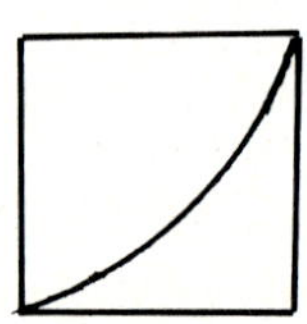

THEOREM 6.4.1. (Rothschild and Stiglitz 1973). *The following are equivalent for two distributions x, y of the same amount of income among n persons:*

(1) the Lorentz curve of x is never below that of y.

(2) x ranks at least as high than y for all social welfare functions u satisfying Axiom DG 1 and $u(tz + (1 - t)w) \geq \min(u(z), u(w))$ for income distributions z, w.

(3) y can be obtained from x by a sequence of transfers of income from poorer to richer individuals.

For a proof see Goldberger (1976). The second condition of this theorem can be replaced by

(2') x ranks at least as high as y for all social welfare functions satisfying Axiom DG 1-DG 5 together with the following axiom and continuity (Axiom KR 2, p. 207).

AXIOM KR 1. *If x is obtained from y by permuting the individuals then* $u(\frac{1}{2}(x + y)) \geq u(x)$.

The reason is that firstly, functions satisfying (2') will satisfy (2) and that to prove the theorem it suffices to use the functions $u(x) = \Sigma\, g(u_i(x))$ where $g(s) = s$ for $s \leq a$, $g(s) = a + \varepsilon(s - a)$, $s > a$, satisfying (2').

The partial order defined by the theorem also satisfies Harsanyi's Bayesian rationality condition: *if x is preferred to y then* $tx + (1 - t)z$ *is preferred to* $ty + (1 - t)z$ *for* $t > 0$. It is not complete, but also satisfies Axioms DG 1-DG 6.

A frequently used measure of inequality is the Gini index.

DEFINITION 6.4.2. The *Gini index* of an income distribution w is twice the area between the Lorentz curve of w and the line y = x.

EXAMPLE 6.4.6. If everyone has the same income, the Lorentz curve is y = x so the Gini index is zero.

EXAMPLE 6.4.7. If one individual has all the income, the Lorentz curve is y = 0 so the Gini index is 1.

The Gini index is given by

$$\frac{\Sigma\,(2i - n - 1)x_i}{n\,\Sigma\,x_i}$$

where x_i is the ith income in the group, in increasing order. It can be characterized by a linearity property.

Suppes earlier had introduced a concept of *Justice*. As Sen argues that this concept is not meaningful unless we introduce interpersonal comparison of utilities, we will consider it only in such a form.

Justice is then the result of two assumptions: (i) if two states differ only by reassigning the utilities to different people, they are indifferent to one another, (ii) one state is at least as good as another if the utility of each person is at least as high. It is a generalization of Pareto optimality in which the identities of individuals are ignored.

EXAMPLE 6.4.8. Suppose in state x, voter 1 has utility 2 and voter 2 has utility 4. Suppose in state y, voter 1 has utility 3 and voter 2 has utility 1. Then x is juster than y even though voter 1 has higher utility in state y. The reason is that if we ignore the identities of the individuals (2, 4) is higher than (1, 3).

One puzzle is that justice is compatible with the "leximax" social welfare function. In the welfare of a group would depend on the welfare of the individual who was best off. In a dictator could improve his own well-being to a high level by oppressing all his people, this is a good thing by the leximax social welfare function. This is contrary to most human concepts of ethics, yet the leximax social welfare function satisfies the two conditions mentioned above.

Sen has introduced a *Weak Equity Axiom*, that if at each level of income a's utility is less than b's (for instance if a needs costly medical care) then it is better to divide a given sum of money so that a receives more than b. Kim and Roush (1980) showed this assumption leads to the leximin social welfare function.

6.5 SOCIAL ARBITRATION FUNCTIONS

By *social arbitration function* we mean a function similar to the social welfare functions considered in the last section, but which could actually be used in practice to decide which of two economic states is better. This is related to the meaning of the term social welfare function as originally introduced by Samuelson.

There might be certain problems with implementing either the utilitarian or leximin social welfare functions. The utilitarian social welfare function, although it was once considered too egalitarian, may not be egalitarian enough to satisfy people today. That is, to consider a utility of 0 for one person and 4 for another person equal to utilities of 2 for both, would not be agreeable to the one who received 0. For this reason we will introduce an element of bargaining in social arbitration functions.

One difficulty with the leximin social welfare function in practice is that it is not continuous, in the sense of the following axiom:

> AXIOM KR 2. CONTINUITY. *The set $\{u: x\ R(u)\ y\}$ is closed for any x, y.*

That is, utilities (1, 1) are considered better than (10, 0.999), for instance. Another is that in the situation a voter with a possible utility of 10 might feel strongly about being reduced to a utility of 1 in order to raise the other from 0.999 to 1. Here too we feel that an element of bargaining is needed.

To use bargaining, we need a disagreement point. We propose that this be done by politically deciding on a minimum utility level u_0. Each person in effect (as far as economic questions are considered) is guaranteed a utility of at least u_0. The level u_0 could be very negative, or zero, or at the minimum utility level in a maximin solution. This freedom in choosing u_0 means that we can range from nearly a utilitarian society to nearly a leximin society according to the ethical views of its members.

Moreover the disagreement point should perhaps be equal for all member of society.

Given this disagreement point u_0, we use essentially the Nash bargaining solution. That is, we take as our social welfare function the product of $u_i - u_0$ where u_i is the utility level of person i. Our reasons for using the Nash bargaining solution are that (1) it is independent of irrelevant alternatives which is needed in a social welfare function, (2) it is invariant under individual utility transformations, so it depends only on things related to the behavior of the individuals, (3) the argument from *risk-dominance* (Zeuthen's principle).

Kaneko and Nakamura (1979), Brock (1979) and Wagoner (1980) have proposed similar ideas. If Kalai's bargaining solution (or a generalization) were used instead of the Nash solution the leximin social welfare function would result.

EXAMPLE 6.5.1. Suppose we set u_0 at -1. Let state x give various people utilities (2, 3, 4) and state y give utilities (3, 3, 3). Then we form the products $(2 - (-1))(3 - (-1))(4 - (-1)) = 3 \cdot 4 \cdot 5 = 60$ and $(3 - (-1))(3 - (-1))(3 - (-1)) = 4 \cdot 4 \cdot 4 = 64$. Thus state y is preferable.

The social arbitration function based on the Nash bargaining solution can be characterized by Axioms DG 1-DG 4, Axiom KR 2 and

AXIOM KR 3. INVARIANCE UNDER SEPARATE UTILITY TRANSFORMATIONS PRESERVING u_0. If $a_i > 0$ and b_i are such that $u_0 = a_i u_0 + b_i$ and if $v(i, x) = a_i u_i(x) + b_i$ then $R(u) = R(v)$.

We must restrict to the domain $\{u: u(i, x) > u_0$ for all $i, x\}$. The concavity property mentioned in connection with the Lorentz curve also holds.

6.5 CONCLUSION

Methods of group choice using individual preferences cannot be strategyproof but can satisfy certain weaker conditions: strong and exact consistency, strong implementability, strict strategyproofness (Type IV), and d-solvability. In order to measure in some sense the benefit to society of a particular alternative, we feel interpersonally comparable utilities are necessary. Many workers favor Harsanyi's social welfare function and some favor that associated with Rawls. For practical use by government, we think that social arbitration functions constructed using the Nash bargaining solution and an assumed minimum utility level may be preferable to either.

CHAPTER 7

INCENTIVE COMPATIBILITY

7.1 INTRODUCTION

Incentive compatibility continues and generalizes the idea of strategyproofness mentioned in Chapter 6. The problem of implementation is to design a mechanism which takes inputs of information (or actions) from a set of agents and then determines the distribution of goods to them or a public choice of a goods, or some thing similar. The mechanism is said to be *incentive compatible* for a game theoretic solution or to implement the social choice with that solution if when players choose their inputs according to self-interest, as a game, the outcome according to the solution concept is the desired social choice.

For example majority rule implements the set of Pareto efficient outcomes by dominant strategy if there are two alternatives, and (using pairwise voting between alternatives) if preferences are single peaked. It will be a dominant strategy for each individual to vote honestly, and the outcome is always Pareto efficient. Assuming a continuum of individuals, the market system is also incentive compatible. For a small group of traders however, the market system is not incentive compatible (monopolists can raise prices above equilibrium), and in fact no economic system can be incentive compatible without being dictatorial or otherwise giving some individual arbitrary power over the goods received by others.

If it is assumed that money represents transferable utility there exist dominant strategy mechanisms for public decision-making. Each individual votes by stating the value of the good to him, in money terms. The alternative with highest total value is chosen. To make sure voters have no incentive for dishonesty they are taxed according to a certain formula, depending on the votes of the players.

These schemes have certain limitations, and have not been used so far in any significant practical situation. Probabilistic concepts of incentive compatibility have been used to solve problems like how can a utility company best be regulated by the public, and when authority should be delegated.

Incentive compatibility is significant for a number of major questions: *to what extent should the market be regulated ? how can welfare be given without destroying incentive ? how can decisions be made about the environment, about education, or defense ? what should be government policy towards monopoly ?*

Many general results of a mathematical nature have been proved, but there are also many open problems.

7.2 THEORY OF IMPLEMENTATION

The terms strategyproofness, implementation, incentive compatibility refer to roughly the same thing, a system which solves the principal agent problem. The principal enters into some sort of contract possibly one-sided with the agents, but does not have enough information about them to be sure they will perform their part fully. Instead, he tries to design a system so that it will be in their own interest to fulfill the contract. For instance,

(1) *In voting theory, the government (principal) would like to find a voting method which the voters (agents) cannot manipulate.*

(2) *The president of an organization (principal) would like a system which encourages his subordinates (agents) to be as productive as possible.*

(3) *Regarding public goods, such as education or freedom from pollution, a government administrator (principal) would like to find out the preferences of the people (agents) in such a way that it would not be in their interest to be dishonest.*

(4) *The planners (principal) of a centralized economy would like to set production quotas in such a way that plant managers have no incentive to say their production capacity is less than it is.*

(5) *An insurance company (principal) wants honest behavior on the part of its clients (agents), i.e., that they don't have an incentive to harm the insured object and collect insurance.*

Implementation presents this situation in a simple, abstract way. Recall that a game form is a function from a product $A_1 \times \dots \times A_n$ of strategy sets to an outcome set T. Individual is preferences R_i on T belong to a set H_i of binary relations.

DEFINITION 7.2.1. A *social choice rule* is a function from $\times H_i$ to nonempty subsets of T.

EXAMPLE 7.2.1. The Pareto set is a social choice rule.

DEFINITION 7.2.2. The *game form g implements* f by a given equilibrium concept if the game obtained from g for any choice of preferences from $H_1 \times \dots \times H_n$; (1) always has an equilibrium, (2) any equilibrium of the game lies in $f(R_1, \dots, R_n)$.

This means that if the principal makes its decisions by the given game form, and the agents act strategically in their own interest according to the equilibrium concept, then the outcome will be the presumably desired social choice rule f.

EXAMPLE 7.2.2. For two alternatives majority voting implements both itself and the Pareto set by almost any equilibrium concept-dominant strategy equilibrium, Nash equilibrium, maximin equilibrium, Stackelberg equilibrium for any order of the voters.

EXAMPLE 7.2.3. For single peaked preferences and an odd number of voters the median (which is preferred by a majority of voters to any other) implements itself and the Pareto set by dominant strategy equilibrium, etc.

Game forms for the principal agent problem are called *mechanisms*. A mechanism is direct if $A_i = H_i$, i.e., agents report their preferences as a strategy. A direct mechanism is straightforward if truth is a dominant strategy for each agent.

DEFINITION 7.2.3. A direct mechanism g *truthfully implements* a social choice rule f if truth is always an equilibrium and $g(R_1, \ldots, R_n) \subset f(R_1, \ldots, R_n)$.

This does not imply implementation since there may be equilibria other than the truth not lying in f. However if truth is an equilibrium we assume it is the equilibrium which actually occurs.

Strategyproofness of a social choice function means that it truthfully implements itself by Nash equilibrium.

The survey paper (Partha Dasgupta, Peter Hammond, and Eric Maskin 1978) gives a number of general conditions for implementability of f on a given domain.

DEFINITION 7.2.4. That a social choice rule f is *monotonic* means for all profiles $(R_1, \ldots, R_n)$, $(S_1, \ldots, S_n)$ and outcomes $a \in f(R_1, \ldots, R_n)$ if for all i, for all $x \in T$, $a R_i x$ implies $a S_i x$ then $a \in f(S)$.

EXAMPLE 7.2.4. The Pareto set is monotonic.

EXAMPLE 7.2.5. For a market, the set of core allocations is monotonic.

This property is stronger than the usual monotonicity property. In fact Moulin (1981) calls it stronger positive association and Peleg (1980) proves it is equivalent to a property called *strong monotonicity*, when the domains are not restricted.

Muller and Satterthwaite (1977) proved that for a set of at least three alternatives and all linear orders (unrestricted domain) there exists no single valued strategy monotone social choice rule which attains every member of the set T.

DEFINITION 7.2.5. That a single valued social choice rule satisfies *independent person-by-person monotonicity* (IPM) means for all i, for all $S_i \in H_i$ for all profiles $(R_1, \ldots, R_n)$ for all a, b $\in$ T such that a $\in F(R_1, \ldots, R_n)$ if a R_i b implies a S_i b and not b S_i a then b $\notin F(R_1, \ldots, S_i, \ldots, R_n)$.

This says if i changes his preferences so if a was previously as high as b then it is now strictly higher then the social choice cannot change from a to b.

For linear orders, IPM implies monotonicity.

EXAMPLE 7.2.6. Majority rule for two alternatives satisfies IPM.

PROPOSITION 7.2.1. (Dasgupta, Hammond, Maskin 1978). *A single valued social choice rule F can be truthfully implemented in dominant strategies if and only if it satisfies IPM.*

Proof. Suppose F can be truthfully implemented but IPM fails. We must have a R_i b, else voter i could gain by pretending his preferences were S_i, if his preferences were R_i. We must have b S_i a, else voter i could gain by pretending his preferences were R_i if they are really S_i. But a R_i b implies not b S_i a. This is a contradiction.

Suppose F satisfies IPM. Let G be the unique element of F. If g does not implement f, there exists a profile $R_1, \ldots, R_n$ and $S_i \in H_i$ such that $F(R_1, \ldots, R_n) = a$, $b = F(R_1, \ldots, R_{i-1}, S_i, R_{i+1}, \ldots, R_n)$ and b R_i a but not a R_i b. Now apply IPM in reverse, going from $F(R_1, \ldots, R_{i-1}, S_i, R_{i+1}, \ldots, R_n)$ to $F(R_1, \ldots, R_n)$. Then we must have b R_i a and a R_i b. This is a contradiction. □

COROLLARY. *A social choice rule F is truthfully implementable in dominant strategies if and only if there exists a single valued social choice rule $F^* \subset F$ satisfying IPM.*

PROPOSITION 7.2.2. *A social choice rule can be truthfully implemented by Nash equilibrium if and only if it can be truthfully implemented by dominant strategies.*

Proof. Every dominant strategy equilibrium is a Nash equilibrium. Conversely let G implement F by Nash equilibrium. Then for any profile $R_1, \ldots, R_n$ and any $S_i \varepsilon H_i$, $G(R_1, \ldots, R_n) R_i G(R_1, \ldots, S_i, \ldots, R_n)$ which verifies that R_i is a dominant strategy for player i. □

For dominant strategies any mechanism is equivalent to a straightforward mechanism. The same is true for a number of other types of equilibrium.

DEFINITION 7.2.6. Let each player have a probability distribution on $H_1 \quad \ldots \quad H_n$ giving his subjective estimates of what the preferences of all players are. Let the probability distribution be a known function of R_i. A *Bayesian equilibrium* is a strategy n-tuple $(x_1, \ldots, x_n)$ such that x_i yields the highest expected utility for player i, according to his subjective probability distribution.

That is, each person simply takes the other players as random variables. There is no strategic interaction for Bayesian equilibrium. For Bayesian equilibrium the fact that every mechanism can be replaced by an equivalent straightforward mechanism is called the *revelation principle*.

However for Nash equilibrium the revelation principle does not always hold.

EXAMPLE 7.2.7. Groves and Ledyard constructed a mechanism described below in order to make a Pareto efficient of a public good, with balanced budget. No such mechanism with balanced budget exists for dominant strategies.

DEFINITION 7.2.7. That a social choice function F *has no veto power* means for all $a \in T$, for all i, for all profiles $R_1, \ldots, R_n$ if for all $b \in A$, for all $j \neq i$, $a R_j b$ then $a \in F(R_1, \ldots, R_n)$.

This means that if all players but one like a certain alternative at least as well as any other, it will be in the choice set.

EXAMPLE 7.2.8. In the rank sum method of social choice there is no veto power if and only if $n \geq m$.

DEFINITION 7.2.8. An *implementation is full* if every value of F is an equilibrium of G.

EXAMPLE 7.2.9. For single peaked preferences, majority rule implements the Pareto set by dominant strategies but this implementation is not full, since the Pareto set usually contains more than one element.

This is Dasgupta, Hammond, and Maskin's terminology. Others refer to *full implementation as implementation and implementation here as partial implementation*, considering full implementation the more important concept. As the previous example indicates, an implementable social choice rule will be a subset of a fully implementable one.

THEOREM 7.2.3. (Maskin). *If F is fully implementable by Nash equilibria, it is monotonic. Conversely if F is monotone and has no veto power, it is fully implementable.*

For a proof, see Maskin (1977).

The appropriateness of various types of implementation is arguable. Moulin (1981) has pointed out that implementation by Nash equilibrium (or d-solvable equilibrium) is not appropriate unless (1) everyone knows everyone else's payoffs or (2) the game is played many times with nearly identical payoffs.

Dominant strategy and Bayesian equilibrium have wider applicability. A weaker concept for the case of a game played only once (or Pareto optimal security levels) is *maximin equilibrium*, that is, maximin strategies for each player. Dasgupta, Hammond, and Maskin (1978) study a quite different maximin concept, related more to Nash equilibrium, and relate it to a strong no veto condition. They also show that implementation by Stackelberg equilibrium valid for all orderings of the players is possible only if there is implementation by dominant strategies. This would cover for example implementation by Nash equilibria of Moulin's (1981) *inessential games*. For two person societies this concept would include the two person games with strictly opposed interests. We mention this only to show that this type of solution concept does not provide anything really new.

A number of implementation results have been obtained in the specific context of voting theory. Implementation by dominant strategies is the previously considered topic of strategyproofness. Strategyproof social choice functions exist only on special domains. E. Kalai and E. Muller (1977) gave conditions for a domain of preferences to admit a social welfare function and showed that such a domain also admits a social choice function, i.e., a nondictatorial implementation of the Pareto set by dominant strategies. Kim and Roush (1980) gave some necessary conditions.

EXAMPLE 7.2.10. A pair of alternatives x, y is called an *inseparable pair* if in every ordering of the domain D, either x, y occur together or y proceeds x, i.e., x P a P y never happens. An Arrow social welfare function is given by letting person 1 decide all choices except between {x, y}. We let the choice between x, y be the choice of persons 1, 2 if they agree, and if not we always choose y over x. See E. Kalai, Z. Ritz (1978).

This gives a nonmanipulable social choice function whose value is the first choice of voter 1 unless voter 1 ranks x first and y second, and voter 2 ranks y over x. In that case y is chosen.

EXAMPLE 7.2.11. The domain of preferences on 1, 2, ... , m consisting of all preferences P such that if $x < y < z$ then it is false that x P z P y is called the *set of increasing peaked preferences*. This contains the single peaked preferences as a subset. Define an Arrow social welfare function by given $x < y$, choosing y unless the choice of x over y is unanimous. This is symmetric in the individuals, but not the alternatives.

This gives a nonmanipulable social choice function such that the social choice is the highest numbered element of the Pareto set.

EXAMPLE 7.2.12. If a domain contains the 2m preferences

1 2 ... m	m ... 2 1
2 3 ... m 1	1 m ... 3 2
m 1 2 ... m-1	m-1 ... 2 1 m

obtained by inversion and cyclic permutation from 1 2 ... m, then no nondictatorial, nonmanipulable social choice function has at least 3 values.

We have mentioned work of B. Peleg and P. Pattanaik by cooperative equilibria involving retaliation. L. Hurwicz and D. Schmeidler studied implementation by Nash equilibrium. Their work is related to that of H. Moulin on implementation by d-solvability. Moulin showed that a necessary condition for implementation by d-solvability is that if any two players either have identical, or strictly reversed preferences, then the social choice function must have truth as a Nash equilibrium point of the two person game between the coalitions formed by all players having a given preference type. A social choice function with this property is said to be *coalitionally easy*.

EXAMPLE 7.2.13. Suppose we assign a score of log k to an alternative for being k^{th} in an individual preferences and add up points. The resulting social choice with some type of *tie-splitting rule* will not in general be coalitionally easy, since for two opposite coalitions of n, n + 1 individuals, the social choice will be near the middle of the preferences of both coalitions, but usually the majority coalition can do better.

A d-solvable equilibrium must also have the property that if everyone prefers any outcome in a set S to any outcome not in S, and the social choice function is onto, the outcome will be in S.

EXAMPLE 7.2.14. The following seems to show that even the weakest monotonicity property, defined for a single individual, may not hold for d-solvable implementation.

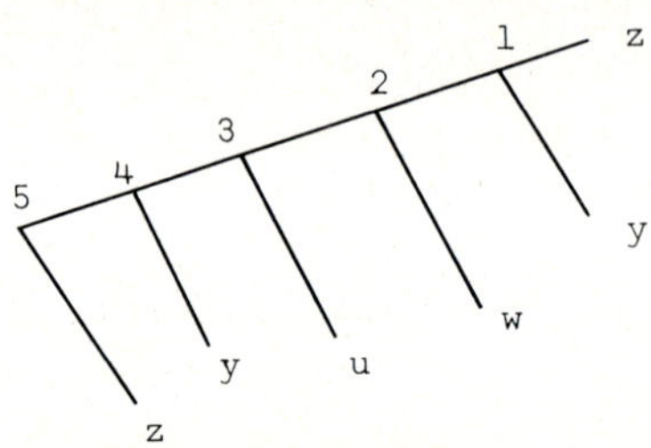

Here at each stage of the game of perfect information, indicated by a tree, the labelled player makes the choice between the two indicated branches. Let the preferences of voters 2-5 be

2	ywz
3	wuy
4	uyw
5	yzu

Then whenever voter 1 prefers z to y the outcome will be y. (Start from the end: voter 1 will so choose z so voter 2 will choose w so voter 3 will choose w so voter 4 will choose y so voter 5 will choose y). But if voter 1 prefers y to z the outcome is z (the choices are y, y, u, u, z from the end).

It is unknown whether there exists a neutral, anonymous, and d-solvable game form for at least three alternatives. Moulin has shown that neutral, anonymous, and d-solvable social choice functions can be implemented by d-solvability for n prime > m.

EXAMPLE 7.2.15. Let rm - sh = 1. Arrange the voters in a fixed order. Let each voter in turn cast a vote against an alternative in sequence, going through the list of voters s times. Any alternative is deleted as soon as it accumulates r votes against it. The remaining alternative is selected. Moulin (1980) proved for r, s sufficiently large gives an anonymous social choice function. Neutrality and efficiency are straightforward to prove.

Moulin and Gabay (1980) studied local d-solvability in a continuous setting. Let x_i be the strategy of player i, a non-negative real number, and $u_i(x_1, \ldots, x_n)$ his utility. Let T be given by

$$t_{ij} = \frac{\dfrac{\partial^2 u_i}{\partial x_i \partial x_j}}{\dfrac{\partial^2 u_i}{\partial x_i^2}}$$

Then an equilibrium point is a d-solvable solution in a neighborhood of itself, if all eigenvalues of T have absolute values less than one (i.e., T^k for large k will reduce the length of all vectors). It is necessary that no eigenvalue exceed one.

7.3 ALLOCATION OF PRIVATE GOODS

The case of purely private goods has different answers for perfect competition and for oligopoly. Suppose that there are a continuous infinity of agents, each too small to affect the market by his own actions. Manipulation of the competitive equilibrium would involve some combination of an agent pretending his initial allocation is less than it actually is and that his utility function is different from what it really is. This means he cannot increase the monetary value of his consumption bundle above what it is at equilibrium, at a set of equilibrium prices.

But within the budget set, the competitive equilibrium allocation is strategyproof. Moreover, no finite set of agents (more generally set of measure zero) can manipulate the competitive equilibrium, since they cannot increase the total value of their goods. A theorem of Hammond states that under differentiability, monotonicity, and concavity conditions the only allocation mechanisms which are Pareto efficient, anonymous, and incentive compatible are those resulting from competitive equilibrium. Douglas Gale (1980) later showed that a similar result is true in an intertemporal model and that it is necessary to introduce money.

This means Pareto efficiency and incentive compatibility cannot both be realized for any centralized economy or even for a market system if the government redistributes income to a significant extent. One system which is incentive compatible but not Pareto efficient is to let everyone keep his initial allocation. More generally such systems can be obtained by letting people trade at will but according to certain restrictions.

If the utility functions only were unknown but the initial allocations known, there can be centralized systems which are Pareto-efficient and incentive compatible, if the total distribution of utilities is known. Set prices equal to marginal utilities at a Pareto optimum and give people an amount of money dependent only on their initial allocation. This can realize for example, all Pareto optimum points at which everyone's consumption bundle has equal monetary value, including *envy-free allocations*.

In the former case when an individual can keep part of his initial allocation to himself and the government redistributes the rest there can be incentive compatible systems which improve the *leximin social welfare* provided that the rich prefer to trade. If the rich prefer their initial allocations, then no incentive compatible system can effectively redistribute wealth, as the rich can pretend to have nothing. But if the rich prefer to trade, the government can assess a tax on the value of all traded goods, and then divide the proceeds of the tax equally among all traders, letting there be free trade subject to the tax.

If trading itself could be concealed then the only allocations that could result would be in the core and therefore they would be competitive outcomes.

EXAMPLE 7.3.1. The present U.S. system is somewhat analogous to the taxation on trade. Individuals can conceal their initial bundles (mainly consisting of a work skills). Trading represents working for a salary, and an income tax taxes this. However the income tax is not divided equally, which might leave room for manipulation.

The Soviet system is an attempt to realize the case where initial allocation cannot be concealed, i.e., quotas are assigned. However prices are set somewhat arbitrarily, and in practice unequal pay is used for incentives to about the same extent as in the West.

Within the set of allocations attainable by incentive compatible systems, it might be of interest to know which maximize the Harsanyi, Nash, or leximin social welfare functions, or to characterize allocations Pareto efficient within the subset of those achievable by strategyproof mechanisms.

P. Samuelson (1954) showed the possibility of manipulation for an economy with public goods. L. Hurwicz (1972) showed that for a finite number of traders the competitive equilibrium is manipulable, i.e., not incentive compatible. We assume the initial allocations are known, and manipulation is misrepresentation of utility functions.

EXAMPLE 7.3.2. Consider two goods, and two traders. Let the initial allocations be (0, 1), (1, 0). Let each trader's true utility function be x_1x_2. Suppose trader 1 represents his utility function as $x_1x_2^{\alpha}$. Then by ratio of marginal utilities, where

$$\begin{cases} p = \dfrac{p_2}{p_1} \\ p = \alpha \dfrac{x_1}{x_2} = \dfrac{1 - x_1}{1 - x_2} \end{cases}$$

and the budget equations are

$$\begin{cases} x_1 + px_2 = p \\ (1 - x_1) + p(1 - x_2) = 1 \end{cases}$$

From the second of each equation, $x_1 = \frac{1}{2}$. Then $p = \frac{1}{2}(1 + \alpha)$ from the first of each set of equations. And

$$x_2 = \frac{\alpha}{p} x_1$$

Thus it is completely in player 1's advantage to pretend his good is more valuable, or his opponent's is less valuable to him, than they really are.

L. Hurwicz also showed that for two traders and two goods, no allocation method is Pareto efficient, straightforwardly incentive compatible, and individually rational for all pairs of convex utility functions. Dasgupta, Hammond, and Maskin extended this result to arbitrary finite sets of traders and goods, without requiring differentiability of the allocation or individual rationality. Satterthwaite and Sonnenschein (1979) then proved a general theorem in which differentiability of the allocation is required (though it seems this could be removed) but the domain consists simply of any nonempty open set of utility n-tuples in the C^2 topology, that is any utility functions such that they, and their first two derivatives are sufficiently close to those of a given n-tuple of utility functions.

EXAMPLE 7.3.3. This assumption is necessary. For instance if we take equal total amounts of all goods and equal utility functions, then the allocation which gives everyone identical bundles would be satisfactory. However in an open set there can always be variations in the utility functions, so they can be at most approximately equal.

It is not assumed that the allocation is Pareto efficient. But two assumptions are made: *nonbossiness and nondictatorship*. An allocation is bossy if an agent could by changing his stated preference, change the bundles of the other players without changing his own. Such a mechanism is undesirable because this gives incentives for under-the-table deals and corruption as well as giving people arbitrary power over another.

EXAMPLE 7.3.4. For three players, let player 3 decide the ratio between the utilities of players 1 and 2, and let player 2 decide the ratio between the utilities of players 1 and 3. Pick a Pareto efficient point such that the utilities are in the given ratio. This mechanism which will be well defined in an open set of utility n-tuples, is bossy, but strategyproof.

In a *serial dictatorship* one player chooses his allocation from a set a second chooses his allocation from a set depending on the first player's choice, and so on. These are also strategyproof. Serial dictatorship do not generally give Pareto efficient allocations.

THEOREM 7.3.1. (Satterthwaite and Sonnenschein). *Any nonbossy, strategyproof differentiable allocation mechanism defined on a connected open set of regular utility n-tuples in the C^2 topology is a serial dictatorship.*

The set of allocations involved need not be different distributions of a collection of private goods. They need only be the image of the allocation mechanism which is required to be continuously differentiable and have various regularity properties. Therefore the Satterthwaite and Sonnenschein theorem applies to cases of pure public goods, pure private goods, mixtures of public and private goods, economies with production, and cases in which externalities occur.

Can any satisfactory allocation mechanism ever be found, considering this general impossibility result ? First, it applies only if the set of agents is finite. In the case of a continuum of agents, the market is generally strategyproof. Second if an administrator knew the distribution of utility functions in the population (but not who had which), he could construct an allocation mechanism. More generally as we will later see, if the utility functions have a special form, mechanisms can be constructed. Thirdly mechanisms might be constructed using alternative equilibrium concepts or a weakend nonbossiness.

We have already taken up the first method. The second will take up a separate section. For a one-time decision, Bayesian or maximin equilibrium is a possibility, especially the former. For the type of continuous-time situations occuring in economics nothing which is not a Nash equilibrium is plausible. The Nash equilibrium should also have some additional properties such as local d-solvability in order to be attractive.

EXAMPLE 7.3.5. Let each agent's message be to state the set of bundles which are minimally acceptable to him. If there exist bundles acceptable to everyone, one is chosen at random. Otherwise everyone receives zero. Then the set of Nash equilibria generally coincides with the Pareto set. However since a Nash equilibrium is unlikely to occur this is not a good allocation mechanism.

Existence of allocation mechanisms having local d-solvability or being otherwise locally stable under best response functions is unknown. Hammond, Dasgupta, and Maskin (1977) showed that for a wide variety of domains occurring in economics unique Nash implementability implies dominant strategy implementability. Thus the prospects for locally unique allocation mechanisms using Nash equilibrium do not seem good, by the Satterthwaite and Sonnenschein theorem. A general method of implementing allocations by nonunique nonlocally stable Nash equilibrium is given in Raphael Rob (1981).

Crawford (1979) and Crawford and Heller (1979) have studied "*divide and choose*" mechanisms. A simple case is the well known method of cutting a cake in two fairly. One person cuts but the other can choose whichever piece he like. An n-person version exists in which the cutter increases the size of the proposed cut continuously and any of the other player says "cut" as soon as he is satisfied with the proposed piece. See Luce and Raiffa (1957).

Crawford and Heller study the problem for 2 players of dividing one divisible good (money) and a set of indivisible goods. The divider splits the total in two and the chooser chooses. We assume each player knows the other's preferences. This method will always be fair in the sense that no one prefers another's bundle to his own but may not be Pareto efficient if the preferences of the two players differ and there is more than one indivisible good. The allocation will be Pareto efficient in the set of fair allocations. The divider has the advantage.

We have mentioned before that for n players fair allocations can be obtained by giving everyone equal initial bundles and letting them trade to a competitive equilibrium, provided preferences are convex and there is no production. This procedure is not strategyproof. Crawford (1979) gives a divide and choose method for obtaining fair Pareto efficient allocation. An auctioneer (divider) is chosen by bidding for the job. He offers each player an allocation z. If everyone elses takes z it is chosen. Else the equal division allocation is chosen.

7.4 PUBLIC GOODS AND TRANSFERABLE UTILITY

Allocation of public goods is particularly likely to have problems with manipulation, since there is little incentive to be honest, but rather to apply as much pressure as possible for one's own viewpoint. If preferences are single peaked, majority voting is generally strategyproof, as in social choice theory, but it is not Pareto efficient without additional assumptions. E. C. Zeeman (1979) gives an argument using catastrophe theory as to why a four-dimensional political model with dimensions of liberty, equality, fraternity, and opportunity should reduce to a linear scale:

Authoritarian Left	Liberal Left	Center	Liberal Right	Authoritarian Right

together with the isolated point of anarchy. The outcome from majority voting is always Pareto efficient for single peaked preferences, within the set of alternatives only.

If there exists another good, money, by which utility can be transferred from one agent to another then Pareto in the set of allocations involving transfer of money and choice of the public good, Pareto efficiency becomes a much stricter condition. In fact an alternative is Pareto efficient if and only if it maximizes the sum of utilities to the agents. If y does maximize the sum of utilities to the agents, no monetary transfer can affect this, and it will be Pareto efficient. If it does not maximize the sum of utilities, let x be have greater sum of utilities. That is

$$\Sigma\ u_i(x) > \Sigma\ u_i(y)$$

Let person i have quantity w_i of money for the allocation associated with y, $\Sigma\ w_i = 0$. Then associate with x the allocation where person i has quantity of money

$$u_i(y) - u_i(x) + w_i + \frac{\Sigma\ (u_i(x) - u_i(y))}{n}$$

This is better for everyone than the original. So an allocation associated with y could not be Pareto optimal.

THEOREM 7.4.1. *Suppose single peaked utility functions have the form $f(x, a)$ where $f(x, a)$ is continuous in x and differentiable in x except possibly at a, strictly increasing in x for $x < a$ and strictly decreasing for $x > a$. Then for any odd number of voters, majority rule maximizes the sum of utilities* *if and only if f(x, a) = |s(x) - s(a)| for some monotone continuous function s.*

Proof. If f(x, a) has this form, divide the voters into the median voter and sets of voters above and below the median. As we move away from the median the utility of the median voter decreases. For every voter whose utility increases there will be a voter on the opposite side whose utility decreases by an equal amount. So the total utility can only decrease as we move away from the median. Thus the sum of utilities is highest at the median.

Suppose conversely f(x, a) is such that the median maximizes the sum of utilities. Suppose for $a < x < b$, $f'(x, a) + f'(x, b) \neq 0$. Then for 1 voter at x, n voters at a, n voters at b, for n sufficiently large, the median will not maximize utility, since a slight shift up or down will be better. Therefore $f'(x, a) + f'(x, b) = 0$. This implies the given property for

$$s(x) = \int_o^x |f'(x, 0)| \, dx$$

(As far as we know this result is new, but there may be some reference in the literature of which we are unaware). □

If this assumption on preferences is true, then Harsanyi's social welfare function is maximized, and also the Lorentz curve of the utility distribution is not below any other Lorentz curve. H. R. Bowen (1943) showed that as the number of voters tends to infinity, if the utilities of a single alternative x are normally distributed, then a majority vote of x versus the status quo will maximize the sum of utilities.

If utilities are such that majority voting will not in general be Pareto efficient, given transferable utility, then the only reasonable alternative is a method of voting that indicates intensities of preference. However a voter would gain in utility by exaggerated the intensity of his own preference over the chosen alternative, in general, unless he paid a price that increased with the stated intensity.

Consider selection of an alternative from a set K. The voters state the monetary value $w_i(x)$ of each alternative $x \in K$ to them. From these votes, a project d(w) is chosen and an amount $t_i(w)$, positive or negative, of money are given to each agent i.

DEFINITION 7.4.1. A *Groves mechanism* is a mechanism in which the chosen alternative d(w) maximizes the sum $\Sigma\, w_i(d(w))$ of stated utilities, and the transfer is

$$f_i(w) = \sum_{j \neq i} w_j(d(w)) + h_i(w)$$

where h_i is an arbitrary but fixed function which does not depend on w_i but does depend on the stated utilities of the other voters.

EXAMPLE 7.4.1. The *Clarke mechanism*, or *pivotal mechanism*, is the Groves mechanism such that

$$h_i(w) = - \max_{x_1 \in K} \sum_{j \neq i} w_j(x_1)$$

EXAMPLE 7.4.2. Suppose we have two alternatives, x, y where x has value 0 to all voters and y has values as follows

voter	1	2	3
utility	2	-3	4

Then if the voters are honest, alternative y will be chosen, since 2 + (-3) + 4 > 0 + 0 + 0. The transfer payments are as follows

voter 1	-3 + 4 + (-(-3 + 4)) = 0
voter 1	2 + 4 + (-(2 + 4)) = 0
voter 3	2 + (-3) + (0 + 0) = -1

The final utilities including transfer payments, are 2, -3, 3.

The total payment is -1.

THEOREM 7.4.2. *The Grove mechanisms implement the Pareto set by dominant strategy equilibrium.*

Proof. We need to show truthful statement of $w_i(x)$ is a dominant strategy for each voter. Suppose the voter were instead to state $v(x)$. Then h_i is unaltered. Let a be the chosen alternative. His new total utility is

$$w_i(a) + \sum_{j \neq i} w_j(a) + h_i \leq w_i(d(w)) + \sum_{j \neq i} w_i(d(w)) + h_i$$

since $d(w)$ maximizes $\Sigma\, w_i(d(w))$. Therefore his utility for v is less than or equal to his utility for w_i so w_i is a dominant strategy.

Conversely it can be shown that the Groves mechanisms are the only ones which truthfully implement the Pareto set by dominant strategy equilibrium. K. Roberts (1979) proved a stronger result for finite alternative sets. □

DEFINITION 7.4.2. A *game form for transferable utility* is a function which to given a statement $w_i(x)$ of the utility of alternative x to player i for all i, x, assigns an alternative $d(w)$ and transfer payment $t_i(w)$ for all i.

EXAMPLE 7.4.3. The Groves mechanisms are game forms for transferable utility.

EXAMPLE 7.4.4. A strategyproof social choice function is a strategyproof game form with transferable utility such that $t_i = 0$.

THEOREM 7.4.3. (Roberts). *Let the alternative set be finite. Suppose d, t give a strategyproof game form such that d can take on any alternative as a value. Then there exist nonnegative numbers k_i not all zero, and numbers $v(x)$ for alternatives x such that $d(w)$ maximizes $g(d(w)) = v(d(w)) + \Sigma\, k_i w_i(x) d(x)$ and*

and for all i such that $k_i > 0$, $w_i(d(w)) + t_i(w) - \frac{1}{k_i}g(d(w))$ *does not depend on* w_i.

There are a number of limitations on the Groves mechanisms: (1) as the example shows, some individuals may be worse off than if no decision were taken, even though the utility sum is positive (individual rationality), (2) the budget will not in general balance, that is, the sum of the transfer payments is nonzero, (3) an individual may be required to pay more than he has, (4) coalitions can cooperatively manipulate the process, (5) there must be transfer utility (additive separability).

The book Green and Laffont (1979) is largely concerned with the question of overcoming these problems. The Clarke mechanism essentially solves problem (3) in that individuals whose total utility is reduced will have zero transfer payments. However the other problems cannot be solved for dominant strategy mechanisms.

EXAMPLE 7.4.5. For the Clarke mechanism with utilities 4, -5, 4 voters 1, 3 can manipulate by stating their utilities as 3. This reduces their transfer payments from $-5 + 4 = -1$ to 0.

The need for separable utility (5) means that Groves mechanisms cannot be used to decide questions in which the distribution of income is an important consideration, such as taxation plans, decisions on how to finance public projects, and projects designed to help overcome poverty.

Some of the above problems are statistically insignificant for large number of voters or repeated applications. If tastes are normally distributed with mean zero, then in repeated applications the pivotal mechanism will be individually rational in that the expected value is nonnegative for a voter. The budget imbalance tends to zero in proportion to the number of voters as that number tends to infinity. And for large numbers of voters the incentive for small coalitions to cooperatively manipulate tends to zero.

Groves and Ledyard (1975) constructed a mechanism implementing the Pareto set by Nash equilibrium and having balanced budget. Their mechanism is based on the existence of a Groves mechanism with balanced budget when the utility functions of individuals are restricted to quadratic functions of a real variable ranging over the alternative set. Voters state quadratic approximations to their utility functions, instead of their entire utility functions, and the special Groves mechanism is used. Hurwicz (1976) implemented the Pareto set by Nash equilibrium with balanced budget in a different way, but his mechanism is highly unstable.

Laffont and Maskin (1982) have characterized Nash and strategyproof implementation when preferences for a 1-dimensional public good are concave and there is transferable utility.

Hurwicz's method involves each agent i stating the amount k_i of the public good he desires and a price p_i. The amount of public good actually chosen is the average of the k_i and the transfer payment is

$$-k\bar{p}_i - p_i(k_i - k_{i+1})^2 - p_{i+1}(k_{i+1} - k_{i+2})^2$$

where $\bar{p}$ is, for n odd,

$$\frac{1}{N} - \sum_{i=1}^{N} (-1)^i p_i$$

and the other p_j are computed in a symmetrical way.

Dubins (1974) constructed a mechanism using maximin equilibrium with each person i stating the utility $w_i(x)$ of each alternative x, with a constant subtracted from $w_i(x)$ to make

$$\sum_i w_i(x) = 0$$

The alternative is chosen to maximize

$$\sum_i w_i(x)$$

and the transfer payment is

$$-w_i(x) + \frac{1}{n} \sum_i w_i(x)$$

Green and Laffont (1979) constructed a dynamic procedure for the nonseparable case. The public good changes continuously over time. Each agent states a marginal rate of substitution of the public good for him at that point. The public utilities exceeds or falls below the marginal cost of providing the good. Transfer payments are defined in terms of fixed shares of the marginal cost of providing the good, the total surplus of marginal utilities over shares of cost, divided evenly and individual's marginal utility. Agents act myopically that is they maximize their rate of return at each instant without regard to the future. Also it is assumed that the number of agents is large enough that the distribution of the surplus to each agent is not a significant factor in his decision. Green and Laffont then prove that truth is a dominant strategy and if production of some amount of the public good gives total benefits exceeding its cost, the procedure converges to a Pareto efficient outcome. Individual rationality is not, however, valid.

Lack of individual rationality in some cases may be a serious problem from the legal and ethical viewpoint in that it may amount to confiscation of private property. Some Groves mechanisms are individually rational, but they are impractical because the budget imbalance rapidly approaches infinity, as the square of the number of voters. In the pivotal mechanism with a choice between the status quo and the project, if the project gives a higher total utility than the status quo, no one hurt by the project is compensated at all.

7.5 BAYESIAN EQUILIBRIUM, GAMES OF INCOMPLETE INFORMATION, AND ORGANIZATIONS

In Bayesian implementation each agent maximizes his expected utility, assuming the other agents act according to a fixed probability distribution. He does not take into account the impact of his decision on them.

We will derive a special case of a formula of d'Aspremont and Gerard-Varet for *Bayesian implementation* where the choice is between the status quo, (0, 0, ... , 0) and a project with utilities $(v_1, v_2, \dots, v_n)$. Each person states a utility w_i for the project. The project is chosen to maximize Σw_i for any straightforward mechanism, and by the revelation principle we can assume the mechanism is straightforward. Let $t_i(w)$ be the transfer payment to agent i. Let f_{-i} denote the distribution of the votes of all other people, in the estimation of voter i, and w_{-i} their votes. The expected value of the transfer function is

$$\int t_i(w) f_{-i}\, dw_{-i}$$

The expected value of the project is

$$v_i \int_{\Sigma w_j > 0} f_i\, dw_{-i}\, dw_i$$

The derivative of the sum of these will be zero at w_i, assuming w_i is the strategy which maximizes player i's utility. This derivative is

$$-v_i \int_{\Sigma w_{-i} > -w_i} f_{-i}\, dw_{-i} + \int \frac{\partial f_i}{\partial w_i} f_{-i}\, dw_{-i}$$

Since the mechanism is straightforward, when $v_i = w_i$ this expression is identically zero.

$$\int \frac{\partial t_i}{\partial w_i} f_{-i}\, dw_{-i} = w_i \int_{\Sigma w_{-i} > -w_i} f_{-i}\, dw_{-i}$$

Now integrate over w_i. We have

$$E_i(t_i) = c_i + E_i(-\sum_{j \neq i} w_i \mid \Sigma w_i \geq 0)$$

where E_i denotes expected value according to the subjective probability distribution of voter 1 and c_i is a constant. We may choose t_i to be any function

$$E_i(- \sum_{j \neq i} w_i | \Sigma w_i \geq 0) + h_i(w_{-i})$$

By properly choosing h_i it may be arranged that $\Sigma t_i = 0$, for instance

$$h_i = - \frac{1}{n - 1} \sum_{j \neq i} E_j(- \sum_{m \neq j} w_i)$$

More generally h_i could also involve w_i provided $E_i(h_i) = 0$ at each value of w_i. However none of these functions will be individually rational.

B. Holmstrom, R. Myerson, and others have studied a group of *principal-agent problems* related to organization structure, games of incomplete information, and bargaining theory, using Bayesian equilibrium (expected utility equilibrium) as the solution concept. Myerson and Satterthwaite (1981) consider the problem in one of its simplest forms. Individual 1 has an object individual 2 wants to buy. Each individual knows the value of the object to him, but has only a subjective probability distribution regarding the value of the object to the other person.

We consider *incentive compatible mechanisms* which on the basis of the stated values of the object to the two players will assign the object to one of them, and determine its price. A direct mechanism can be described by functions $p(w_1, w_2)$ and $x(w_1, w_2)$ where w_i is the value stated by agent i, p is the probability the object is given to the buyer, and x is the expected payment from buyer to seller. Let f_i be the density of the probability distribution of the value to player i, as seen by the other player.

For this problem the d'Aspremont and Gerard-Varet mechanism amounts to

$$t_1 = E_1(-w_2 | w_2 \geq w_1) - E_2(w_1 | w_2 \geq w_1)$$

since if we set the utilities of the status quo to zero, by subtracting a constant, the utilities of the project are $-w_1$, w_2.

$$t_1 = \int_{w_1}^{\infty} -w_2 f(w_2)\, dw_2 - \int_0^{w_2} w_1 f_1(w_1)\, dw_1$$

EXAMPLE 7.5.1. Let w_1, w_2 range between 0, 1 with uniform distribution. Then

$$t_1 = \int_{w_1}^{1} -w_2\, dw_2 - \int_0^{w_2} w_1\, dw_1 = -\frac{1}{2} - \frac{w_2^2}{2} - \frac{w_1^2}{2}$$

The expected value of t_1 is

$$-\frac{1}{2} - \frac{1}{6} - \frac{w_1^2}{2}$$

The total expected utility of player 1 is

$$-v_1(1 - w_1) - \frac{1}{2} - \frac{1}{6} - \frac{w_1^2}{2}$$

which has a maximum at $w_1 = v_1$, as required. Since this expected utility is negative, the mechanism is not individually rational for player 1.

Myerson and Satterthwaite examine mechanisms which are individually rational, but not necessarily efficient. They show a necessary condition for efficiency is that $f_1 f_2 = 0$ almost everywhere, that is the two traders have completely different ideas of what the good is worth. They show there is a mechanism which maximizes efficiency and derive a formula for it.

EXAMPLE 7.5.2. For the previous example, the following mechanism maximizes efficiency

$$p(v_1, v_2) = \begin{cases} 1 \text{ if } v_1 \le v_2 - \frac{1}{4} \\ 0 \text{ otherwise} \end{cases}$$

$$x(v_1, v_2) = \begin{cases} \dfrac{v_1 + v_2 + 0.5}{3} & \text{if } v_1 \le v_2 - \frac{1}{4} \\ 0 & \text{otherwise} \end{cases}$$

Here as before, p is the probability the buyer receives the object and x is the expected tranfer payment.

This mechanism is not efficient, since to be efficient, the buyer would have to receive the object whenever $v_1 \le v_2$. D. P. Baron and R. B. Myerson (1979) apply Bayesian implementation to the problem of regulating a monopolist, such as government regulation of a utility company, when the government does not know the truth costs faced by the utility, but only a probability distribution. The regulatory mechanism yielding highest expected valued will penalize the company for reporting high costs by forcing it to change a price which can be above the monopoly price.

B. Holmstrom (1980) studies incentive compatibility in relation to organization. The former paper is concerned with delegation. Suppose the agent has information not available to the principal, although the principal can control his actions. When is it advanatgeous to allow the agent freedom to choose his actions (which he will do in his own interest, not necessarily the principal's) ?

Let y be the set of information available to the agent D the set of decisions, and $d_i(y)$ the decision person i would take on the basis of information y. Here i = 1 is the principal, i = 2 the agent. Both y and D are considered intervals of real numbers.

DEFINITION 7.5.1. Let $y_i(d) = \{y \in Y | d_i(y) \ge d\}$. The *preferences of the principal and agent* are coherent provided that for all d either $y_1(d) \subset y_2(d)$ or $y_2(d) \subset y_1(d)$.

EXAMPLE 7.5.3. If the preferences of principal and agent are of the form $d_1(y) = y + a_1$, $d_2(y) = y + a_2$ then they are coherent.

EXAMPLE 7.5.4. The preferences $d_1(y) = y$, $d_2(y) = -y$ are not coherent.

Coherence means that for any d either if the agent would choose an action stronger than d, so would the principal, or vice versa. Under appropriate mathematical conditions, if preferences are coherent and the agent would take actions on either side of the principal's action in the absence of informa--tion, then delegation is beneficial.

If transfer payments are allowed then delegation is beneficial provided that in y the amount of money the agent would pay to increase y is increasing and the amount the principal would accept to increase y is decreasing.

In general principal agent problems there are two separate things not controlled by the principals. Adverse selection is information known to an agent but not the principal, such as the utility of an outcome to him. Moral hazard refers to actions he can perform which the principal cannot control. If there were adverse selection only the previous concept of Bayesian equilibrium is appropriate. For moral hazard only, Nash equilibrium (or d-solvable, etc.) is appropriate.

A situation involving both is modelled as a game of incomplete information (Harsanyi 1967, 1968).

DEFINITION 7.5.2. A *game of incomplete information* consists of a set N of players for $i \in N$, a set A_i of strategies of player i, a set T_i of types of player i, an expected utility function u_i from $A_1 \times \ldots \times A_n \times T_1 \times \ldots \times T_n$ to the real numbers, and probability distribution p_i on $T_1 \times \ldots \times T_{i-1} \times T_{i+1} \times \ldots \times T_n$.

EXAMPLE 7.5.5. If each T_i contains only one element we have a game in the usual sense.

EXAMPLE 7.5.6. If each A_i for $i > 1$ contains only one element, player i has the decision theory problem of maximizing his expected utility.

DEFINITION 7.5.3. A *Bayesian Nash equilibrium* of a game of incomplete information consists of a strategy n-tuple

$a_1, \ldots, a_n$ such that for all i, for all $b_1, \ldots, b_n$ such that $a_j = b_j$ for $i \neq j$

$$E_i(u_i(a_1, \ldots, a_n, t_1, \ldots, t_n)) \geq E_i(u_i(b_1, \ldots, b_n, t_1, \ldots, t_n))$$

where E_i is expected utility computed using the probability distribution p_i on $T_1 \times \ldots \times T_{i-1} \times T_{i+1} \times \ldots \times T_n$ and t_i is player i's true type.

This reduces to the usual Nash equilibrium in case each T_i has only one element. In fact we can generally reduce the problem of finding Bayesian Nash equilibria to that of finding Nash equilibria by replacing u_i by its expected value.

Cooperative games of incomplete information may also be considered. Harsanyi-Selten (1972) proposed a generalization of the Nash bargaining solution to games of *imperfect information.* Myerson (1980b) presents a modified version of this, and another paper (Myerson 1980c) gives a generalization of the Shapley λ-transfer value as a solution concept for cooperative games of incomplete information.

Myerson (1980a) takes up problems involving several principals, such as several firms in related industries. He shows that it may not be possible for principals to simultaneously choose mechanisms maximizing their expected returns giving the mechanisms of other principals but that a limiting concept of quasi-equilibrium will exist.

Myerson (1981) takes up the problem of finding the best incentive compatible mechanism when the principal has information he desires to conceal from the agents. That is, he has several different types, which would affect the payoffs both to him and to the agents.

For instance the government might wish to conceal the criteria it uses for auditing tax returns. Yet the mechanism itself may reveal information about the principal's type.

EXAMPLE 7.5.7. Myerson (1981) calls this the *principal's dilemma*. The principal has only 1 strategy and the agent has only one type.

		Agent's action			
		2a	2b	2c	2d
Principal's type	1a	(4, 4)	(3, 3)	(1, 5)	(0, 0)
	1b	(3, 3)	(4, 4)	(0, 0)	(1, 5)

Consider a mechanisms where in π_1 the agent is to play strategy 1 regardless of the principal's type. This is incentive compatible as long as the agent thinks there is a 50-50 chance the principal has either type, yielding the agent a return of 3.5. The mechanism π_2 in which the agent agrees to play always strategy 2 is also incentive compatible, yielding the agent a return of 3.5. Yet if the principal has type 1a he will prefer π_1 and if he has type 1b he will prefer π_1. Thus the agent can figure out his type from the mechanism.

If the agent knows the principal's type, the mechanism is no longer incentive compatible, since he would then play 2c or 2d. Thus the mechanisms π_i are not incentive compatible from this broader viewpoint.

Myerson models this situation as a sort of cooperative game among the different types of the principal, and develops a solution analogous to the core, and a stronger concept called *neutrality*.

EXAMPLE 7.5.8. There are 3 neutral mechanisms for the principal's dilemma, π_1, π_2 and the mechanism π_3 such the probabilities of the agent's actions given the principal's types are

	Action	
Type	2a	2b
1a	0.75	0.25
1b	0.25	0.75

The *principal's core* is the set of mechanisms x such that there is no collection S_1 of types such that all types in S_1 prefer the mechanism y, and y is incentive compatible for any set of types containing S_1. Else when the principal was of one of these types, he would always prefer to use a different mechanism. Myerson shows the principal's core and even the subset of neutral mechanisms defined as those which cannot be blocked by any solution concept satisfying four axioms, are nonempty.

7.6 CONCLUSION

In cases in which the individual can conceal his true condition and can gain from lying, economic mechanisms should have some degree of strategyproofness, or incentive compatibility. There are different concepts of incentive compatibility or implementation, corresponding to different game theoretic solutions: dominant strategy, Bayesian equilibrium, maximin equilibrium, d-solvability, Nash equilibrium, and various cooperative solution concepts. The strongest and most important is dominant strategy implementation. Dasgupta, Maskin, and Hammond showed that dominant strategy implementation is equivalent to a very strong monotonicity condition, related to existence of social welfare functions. On sufficiently inclusive domains, existence of a single-valued Nash equilibrium implementation is equivalent to existence of a dominant strategy implementation, and more generally single-valued Nash implementation is equivalent to another monotonicity condition. Nonunique Nash implementation is of doubtful significance without some type of local stability. Bayesian implementation seems mainly appropriate for discrete processes for which conditions do not exactly repeat themselves. For Bayesian and dominant strategy implementation the revelation principle asserts that every implementation is equivalent to a straightforward implementation in which the agents tell the truth.

In social choice theory dominant strategy mechanisms (strategyproof mechanisms) exist only on restricted domains, such as domains on which social welfare functions exist. Various cooperative solution concepts have been used by Peleg, Dutta, and Pattanaik. H. Moulin has shown that interesting social choice functions can be implemented by d-solvability.

For allocation of goods, the market is strategyproof provided that no individual can influence prices by his actions and that the government does not play a significant role. If the set of preferences of individuals is sufficiently general, it is the only mechanism which is incentive compatible, anonymous, and Pareto efficient. However there are other, more egalitarian mechanisms, which may be Pareto efficient restricted to the subset of allocations achievable by incentive compatible mechanisms, in which the government taxes trade and redistributes the revenue.

For small numbers of agents Sonnenschein and Satterthwaite proved a very general impossibility theorem, applying both to private and to public goods, for dominant strategy mechanisms. However dominant strategy mechanims do exist for transferable utility, called *Groves mechanisms*. They have certain limitations: the budget does not balance, except asymptotically, coalitions can manipulate them, they cannot be used in cases in which distribution of wealth is a serious problem. Moreover individuals may receive less than in the status quo even though society as a whole benefits. In some cases this might cause legal and ethical problems. This defect is known as *lack of individual rationality*. Green and Laffont propose a *dynamic mechanism* which may allow questions of distribution to be taken into account. Perhaps mechanisms can be found which subject to individual rationality constraints maximize the sum of utilities even though they are not strictly efficient.

Myerson, Holmstrom, and others have applied Bayesian equilibrium to variety of problems related to management and regulation. Green and Laffont showed that Bayesian mechanisms cannot in general reconcile Pareto efficiency and individual rationality. A paper of Myerson and Satterthwaite finds the most nearly efficient Bayesian mechanisms satisfying individual rationality for a two person bargaining problem.

The theory of Bayesian mechanisms is still in its initial stages, and much remain to be discovered.

CHAPTER 8

APPLICATIONS

8.1 INTRODUCTION

In this chapter we outline possible applications of the preceding theory. First we take up the problem of deciding what public goods, such as education and environmental quality a community is to have. Both social arbitration functions and incentive compatible mechanisms can potentially be applied. *Lindahl equilibrium* is an equilibrium concept which generalizes the competitive (market) equilibrium to public goods, and can be implemented by incentive compatible mechanisms. Pigou tax subsidies in principle provide a simple means of inducing efficient pollution control by taxing emission of harmful substance.

Social arbitration functions, generalized to a situation of more than one time period allow optimum rates of use of nonrenewable resources such as oil to be calculated. If everyone's utility function were identical, the market system under perfect competition would achieve this rate.

The business cycle and inflation can be analyzed by methods related to equilibrium theory. It is unknown the extent to which the inflation of the seventies is made up demand-pull, cost-push, or an inflation due to expectations of inflation. The second is a game theoretic problem in which each agent could gain by raising his prices if the other's prices are taken as fixed. This is related to monopoly power and can only be controlled by some type of government regulation.

Redistribution for instance income tax rates is also a question which can be studied by social arbitration functions, though complex tax systems have serious drawbacks.

8.2 PUBLIC GOODS AND EXTERNALITIES

Public goods ideally are owned by separate individuals and each affects his utility alone. Public goods are goods which are held by the society as a whole, and the choice of which affects everyone's utility. If each farmer in a village owns his own land, that land is a private good. But if there is a range on which any one may graze his animals, that land is a public good.

Public goods cannot be effectively allocated by the market, so they are traditionally the domain of government. Examples usually considered public goods include defense, public education, polic protection, a healthful and attractive environment, game birds, fish in the ocean, liberties quaranteed by law, scientific knowledge, recreational facilities such as parks and art museums, the possibility of adequate food and water supplies.

Externalities reflect the same basic interdependence of utilities, that one person's utility is affected by his neighbor's bundle of goods (consumed). The usual example is that a factory's production affects by noise and pollution those living near by. A frequent difference between public goods and externalities is that externalities are ordinarily privately controlled, except as constrained by law, but public goods are a matter of group choice. However there is much overlap and the two concepts may be considered different ways of looking at the same thing.

While private goods are chosen noncooperatively by the market, public goods are often chosen by cooperative game processes such as majority rule.

The central problem of public goods is to choose a level of public goods which is Pareto optimal and in some sense fair. In the case when the utility functions of individuals are adequately known and the government has free power to make the choice, this function is solved by social arbitration functions. The government need only choose a levels of public goods maximizing the social arbitration function (the affect on private goods bundles can be allowed for approximating by considering the utility of money for the value of a citizen's income).

The *voucher method* is implicitly an application of this concept. In that method the individual must purchase a voucher, a ticket for some public service such as education. Proces and services may vary from household to household, but are chosen so as to achieve a social optimum.

Alternative methods of achieving a somewhat similar goal include use of a game theory solution as a *fair arbitration method*. For instance the Shapley value (E. Bres, A. Charnes, D. Cole Eckels, S. Hitt, R. Lyders, J. Rousseau, K. Russel, and M. Schoeman (1979)) has been used to assess the costs of a medical library and to study a transportation system (H. Diaz and G. Owen (1979)).

Much theoretical work has been done on the case when instead of the government prescribing a method it prescribes a game which the agents play and the outcome is the result of the game.

Beyond majority rule, the simplest techniques of this kind may be *(1) tax subsidy methods*, and *(2) bargaining among concerned parties*. In tax subsidy methods, going back to Pigou, polluters are charged emissions fee. These are arranged so that a Pareto optimum results. Each person's tax may have to vary with another's consumption levels unless there is a strong separability of costs.

EXAMPLE 8.2.1. (J. M. Henderson and R. E. Quandt (1958)). Suppose there are two producers of a good, having costs given by $C_1(q_1, q_2)$, $C_2(q_1, q_2)$ where q_i is production level of person i. To maximize total profit (Pareto optimum) is to maximize

$$T = p(q_1 + q_2) - C_1(q_1, q_2) - C_2(q_1, q_2)$$

The unique constant tax rates which do this are

$$\frac{\partial C_2}{\partial q_1}, \qquad \frac{\partial C_1}{\partial q_2}$$

Other variable tax rates exist.

It has been estimated that use of emissions fees in place of fixed standards could achieve a 50% reduction in pollution control costs in the United States, because industries finding it more costly to control pollution would pay the bill and emit as they have, but industries which can efficiently control pollution would cut down on emissions to balance out the total. Thus funds spent on pollution control would be spent efficiently.

Bargaining among concerned parties is feasible if there are only two but where many people are involved bargaining could be unwieldy.

Incentive compatible mechanisms such as were taken up in the last chapter are a possibility although questions such as individual rationality and fairness remain. These cannot achieve allocations involving interpersonal comparison of utilities but in some cases may achieve envy-free allocations.

Several equilibrium concepts have been devised generalizing or related to the competitive equilibrium for purely private goods. M. Kaneko (1977) developed the ratio equilibrium, which can be implemented as the core of a cooperative game related to majority rule. The government sets ratios by which the costs of public goods are divided among the agents.

A Lindahl equilibrium, for a consumers having initial private goods bundles $w\langle i\rangle$ and an initial public goods bundle $w\langle 0\rangle$, consists of a price p_j for each private good, a positive number $p_k\langle i\rangle$ for each consumer and public good, a private goods bundle $x\langle i\rangle$ for each consumer and a public goods bundle $x\langle 0\rangle$. These are required to satisfy (1) the bundle $x\langle 0\rangle$ and $x\langle i\rangle$ are simultaneously feasible, (2) the vectors $x\langle i\rangle$ and $x\langle 0\rangle$ maximize agent i's utility function u_i subject to the budget constraint

$$p \cdot x\langle i\rangle + p\langle i\rangle \cdot x\langle 0\rangle = p \cdot w\langle i\rangle + p\langle i\rangle \cdot w\langle 0\rangle$$

and (3)

$$p \cdot \Sigma\, x\langle i\rangle + \Sigma\, p\langle i\rangle \cdot x\langle 0\rangle \geq p \cdot y + \Sigma\, p\langle i\rangle \cdot z$$

for all bundles y of private goods and z of public goods which are simultaneously feasible.

The second condition implies that prices are proportional to marginal utilities. The third condition is a Pareto optimality condition. If we could find y, z differing only slightly from $x<i>$, $x<0>$ yielding a higher total in (3) then the sum of the changes in of all agents could be increased since marginal utilities are proportional to prices. The private goods bundles summing to y can be chosen so that no individuals 1, 2, ... , n - 1 have constant utility plus a very slight increase. Then individual n's utility by the sum condition, will increase.

EXAMPLE 8.2.2. Suppose there is only one private good money which is separable so that utilities have the form $u(x<0>) + m<i>$ where $m<i>$ is the money agent i has. Let $w<0> = 0$. Set $p = 1$. A Lindahl equilibrium must be a feasible Pareto optimum. We have

$$p<i> = \frac{\partial u_i}{\partial x_k<0>}$$

by the maximum in (2). Individual (i) must be able to afford his share of the Pareto optimum in the sense that

$$w<i> = p<i> \cdot x<0> + m<i>$$

Thus an Lindahl equilibrium is an individually affordable Pareto optimum.

For a given initial allocation there will generally be a finite set of Lindahl equilibrium. As $w<i>$ range over all possibilities, the Lindahl equilibria should range over all individually rational Pareto optima.

L. Hurwicz (1979) proved that every continuous mechanism implementing individually rational Pareto optima must include the set of Lindahl equilibria provided the domain contains various linear and logarithmic utility functions. He had earlier found a mechanism implementing Lindahl equilibria, which, however, is not locally stable. M. Nakayama (1980) gave a mechanism which has some local stability properties.

The outcomes may not be feasible and there exist extraneous equilibria with zero production. E. Kalai, A. Postlewaite, and J. Roberts (1980) gave a cooperative game mechanism for implementing core or Lindahl equilibrium by strong equilibrium. However no bargaining mechanism is specified, and all players must precisely agree on the allocations.

The question remains open: *are there distributionally fair, individually rational, efficient, locally stable mechanisms which are incentive compatible in a plausible way and are simple enough to be practicable, and can they be used to solve actual public goods questions as construction of schools, power plants, or other community facilities ?* However knowledge about the possibilities has been greatly increased.

8.3 RESOURCE EXPLOITATION

Two problems frequently studied in connection with energy economics are the *rate of exploitation and the nature of demand.* To analyze the former, we extend our previous social arbitration functions to the case of different times. One way to treat utilities at different times is as if they represented different person's utilities. In the case of zero discount rate this gives

$$\sum_{i,j} \log (u_i(j) - a)$$

where $u_i(j)$ is the utility of person i at time j. The formula should have as its term in player i, the total utility to him over all time periods. Another argument yielding a different result would be that if the person does not know ahead of time what his utility would be, this would not affect his choice. And a sequence of unexpected events giving an average utility of u is the same as a constant situation of expected utility u.

This would give a different formula

$$\sum_{i} \log \left(\sum_{j} (u_i(j) - a)\right)$$

The two principles would agree for Harsanyi's utilitarian social welfare function to give the simple $\sum_{i,j} u_i(j)$. Of these three possibilities the first could be argued on the basis that people at different times are comparable to different people, and that probability theory being in principle nonverifiable is not so fundamental as other ideas. However we will choose the second on the basis that (1) unless we regard a sequence of events in a probabilistic way the idea of expected utility is meaningless and (2) equal distribution between persons is a positive value.

The sum can be replaced by an integral, which for infinite time periods should be averaged

$$\sum_i \log \left(\int_0^T (u_i(t) - a)dt\right)$$

or

$$\sum_i \log \left(\lim_{T\to\infty} \frac{1}{T} \int_0^T (u_i(t) - a)dt\right)$$

It can be noted that with this function the past may affect what is the best decision, even when the choices are independent at different times.

EXAMPLE 8.3.1. Suppose there are two individuals, two choices x_i, y_i at each time i and two times and the utilities are as follows.

Individual	x_1	y_1	x_2	y_2
a	40	40	10	1
b	40	40	10	30

Let a be zero. The choice at time 1 makes no difference. The choice at time 2 must be y_2 since

$$(40 + 30)(40 + 1) > (40 + 10)(40 + 10)$$

Yet if we consider time 2 alone, choice x_4 would be better since

$$10(10) > (30)$$

This reflects the idea that if we consider the total utility over time the past plays a role. Also it reflects the idea that the Nash formula for a social arbitration function is a compromise, an outcome of bargaining rather than a theoretical ethical ideal.

Since the future is uncertain, positive discount rates are usually employed with future utilities. One way to introduce them is to assume that given the system has lasted to time j there is probability (1 - r) it will last to time (j + 1) and probability r it will cease. This discount applied to each individual's utility gives

$$\sum_i \log \left(\sum_j (1-r)^j (u_i(j) - a)\right).$$

or

$$\sum_i \log \left(\int e^{-rt} (u_i(t) - a)dt\right)$$

The last integral is the basic formula for *intertemporal social arbitration*. If Harsanyi's theorem were used instead, the logarithm would be deleted and a would be 0.

Suppose we have a known, fixed amount A of a resource and assume the population and technology are constant. As an approximation here take everyone's utility function to be the same. The problem is to choose a function $x(t) \geq 0$ so as to maximize

$$\int e^{-rt} u(x(t))dt$$

subject to the constraint

$$\int x(t)\, dt = A$$

This can basically be solved in an elementary way. For two times t_1, t_2 we must not be able to gain by shifting consumption from t_1 to t_2 or vice versa. This means

$$u'(x(t_1)) = u'(x(t_2))e^{-r(t_2-t_1)}$$

Therefore $u'(x(t)) = u'(x(0))e^{rt}$ where $x(0)$ is determined from the condition that total consumption is A. In other words, the marginal utility of increasing consumption, discounted at rate r, must be constant. This holds true until consumption is zero.

There are a number of complications in actuality. The amount of the resource is unknown. Fifty years ago people were predicting we would shortly run out of oil. If estimates are so inaccurate, mathematical planning can be meaningless. There is a maximum rate at which oil can be extracted from an oil field without injuring it. Exploration for new fields is an important consideration.

In the market system, profit maximization decides how rapidly oil is used. For perfect competition the excess of selling price over cost of extraction, discounted at rate r, should be constant. This does maximize the social arbitration function if everyone's utility is taken to be the same.

A monopolist would maximize his total expected profits. This differs from perfect competition in that he can affect prices by restricting supply. Thus a monopolist would tend to conserve the resource, but this would not be a social benefit.

Demand for energy is mainly an empirical question. The main measurement studied is elasticity of demand with respect to price and income. One complication is that elasticity varies greatly with the time period. In the short run gasoline is a necessity and except for cutting down on vacation and pleasure driving, there is little people can do to reduce consumption. Estimates of short-run price elasticity of demand, given in L. D. Taylor (1977) vary from 0.1 to 0.55. The long-run elasticity is much greater, since people can buy fuel-conserving cars and heaters, plan car pools, insulate homes. New energy saving devices may be invented and marketed to meet demand. The long-run elasticity (L. D. Taylor (1977)) has been estimated as being from 0.25 to 1.

8.4 THE BUSINESS CYCLE, INFLATION, AND UNEMPLOYMENT

A number of cycles of varying lengths are generally accepted as existing in the U.S. economy. The *National Bureau cycle* of

40 months, due to W. C. Mitchell and his colleagues, and the *Kuznets cycle* of 20 years are well accepted. The *Juglar 8-year cycle* and *Kondratieff 50-year cycle* are more debated.

Many theories have been proposed to explain them. Most depend on the idea that the future can be imperfectly foreseen and calculated for. We have previously noted that a cycle has higher discounted expected utility than a constant function with the same average value. Most detailed mathematical models involve lags in economic response such as lags between supply and demand.

Keynesian theory involves lags involving the multiplier and accelerator. The theory of the multiplier states that additional investment has an effect on national income much greater than the amount of the investment. This is because increased demand increases wages which in turn increases demand in other sectors. Let I denote total investment, Y total income, C total consumption. Then Y = C + I. An important assumption in Keynesian theory is that a constant proportion of increases in income is consumed as opposed to that saved. Therefore $c\Delta Y = \Delta C$ where ΔY, ΔC are increases in income and consumption and c is constant called the *propensity* to consume. From the previous equation,

$$\Delta Y = \Delta C + \Delta I$$

so

$$\Delta Y - \Delta C = \Delta Y - c\Delta Y = (1 - c)\Delta Y = \Delta I$$

$$\Delta Y = \frac{1}{1 - c}\Delta I$$

The quantity $\frac{1}{1 - c}$ is called the *multiplier*.

The *accelerator principle* is that investment equals the change in capital from one time period to the next.

$$K_{t+1} - K_t = I_{t+1}$$

where K is capital, that is, ability to produce: factories, equipment, trained personnel, I is investment, and t is time.

Assuming a fixed capital-output ratio v, K = vY. Therefore

$$v(Y_{t+1} - Y_t) = I_{t+1}$$

The multiplier and accelerator act to amplify existing fluctuations. It is known that capital goods tend to fluctuate more than consumer goods during business cycles.

Other theories of the business cycle involve some sort of increase towards a catastrophic collapse: increase in debt, speculative bubbles, the social climate becoming less thrifty, perhaps instability related to multiple equilibria.

A. Lerner (1972) has classified inflation as follows. *Type I* or *demand-pull inflation* is due to supply shortages or demand excesses, as shortages of oil or food, too rapid expansion of the money supply, release of previously restrained demand being released as at the end of a war. Most countries have found it impossible to finance war except by increasing the national debt or the money supply so that inflation has typically followed the war's end. The debts are rarely paid except by debasing the coinage or currency. The productive capacity exists, but not the incentive. If the money supply increases 10%, prices will increase 10%. A shortage of goods will raise prices at least to the new equilibrium level. The price elasticity of demand for the good is the most important factor, which depends on such factors as the availability of substitutes, its use in producing other goods, and how much of a luxury it is. In a calculation it might be assumed that the price of that good least affected by the shortage will remain constant, and other prices will be such that there is an equilibrium.

Related explanations of inflation include increases in costs, such as for pollution control, paperwork, or legal problems. Lerner describes Type I inflation as an attempt of buyers to buy more than 100% of the available goods, and *Type II inflation* as the attempt of producers to get more than 100% of the income spent on such goods.

Type II inflation is inflation due to the absence of Nash equilibrium: each of a set of agents can increase its income share by raising prices, and attempts to do so. Under perfect competition this should not happen but in Chapter 5 we give a model indicating that it will typically happen for monopolistic competition. Whether it does or not is a matter of controversy. Are prices in oligopolistic industries significantly above the competitive level ? It has been argued that if this were the cause of the inflation of the 1970's that it would have occurred also in the 1960's when the degree of oligopoly was nearly the same. There are also opposing arguments: that Vietnam deficits were not that great and that only Type II inflation is consistent with recession. Type II inflation can involve in theory unions and other groups as well as corporations.

Type III inflation is inflation due to people's expectation of inflation. People ask for contracts including future increases to allow for inflation.

Type I inflation can be limited by controlling the money supply and encouraging industry to produce (*supply-side economics*). Type II inflation perhaps require, government action, as in J. Galbraith's proposal to regulate the largest firm in an industry, or anti-trust action. Type III inflation requires control of the other two types.

Government attempts to combat unemployment may be related to inflation. During the *Depression*, the Civilian Conservation Corps, and Works Projects Administration accomplished quite a bit of useful work, but hired only about $\frac{1}{3}$ of the unemployed. However government spending in World War II quickly ended the unemployment problem.

Experience has confirmed since that the Keynesian policy of deficit spending can ease recessions. Conservatives have argued that there is a causal relationship between the first acceptance of large government deficits and the first occurrence of stagflation. H. Stein in W. Fellner (1976) argued that sharp increases in government deficits do cause inflation. However the econometric study by G. L. Perry in A. M. Okun and G. L. Perry (1978) did not shown deficit, as a major cause of inflation.

The national debt has caused concern as of 1981-1982 that government borrowing to pay it competes with private borrowing to drive up interest rates. If it should be necessary to pay off a sizeable fraction of it the least catastrophic method appears to be for the government print enough extra money to pay it thus in effect devaluing the currency by up to 50%. Other countries have undergone devaluations this severe.

A major question regarding the unemployment of the 1970's is its basic nature: is it structural, due to a lack of jobs skills, cyclical, due to a depressed economy, is it caused by the entrance of illegal aliens and women into the job market, a decline in the work ethic, or is in part an artifact due to generous unemployment benefits which enable people to stay out of work for long periods ?

G. Melloan and J. Melloan (1978) cite D. Yankelovitch polls finding that in 1967 69% of those polled answered "yes" to "Does hard work pay off ?" Whereas in 1975 75% replied "no." U.S. unemployment has been about twice as great for blacks as for whites and three times as great for teenagers. Most job openings require skill or experience, and unskilled jobs when available pay hardly enough to support a family, very little compared with wages for skilled labor.

The *Phillips tradeoff curve* is a proposed inverse relationship between unemployment and inflation. If the Phillips curve exists, it is a short-term phenomenon since the curve itself changes. It has been getting higher. The Phillips curve may reflect the fact that large increases in government spending and expansionary monetary policy reduce unemployment but increase inflation. It is also true that an increase in demand tends to decrease unemployment but raise prices.

8.5 REDISTRIBUTION AND WELFARE

Poverty, rather than inequality itself, is an economic evil. However inequality which has been institutionalized may be a cause of poverty. It may be that if surplus production goes to the poor, they use it in ways that are economically more constructive, i.e. building infrastructure, supporting those who produce their necessities, than if it goes to the rich. However the character of the wealthy varies widely from society to society, from those who form philanthropic foundations or invest their wealth in corporate stock to those who hoard or spend it extravagantly.

Inequality can be measured by the previously mentioned Lorentz curve which at $x = \frac{a}{N}$ gives the proportion of total income received by the lowest a members of the population. There are also measures such as the Gini index, $\frac{1}{2} - A$ where A is the area under the curve. Quintiles are often used, the fraction of income received by the lowest fifth, the second lowest, etc. These give a more complete picture than any single number. The 1950 Gini indexes as computed by S. Kuznets for the United States and Great Britain were 0.33 and 0.35. There are differences of opinion as to whether the unit should be the individual or the household, and as to how new households should be treated as concerns their income last year. Kuznets used households, while Wiles in Krelle and Shorrocks (1978) argues that the person should be the unit and new households should not be treated as if they had zero income last year. According to Wiles's figures the least unequal nations are those of Eastern Europe, followed by the welfare states such as Sweden and the United Kingdom than the United States, Canada, and the Latin countries of Europe. Others may disagree with the figures on socialist countries. It has been argued that differences between compensation for workers and management are greater in the Soviet Union than in the U.S.

The primary methods of redistribution are taxation at higher rates of those with high income, direct payments to those who cannot support themselves, and provision of social services such as retirement income, medical insurance, education, subsidized transportation, low-income housing, food stamps, and fuel allowances.

In the U.S., D. Kershaw and J. Fair (1976) state that those with less income pay more in taxes than the upper middle class because of local sales and excise taxes.

Rowley and Peacock (1975) argue for a fixed income tax rate with no exceptions as fairest and as avoiding loopholes. As of 1982 this has become something of a popular cause. Results of M. Kaneko (1981) obtained by using the Nash social welfare function indicate that the optimum tax rate should approach 100% as income tends to infinity. However the effects caused by such a complicated system as the United States has at present are hard to gauge. L. Thurow (1980) argues against corporation income taxes as (1) being double taxation, (2) being passed on to the consumer in many cases.

A *negative income tax* has been proposed as a method of redistribution which could reduce the costs of administering welfare. It has actually been tried on a small-scale in a number of experiments. The initial experiment showed no significant decrease in hours worked by adult men, but later experiments have pretty much yielded the opposite result, that there is a significant reduction in incentives to work, which would make the program a failure. The Seattle-Denver experiment also reported a 43% increase in breakups of marriages during the experiment (M. Anderson (1980)).

The theory of taxation and redistribution can be handled by social arbitration functions provided that effects on incentives and the use of tax shelters can be adequately allowed for.

Welfare is redistribution to those with need because of special circumstances. W. C. Cates (1980) states that for the past decade exports have done their best to reconcile these three goals: *adequate welfare levels*, *costs that are not out of the question*, and *incentives for those on welfare to become self-supporting*, but have concluded this is an impossibility. The problem is that to provide reasonable incentives, someone on welfare who takes a job must not have his payments reduced by more than, say, half of what the job pays. This is already a very high, 50% marginal income tax rate. But this means welfare must be paid to those earning anything less than twice the welfare support level. The costs of such a program would be too great. He concludes that effective policing of who is allowed to receive welfare is the best that can be done.

The poverty level in the United States has been defined by taking the minimum cost of an adequate diet and multiplying by three, on the assumption that the poor spend about $\frac{1}{3}$ of their income on food. Census statistics gave the official proportion o of U.S. citizens in poverty as remaining near 12% during the period 1968-1975 of the *Great Society Programs*. This did not consider nonmonetary aid such as food stamps, housing, and medical benefits. The Congressional Budget Office found out that federal programs, counting these benefits, had reduced poverty from 11% to 6% (M. Paglin (1977)).

Regarding the mathematical form of the distribution of incomes the two simplest forms generally used are the Pareto distribution in which the income density is given by

$$\begin{cases} am^a x^{-a-1}, & x \geq m \\ 0, & x < m \end{cases}$$

where a, m are constants and x is income level, and the log-normal distribution with density function

$$f(x) = \frac{1}{x\sigma\sqrt{2\pi}} e^{\frac{-(x-\mu)^2}{2\sigma^2}}$$

The latter can be interpreted as a theory that income represents the product of a large number of independent, random factors.

8.6 CONCLUSION

We conclude that social arbitration functions and equilibrium mathematical models might be useful tools in the specific practical problems considered here. Incentive compatibility and game theory offer an explanation of various economic phenomena. Whether incentive compatible mechanisms other than majority rule should be used in public choice is not known, but knowledge has increased to the point that experiments could be made with them.

REFERENCES

A. Achinstein, Introduction to Business Cycles (Crowell Company, New York, 1950).

M. Anderson, Welfare reform, in: P. Ouignan and A. Rabushka (ed.), The United States in the 1980's (Hoover Institute, Stanford, 1980).

K. Arrow, Political and economic evaluation of social effects and externalities, in: M. Intriligator (ed.), Frontiers of Quantitative Economics (North-Holland, New York, 1975).

A. Askin (ed.), How Energy Affects the Economy (Lexington Books, Lexington, Massachusetts, 1978).

C. d'Aspremont and L. A. Gerard-Varet, Stackelberg solvable games and preplay communication, Journal of Economic Theory 23 (1980) 201-217.

R. J. Aumann, Acceptable points in general cooperative n-person games, in: A. W. Tucker and R. D. Luce (eds.), Contributions to the Theory of Games, IV (Princeton University Press, Princeton, 1959).

R. J. Aumann, Acceptable points in games of perfect information, Pacific Journal of Mathematics 10 (1960) 381-417.

R. J. Aumann, The core of a cooperative game without side payments, Transactions of the American Mathematical Society 98 (1961) 539-552.

Y. Balasko, Number and definiteness of economic equilibria, Journal of Mathematical Economics 7 (1980) 215-225.

D. Baron and R. Myerson, Regulating a monopolist with unknown costs, Economics and Management Science Discussion Paper 412, Northwestern University (1979).

J. P. Benassy, The disequilibrium approach to monopolistic price setting and general monopolistic disequilibrium, Review of Economic Studies 43 (1976), 69-81.

H. R. Brown, The interpretation of voting in the allocation of economic resources, Quarterly Journal of Economics 58 (1943) 27-48.

S. Brams, Paradoxes in Politics (Free Press, New York, 1976).

E. Bres, A. Charnes, D. Cole Eckels, S. Hitt, R. Lyders, J. Russel, and M. Schoeman, Costs and their assessment to users of a medical library, in: S. Brams, A. Schotter, G. Schwödiauer (eds.), Applied Game Theory (Physica-Verlag, Vienna, 1979).

H. W. Brock, A game-theoretic account of social justice, Theory and Decision 11 (1979) 239-265.

E. Burger, Introduction to the Theory of Games (Prentice-Hall, Englewood Cliffs, New Jersey, 1963).

A. Campagna, Macroeconomics (St. Martin's Press, New York, 1981).

W. C. Cates, Where is the Free Lunch (Thomond Press, New York, 1980).

H. Chenery, M. S. Ahluwalia, C. L. G. Bell, J. H. Duloy, R. Jolly, Redistribution with Growth (Oxford University Press, London, 1974).

L. Cohen, Cyclic sets in multidimensional voting, Journal of Economic Theory 20 (1979), 1-12.

V. Crawford, A procedure for generating Pareto efficient egalitarian equivalent allocations, Econometrica 47 (1979) 49-61.

V. Crawford and W. Heller, Fair division with indivisible commodities, Journal of Economic Theory 21 (1979) 10-27.

A. Crockett, International Money Issues and Analysis (Academic Press, New York, 1977).

P. Dasgupta, P. Hammond, and D. Maskin, The implementation of social choice rules: some general results on incentive compatibility, Review of Economic Studies 46 (1979), 185-216.

G. Debreu, Economies with a finite set of equilibria, Econometrica 38 (1970) 387-392.

G. Debreu and H. Scarf, A limit theorem on the core of an economy, International Economic Review 4 (1963) 235-246.

D. N. Dewees, C. K. Everson, W. A. Sims, Economic Analysis of Environmental Policies (University of Toronto Press, Toronto, 1975).

H. Diaz and G. Owen, Fair subsidies for urban transporation systems, in: S. Brams, A. Schotter, and G. Schwödiauer (eds.), Applied Game Theory (Physica-Verlag, Vienna, 1979).

E. Dierker, Topological Methods in Walrasian Economics, Lecture Notes in Economics and Mathematical Systems 92 (Springer-Verlag, Berlin, 1974).

E. Dierker,Regular economies: a survey, in: M. Intriligator (ed.), Frontiers of Quantitative Economics (North-Holland, New York, 1977).

M. Drazen, Recent developments in macroeconomic disequilibrium theory, Econometrica 48 (1980) 283-306.

D. Easley and J. Ledyard, A theory of price formation and excange in oral auctions, Economics and Managment Science Discussion Paper 461, Northwestern University (1981).

F. Edgeworth, Mathematical Psychics (Kegan Paul, London, 1881).

P. T. Ellsworth and J. C. Leith, The International Economy (Macmillan, New York, 1975).

R. E. Ericson, A difficulty with the command allocation mechanism, Economics and Management Science Discussion Paper 464, Northwestern University (1981).

I. Fagerlind, Formal Education and Adult Earnings (Almqvist and Wiksell, Stockholm, 1975).

M. Farrell, Edgeworth bounds for oligopoly prices, Economica 37 (1970) 342-361.

A. Feldman and A. Kirman, Fairness and envy, American Economic Review 64 (1974) 995-1005.

M. Feldstein (ed.), The American Economy in Transition (University of Chicago Press, Chicago, 1980).

W. Fellner, Contemporary Economic Problems (American Enterprise Institute, Wahsington, D.C., 1976).

J. A. Ferejohn, M. P. Fiorina, and E. W. Packel, A nonequilibrium approach to legislative decision theory, Working Paper 202, California Institute of Technology (1978).

J. W. Friedman, Oligopoly and the Theory of Games (North-Holland, New York, 1977).

D. Gale, Money, information, and equilibrium in large economies, Journal of Economic Theory 23 (1980) 28-65.

J. K. Galbraith, The farm problem and the policy choices, in: E. S. Phelps, et. al. (eds.), Problems of the Modern Economy (Norton, New York, 1966).

J. K. Galbraith, Money: Whence It Came, Where It Went (Houghton-Mifflin, Boston, 1975).

A. Gibbard, Manipulation of voting schemes that mix voting with chance, Econometrica 45 (1977) 665-681.

D. B. Gillies, Solutions to general non-zero sum games, in: A. W. Tucker and R. D. Luce (eds.), Contributions to the Theory of Games, IV (Princeton University Press, Princeton, N.J., 1959).

S. Goldberger, Undergraduate Mathematics and the Social Sciences, Mathematical Association of America, Haywood, California (1976).

J. M. Grandmont, Temporary general equilibrium theory, in: M. Intriligator (ed.), Frontiers of Quantitative Economics (North-Holland, New York, 1977).

J. M. Grandmont and G. Laroque, On Keynesian temporary equilibria, Review of Economic Studies 43 (1976) 53-67.

J. R. Green and J. J. Laffont, Incentives in Public Decision-Making (North-Holland, New York, 1979).

R. Gretlein, Dominance solvable voting games: a comment, Econometrica 50 (1982) 527-528 (same as 1980a).

R. Gretlein, Dominance elimination procedures on finite alternative games, Discussion Paper, Carnegie Mellon University (1980b).

T. Groves and J. Ledyard, An incentive mechanism for efficient resource allocation in general equilibrium with public goods, Economics and Management Science Discussion Paper 119, Northwestern University (1975).

F. Hahn, On non-Walrasian equilibria, Review of Economic Studies 45 (1978) 1-17.

J. Harsanyi, An equilibrium point interpretation of stable sets and a proposed alternative definition, Management Science 20 (1974) 1472-1495.

J. Harsanyi, Rational Behavior and Bargaining Equilibrium in Games and Social Situations (Cambridge University Press, New York, 1977).

J. Harsanyi and R. Selten, A generalized Nash bargaining solution for two-person bargaining games with incomplete information, Management Science 18 (1972) 80-106.

J. Henderson and R. E. Quandt, Microeconomic Theory: A Mathematical Approach (McGraw-Hill, New York, 1958).

W. Hildenbrand, Limit theorems on the core of an economy, in: M. Intriligator (ed.), Frontiers of Quantitative Economics (North-Holland, New York, 1977).

W. Hildenbrand and A. P. Kirman, Introduction to Equilibrium Analysis (North-Holland, New York, 1976).

B. Holmstrom, On the theory of delegation, Economics and Management Science Discussion Paper 438, Northwestern University (1980).

H. Houthakker, The farm problem is not hopeless, in: E. S. Phelps, et. al. (eds.), Problems of the Modern Economy (Norton, New York, 1966).

L. Hurwicz, Outcome functions yielding Walrasian and Lindahl equilibria at Nash equilibrium points, Discussion Paper, Berkeley (1976).

L. Hurwicz, On allocations attainable through Nash equilibria, Journal of Economic Theory 21 (1979) 140-165.

J. Kahan and A. Rapaport, Coalition formation in the triad when two are weak and one is strong, Mathematical Social Sciences 1 (1980) 11-37.

E. Kalai, Proportional solutions to bargaining situations: interpersonal utility comparisons, Econometrica 45 (1977), 1623-1630.

E. Kalai, Preplay negotiations and the prisoner's dilemma, Mathematical Social Sciences 1 (1980) 375-379.

E. Kalai and E. Muller, Characterization of domains admitting nondictatorial social welfare functions and nonmanipulable voting procedures, Journal of Economic Theory 16 (1977) 456-469.

E. Kalai, A. Postlewaite, and J. Roberts, Barriers to trade and disadvantageous middlemen: nonmonotonicity of the core, Journal of Economic Theory 19 (1978) 200-209.

E. Kalai, A. Postlewaite, and J. Roberts, A group incentive-compatible mechanism yielding core allocations, Journal of Economic Theory 20 (1979) 13-22.

E. Kalai and Z. Ritz, An extended single peak condition in social choice, Economics and Management Science Discussion Paper 325, Northwestern University (1978).

M. Kaneko, The ratio equilibrium and the core of the voting game G(N, W) in a public goods economy, Econometrica 45 (1977) 1589-1594.

M. Kaneko, The ratio equilibrium and a voting game in a public goods economy, Journal of Economic Theory 16 (1977) 123-136.

M. Kaneko, A bilateral monopoly and the Nash cooperative solution, Journal of Economic Theory 24 (1981) 311-327.

M. Kaneko, The conventionally stable sets in noncooperative games, to appear.

M. Kaneko, The central assignment game and the assignment markets, Cowles Foundation Discussion Papers 563, New Haven (1980).

M. Kaneko, On the existence of an optimal income tax schedule, Review of Economic Studies, to appear.

M. Kaneko, The optimal progressive income tax-the existence and the limit tax rates, Mathematical Social Sciences 3 (1982), to appear.

M. Kaneko and K. Nakamura, The Nash social welfare function, Econometrica 47 (1979) 775-778.

D. Kershaw and J. Fair, The New Jersey Income-Maintenance Experiment (Academic Press, New York, 1976).

K. H. Kim, Juche in international trade, Mathematical Social Sciences 3 (1982), to appear.

K. H. Kim and F. W. Roush, Introduction to Mathematical Consensus Theory (Marcel Dekker, New York, 1980).

K. H. Kim and F. W. Roush, Special domains and nonmanipulability, Mathematical Social Sciences 1 (1980) 85-92.

K. H. Kim and F. W. Roush, Economic planning based on social preference functions, Mathematical Social Sciences 1 (1981), 193-200.

K. H. Kim and F. W. Roush, Social systems analysis, Mathematical Social Sciences 2 (1981), 75-103.

K. H. Kim and F. W. Roush, Dominance solvable games and trees, Mathematical Social Sciences 2 (1982) 245-256.

K. H. Kim and F. W. Roush, Ecological log-rolling, Mathematical Social Sciences 2 (1982) 317-321.

K. H. Kim and F. W. Roush, Juche versus Sadae: game-theoretic approach, Mathematical Social Sciences 3 (1982), to appear.

L. Komisar, Down and Out in the U.S.A., (Watts, New York, 1973).

M. E. Kreinen, International Economics: A Policy Approach (Harcourt, Brace, Javanovich, New York, 1979).

W. Krelle and A. Shorrocks, Personal Income Distribution (North-Holland, New York, 1978).

D. Kreps and E. Porteus, Temporal von Neumann-Morgenstern and induced preferences, Journal of Economic Theory 20 (1979) 81-109.

S. Kuznets, Quantitative aspects of the growth of nations, Economic Development and Cultural Change (1963).

S. Kuznets, Notes on the pattern of U.S. economic growth, in: Fogel and Engermann (eds.), The Reinterpretation of American Economic History (Harper and Row, New York, 1971).

J. J. Laffont and E. Maskin, A different approach to dominant strategy mechanisms, Econometrica 48 (1980) 1507-1520.

A. Lerner, Flation (Quadrangle Books, New York, 1972).

R. D. Luce and H. Raiffa, Games and Decisions (Wiley, New York, 1957).

F. Machlup, International Payments, Debts, and Gold: Collected Essays (New York University Press, New York, 1976).

R. D. McKelvey, General conditions for global intransitivities in formal voting models, Econometrica 47 (1979) 1085-1112.

R. D. McKelvey and P. C. Ordeshook, An experimental test of several theories of committee decision making under majority rule, in: S. Brams, A. Schotter, and G. Schwödiauer (eds.), Applied Game Theory (Physica-Verlag, Vienna, 1979).

R. D. McKelvey, P. C. Ordeshook, and M. Winer, The competitive solution for n-person games without transferable utility with an application to committee games, American Political Science Review 92 (1978) 599-616.

R. B. Mancke, Performance of the Fderal Energy Office (American Enterprise Institute, Washington, D.C., 1975).

E. Maskin, Nash equilibrium and welfare optimality, Discussion Paper, Massachusetts Institute of Technology (1977).

G. Melloan and J. Melloan, The Carter Economy (Wiley, New York, 1978).

M. A. Miles, Devaluation, the Trade Balance, the Balance of Payments (Marcel Dekker, New York, 1978).

H. Moulin, Dominance solvable voting schemes, Econometrica 47 (1979) 1337-1351.

H. Moulin, Implementing efficient, anonymous, and neutral social choice functions, Journao of Mathematical Economics 7 (1980) 249-269.

H. Moulin, The Strategy of Social Choice, CEREMADE, University of Paris IX (1981).

H. Moulin, Game Theory for the Social Sciences, New York University Press, to appear.

H. Moulin, Bargaining and non-cooperative implementation, Discussion Paper, Ecole Polytechnique (1982).

H. Moulin and D. Gabay, On the uniqueness and stability of Nash equilibria in non-cooperative games, in: A. Bensoussan, et. al., (eds.), Applied Optimal Stochastic Control in Econometrics and Management Science (North-Holland, New York, 1979).

H. Moulin and B. Peleg, Stability and implementation of effectivity of functions, Journal of Mathematical Economics (1982), to appear.

R. Myerson, Optimal coordination mechanisms in principal-agent problems, Economics and Management Science Discussion Paper 429, Northwestern University (1980a).

R. Myerson, Solutions for two-person bargaining problems with incomplete information, Economics and Management Science Discussion Paper 432, Northwestern University (1980b).

R. Myerson, A general theory of cooperative solutions for games with incomplete information, Economics and Management Science Disucssion Paper 433, Northwestern University (1980c).

R. Myerson, Mechanism design by an informed principal, Economics and Management Science Discussion Paper 481, Northwestern University (1981).

R. Myerson and M. Satterthwaite, Efficient mechanisms for bilateral trading, Economics and Management Science Discussion Paper 469, Northwestern University (1981).

K. Nakamura, The vetoers in a simple game with ordinal preferences, International Journal of Game Theory 8 (1979) 55-61.

M. Nakayama, Optimal provision of public goods through Nash equilibria, Journal of Economic Theory 23 (1980) 334-347.

H. Nikaido, Introduction to Sets and Mappings in Modern Economics (North-Holland, New York, 1970).

A. M. Okun and G. L. Perry, Curing Chronic Inflation (Brookings Institute, Washington, D.C., 1978).

P. K. Pattanaik, Threats, counterthreats, and strategic voting, Econometrica 44 (1976) 91-104.

P. K. Pattanaik, Counterthreats and strategic manipulation under voting schemes, Review of Economic Studies 43 (1976) 11-18.

P. K. Pattanaik, Strategy and Group Choice (North-Holland, New York, 1978).

J. Pen, Income Distribution: Facts, Theories, Policies, translated by T. S. Preston (Praeger, New York, 1971).

I. Polishchuk, Monotonicity and uniqueness of consistent voting system, Journal of Mathematical Economics, to appear.

J. T. Richelson, A comparative analysis of social choice functions Behavioral Science 23 (1978) 169-176.

R. Rob, A condition guaranteeing the optimality of public choice, Econometrica 49 (1981) 1605-1613.

J. Roberts and H. Sonnenschein, On the foundations of the theory of monopolistic equilibrium, Econometrica 45 (1977) 101-113.

K. Roberts, The characterization of implementable social choice rules, in: J. J. Laffont (ed.), Aggregation and Revelation of Preferences (North-Holland, New York, 1979).

J. C. Rochet, Selection of a unique equilibrium payoff for extensive games with perfect information, CEREMADE Discussion Paper, University of Paris IX (1980).

J. Rosenmüller, The Theory of Games and Markets (North-Holland, New York, 1980).

A. Roth, Axiomatic Models of Bargaining, Lecture Notes in Economics and Mathematical Systems 170 (Springer-Verlag, Berlin, 1979).

A. Roth and M. Malouf, Scale changes and shared information in bargaining: an experimental study, Mathematical Social Sciences 3 (1982), to appear.

M. Rothschild and J. Stiglitz, Some further results on the measurement of inequality, Journal of Economic Theory 6 (1973) 188-204.

C. Rowley and A. Peacock, Welfare Economics: a Liberal Restatement (Wiley, New York, 1975).

K. Sale, Human Scale (Coward, McCann, and Geoghegan, New York, 1980).

M. A. Satterthwaite and H. Sonnenschein, Strategy-proof allocation mechanisms, Economics and Management Science Discussion Paper 395, Northwestern University (1979).

H. Scarf, On the existence of a cooperative solution for a general class of n person games, Journal of Economic Theory 3 (1971) 169-181.

H. Scarf, The Computation of Economic Equilibrium (Yale University Press, New Haven, 1973).

H. Scheiber, H. Vatter, and H. Faulkner, American Economic History (Harper & Row, New York, 1976).

D. Schmeidler, The nucleolus of a characteristic function game, SIAM Journal of Applied Mathematics 17 (1969) 1163-1170.

A. Sen, Collective Choice and Social Welfare (North-Holland, New York, 1970).

A. Sen, On Economic Inequality (Norton, New York, 1973).

A. Sen, Social choice theory: a re-examination, Econometrica 45 (1977) 53-89.

H. Shapley and H. Scarf, On cores and indivisibility, Journal of Mathematical Economics 1 (1972) 23-38.

H. Shapley and M. Shubik, On market games, Journal of Economic Theory 1 (1969) 9-25.

M. Shubik, Games for Society, Business, War (Elsevier North-Holland, New York, 1975).

C. I. Siven, A Study in Inflation and Unemployment (North-Holland, New York, 1979).

R. Solomon, W. M. Martin, and P. A. Southard, The International Monetary System: Progress and Prospects (Westview Press, Boulder, Colorado, 1977).

H. Sonnenschein, Market excess demand functions, Econometrica 40 (1972) 549-563.

P. Taubman, The Relative Influence of Inheritable and Environmental Factors and the Importance of Intelligence in Earnings Functions (North-Holland, New York, 1978).

L. Taylor, The demand for energy: a survey of price and income elasticities, in: W. Nordhaus (ed.), International Studies of the Demand for Energy (North-Holland, New York, 1977).

H. Theil, Theory and Measurement of Consumer Demand (North-Holland, New York, 1975).

E. Thompson and R. Faith, Social interactions under truly perfect information, Journal of Mathematical Sociology 16 (1980) 181-197.

L. Thurow, The Zero Sum Society (Basic Books, New York, 1980).

R. H. Wagoner, Impartiality and equity, Theeory and Decision 12 (1980) 61-74.

M. Walker, A simple incentive-compatible scheme for attaining Lindahl allocations, Econometrica 48 (1980) 65-71.

C. I. Waxman, The Stigma of Poverty (Pergamon Press, New York, 1977).

P. Wiles, Our shaky data base, in: W. Krelle and A. Shorrocks (eds.), Personal Income Distribution (North-Holland, New York, 1978).

E. C. Zeeman, A geometrical model of ideologies, in: C. Renfrew and K. Cooke (eds.), Transformations: Mathematical Approaches to Culture (Academic Press, New York, 1979).

AUTHOR INDEX

INDEX OF DEFINITIONS